International Project
Management

International Project Management

Bennet P. Lientz

University of California, Los Angeles
Los Angeles, California

Kathryn P. Rea

The Consulting Edge, Inc.
Beverly Hills, California

ACADEMIC PRESS

An imprint of Elsevier Science

Amsterdam Boston London New York Oxford Paris San Diego
San Francisco Singapore Sydney Tokyo

Academic Press
An imprint of Elsevier Science
525 B Street, Suite 1900, San Diego, California 92101-4495, USA
http://www.academicpress.com

Academic Press
An imprint of Elsevier Science
84 Theobald's Road, London WC1X 8RR, UK
http://www.academicpress.com

Library of Congress Control Number: 2002111028

International Standard Book Number: 0-12-449985-6

PRINTED IN THE UNITED STATES OF AMERICA
02   03   04   05   06   MB   9   8   7   6   5   4   3   2   1

Contents

v

Chapter 4

Nail Down the Project Organization and Team

Chapter 5

Develop the Project Plan

Chapter 6

Use Technology to Your Advantage

Part II

Manage Your International Effort for Success

Chapter 7

Manage the International Team and the Work

Chapter 8

Manage Outsourcing and Vendors

Chapter 9

Sustain Effective Communications

Chapter 10

Deal with Issues and Use Experience

Part III
Types of Global Projects

Chapter 11

Multinational Software Deployment

Chapter 12

Mergers and Acquisitions

Chapter 13

Marketing of a New Product

Part IV
Issues in Global Projects

Chapter 16
Management Issues

Chapter 17
External Issues

- The Culture in a Country Is Not Compatible with the Results of the
  Project
- There Are Many Different Cultures and Languages in a
  Country

Preface

Globalization, international projects, mergers and acquisitions, implementing international and regional systems and technology are all becoming more common. There are natural reasons for this, including:

- Economies of scale in operations;
- Need to reach global markets;
- Facilitation of integration through the Internet, networking, and common systems;
- Desire by firms to spread risks across different countries.

Yet, with all of these trends, there is an almost unbroken chain of disasters and only partial successes. Surveys indicate that there is less than a 40% success rate of international efforts. International, regional, and global efforts are projects and one would think that standard project management methods would be useful and contribute to success. While this is true in some cases, there are still many failures and problems with existing project management methods. It is not that there must be radical change in project management; there is a need for modern techniques in project management geared and suited to international projects.

International projects are different because of the following factors:

- Culture and social differences within firms;
- Culture and social differences among countries and within countries;
- Languages and dialect variations;
- Religious practices;
- Legal, regulatory, and reporting requirements;
- Technology level differences in different areas;

- Infrastructure variations;
- Time zone differences.

While the attention is on international projects the approach and guidelines also apply to complex national or regional projects as well.

Looking at this list it is no wonder that you can see why managing projects and work in a standard centralized manner while ignoring the above factors leads to failure.

The purpose of this book is to provide specific guidelines for you to achieve greater project success. There are also lessons learned from failures and problems in international projects. The book is the product of work on international projects by the authors over a fifteen-year period in various project areas and industries. Projects and work have included manufacturing, distribution, communications, media, transportation, government, IT, marketing, energy, medical care, tourism, and other industries in forty countries across five continents.

The technical approach of the book is based on the following:

- Collaboration and collaborative approach rather than a strictly hierarchical approach to project management works best.
- Extensive and intensive communications using both traditional and modern technology is a critical success factor.
- In order to achieve project success, you must work to address issues and opportunities.
- There is a need to manage everyday work and other projects in addition to your main project. If you fail to do this, resources may not be available.
- In order to launch a project you must have management support, funding, and an agreement for resource allocation to the project and other work.
- Application to not only projects, but also small projects and on-going programs, must be carried out.

The book is organized into the following parts.

- Setup and launch your international projects;
- Manage the international projects;
- Examples of projects including systems deployment, mergers and acquisitions, and new product introduction; these chapters are organized around three of the themes of the book: issues, templates, and lessons learned;
- How to deal with specific issues involving projects, business, management, government, and external factors.

There is a common chapter structure in each part that emphasizes real world suggestions and tips. Our goal is that you can start using the materials in this book as you read it. This is not a concept book, it is a HOW TO DO IT book. The methods of the book have been tested in many different projects and work.

Here is a list of key features of the book:

- Critical success factors for international projects;
- How to avoid failure and problems;
- Over 150 specific lessons learned and guidelines;
- How to manage vendors and outsource across national boundaries;
- Major examples in different regions and areas;
- How to address cultural, social, and political situations;
- How to set up and coordinate international communications;
- How to address issues, problems, and opportunities;
- Complete coverage of all parts of managing international projects and work from start to finish;
- Written in a down-to-earth style;
- Web sites and references for follow-up;
- Specific suggestions on what to do after reading each chapter;
- A Magic Cross Reference for easy access to the materials in the book.

Part I

Launch Your International Project

Chapter 1

Introduction

WHAT IS AN INTERNATIONAL PROJECT?

A project is directed work that is aimed at achieving specific goals within a defined budget and schedule. An international or regional project is a project that involves multiple locations, entities, organizations, and business units. Examples of international and regional projects are:

- A company is doing a major construction project in a country that involves many subcontractors.
- Two companies are merging their operations.
- An organization is implementing major new systems and technology across all business units.
- A company is deploying a new product in a region.
- There is a new marketing campaign for an innovative consumer product.

What do these projects all have in common? They are all projects, but they are complex projects. They are sufficiently complex that the standard techniques of project management do not work well. Traditional project management targets a single project in one location. That was, after all, the case when many project management methods were conceived.

With globalization, mergers, and acquisitions international projects are more frequent. In this book we will consider a wide range of international projects—based in different industries and multiple countries. The methods and lessons learned here also apply to national projects where you encounter issues in culture, organization, and politics.

Why not use standard project management methods? Because they tend to fail or only partially work in the more complex environment. Statistics show that over half of international projects either fail, fail to be completed, or do not deliver the results that were promised.

EXAMPLES OF INTERNATIONAL PROJECTS

Let's consider some categories of international projects that we see more frequently.

- *International efforts by governments.* The war against terror is one example. Others are international police efforts, foreign aid, government promotion of trade and business, and health care initiatives. Regional government organizations such as APEC, the Organization of African Unity, and others are examples.
- *International nonprofit and aid agencies.* These organizations regularly are involved in small and large scale efforts around the world.
- *Efforts by firms to enter new markets and expand their customer base.* We see this all of the time in supermarkets and other retail establishments as new products appear.
- *Mergers and acquisitions.* Companies for the past decade have moved to acquire other firms across national boundaries.
- *Support for standardization.* With common and more powerful technologies and systems, it is possible now to impose the same systems and methods on all locations of a firm. Implementation of ERP systems in many companies are examples of this.
- *Marketing initiatives.* Companies tend to seek new customers and follow their existing customers around the globe.

However, international projects are not new. Probably the first projects were migrations of peoples across the globe after the Ice Age. More recently, the world has seen conquests and invasions. Alexander the Great is probably one of the first and most successful managers of international projects. He mounted armed forces that conquered a substantial part of the known world. He and his armies perfected the technique of operating far from their home base. In contrast earlier conquerors such as the pharaohs of ancient Egypt operated from their bases on the Nile River.

Moving ahead in history we come to the Phoenicians and the Greeks. While they established remote settlements, these were relatively small projects. The groups that improved on Alexander were the Chinese emperors and the Roman Empire. In each case, they were able to establish remote centers and run an empire that spread across many cultures, time zones, and climates for hundreds of years. How did they do it? Let's create a small list that we can use later.

• *Establishment of communications and roads.* Critical to any international project is the ability to communicate quickly and effectively with remote locations. The Romans, for example, established a road that was second to none until the twentieth century. The elapsed time for a governor to send correspondence to Rome was not equaled until the twentieth century.

• *Sensitivity to local culture.* All empires that have been lasting for many years adapted their regulations and rules to the specific culture. Those that tried to impose their will failed. An example is Attila the Hun. He conquered many lands quickly, but when he died, the empire blew apart.

• *Establishment of an organization that was international.* This is critical to the success of an international project, or even a large project in a single company. Each department has its own style. The organization that carries out projects must be flexible and knowledgeable about what is going on. Techniques and methods that work in one place often fail in other places.

After the Roman and Chinese empires declined, there was a huge time gap before international projects reemerged. Most of the efforts were expeditions. The next wave of international projects occurred during the colonial period that ended in the twentieth century with World Wars I and II. The most successful colonial powers were those that followed the lessons learned and critical success factors listed above. The ones that did not failed in a fairly short time.

TRENDS IN GLOBAL BUSINESS

Over the past decades we have experienced an explosion of international and large-scale projects. Benefits from these efforts have, in turn, spurred on more efforts. Here are some trends.

• *Expansion of individual firms to sell their products and services in other countries.* This began in the nineteenth century, but really accelerated after World War II. Today, you see the same products and services in almost all countries—leading to resentment of the invasion of the local culture.

• *Standardization in government regulations and simplification.* Governments around the world have seen the benefits of expanding trade and business through changing and simplifying regulations through free trade zones and other measures.

• *Mergers and acquisitions.* This will be explored in Chapter 12 in more detail. Today, you can see that the number of individual large companies doing business in just one country or area has greatly diminished.

• *Requirement for a global presence to be viable in an industry.* Whether you look at automobiles, banking, insurance, pharmaceuticals, or one-hundred other industries, you can see that there is drive for global presence.

- *Worldwide manufacturing and distribution.* When you buy any complex product that has multiple components, chances are that individual pieces were made in a variety of locations. Assembly was then carried out somewhere else.

Why have these occurred? A prime reason is improved communications and technology. Another reason has been expansion of transportation. Both of these have lowered the cost of doing business in multiple locations to the point that is affordable to many individuals as well as companies.

What are the benefits that organizations seek in carrying out international and complex projects such as those mentioned above?

- *Economies of scale.* By having one headquarters you achieve administrative economies of scale. By centralizing manufacturing activities of the same type you have additional economies of scale and lower costs of operations.
- *Strength in size.* For many firms there are major benefits to increased size. Retailing is a good example. A Wal-Mart or Carrefour can obtain goods at lower prices and then be more competitive.
- *Penetration of new markets and increased sales.* The elapsed time to enter new markets has been dramatically reduced. In addition, a company can enter a market on a test basis and then later withdraw or retrench if the conditions are not favorable.
- *Access to human resources.* Many firms are challenged with labor problems such as a lack of personnel with specific skills or high labor costs. Operating internationally can help ease these problems.
- *Lower cost of operations.* With economies of scale and flexibility in moving and locating operations to lower cost locales, the cost of doing business is reduced.
- *Maintenance and expansion of the firm's competitive position.* You often either grow or risk dying out. This has been the case in banking, insurance, and the automotive industry. When a competitor has success in expansion, you often have no choice but to copy the move.

What is the impact of these global trends? More international projects. But as you have seen, the results are often mixed. For every case of success, there are many instances of failure and problems. Look at the merger of Chrysler and Daimler-Benz for one example of problems.

TECHNOLOGY AND SYSTEMS TRENDS

There are some specific breakthroughs that have made international projects possible and easier as well as cheaper. Some of these are:

• *Telecommunications*. The middle twentieth century saw the worldwide telephone system being established. Fiber optics and satellite communications greatly increased both the capabilities and the capacity for communications. Costs have been dramatically lowered. A telephone card can let you talk to most of the people of the world for a very low per minute charge.

• *Networking*. Networking technology has taken advantage of the telecommunication advances to allow for high-speed data and image communications.

• *Mobile communications*. Cellular phone use has continued to rise rapidly over the past five years. While the growth is lower today, it is still on the rise. Mobile communications not only offers convenience to people and organizations, but it offers an alternative to standard land-based communications. This increases reliability of communications overall and encourages businesses and individuals to carry out more work overseas.

• *Hardware and systems software*. Twenty years ago, hardware was much more expensive. Further back, there were many incompatible systems. The dominance of first IBM and then Microsoft has created standards for computing and common computing environments. Both of these facilitate and make feasible many international projects.

• *Computer systems*. In the earlier days of IT (information technology), most computer systems were built for a specific firm in a specific company. The emergence of software packages changed the landscape. Many ERP (enterprise resource planning) systems can be tuned and set up to run in many different countries operating with different currencies and different rules and regulations.

• *Internet and World Wide Web*. Probably, nothing has been more dramatic in impact than the use of the Web for communications and supporting the operations of multiple locations. Information is more available and widespread than it has ever been. There is a greater awareness of what is going on around the world. This in turn has fueled the interest in international projects.

What does the technology help an organization do better? How does technology support the global trends mentioned above?

• *Ability to clone the infrastructure and replicate it in many locations*. Look at retailing or manufacturing. Today, you can take the software in one location and establish it in a location thousands of miles away with the same type of hardware and networking technology. You can then adapt it to local conditions more easily due to flexibility. You can obtain vendor support in many countries similar or comparable to what you have at home. One retail firm boasts that they can establish a new remote location within 60 days.

• *Ability to control remote locations on a more or less real time basis*. Going back in time, the method for control was to empower the remote manager with almost all power and discretion of authority. Times have changed. Today, for many firms, there is a daily monitoring of what is going on in each location. Production schedules can be established, fine tuned, and changed overnight.

• *Ability to provide for standardization.* The technology supports standardization. This means that if different locations use similar software or databases, they can share information quickly and effectively without massaging the data.

• *Ability to support some flexibility in offering products and services.* Notice the word "some." Automation and technology provide for limited flexibility and still act to restrain a company from carrying major new changes due to the limitations of the software. However, there is greater flexibility than was the case years ago.

HOW INTERNATIONAL PROJECTS ARE DIFFERENT

Having discussed what international projects are, we can explore differences between standard projects and international or more complex projects. A number of topics will be discussed. This discussion will then be summarized by a table.

One good way to understand the difference is to examine a simple chart. A spider or radar chart is given in Fig. 1.1. In a radar chart each axis represents one dimension. This type of chart is useful in showing multiple dimensions. Keep it in mind and use it as you manage and work with international projects. Let's look at the chart. First, consider the dimensions. There are eight of these. They can be divided into two groups. The first group is the first five. These are variables that describe the project. The second group (the last three) consists of impacts and effects of the project.

Consider the graph. Note that the international project totally dominates the standard project. We recognize that this is just an example and that you have to draw up your own chart. When you look at the chart, you see that there are differences in each dimension. Here are some comments on each factor.

• *Number of locations.* International or regional projects have more locations. They can be in different cities, states, provinces, districts, or countries.

• *Extent of purpose.* You may take on many small projects in the traditional mode. However, there is typically an overriding purpose when you work on an international level. The purpose tends to be wider and more complex.

• *Range of project.* This is also the scope of the project. There are typically more things to change and do in an international project.

• *Number of organizations involved.* In a standard project, there is often only one department involved. The situation is more homogeneous.

Factors
1. Number of locations
2. Extent of purpose
3. Range of project
4. Number of organizations involved
5. Dependence of the organization on the project
6. Risk and complexity
7. Potential benefits
8. Cost of the project

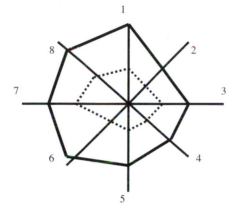

Figure 1.1   Comparative Scope of International Projects

International projects are almost the direct opposite. You can have headquarters, regional headquarters, and local offices involved—all separate and individual entities.

• *Dependence of the organization on the project.* In a standard project, if there is failure, the people and the organization go on. However, international projects tend to be more visible. The project is much more important and more at stake with the international project.

• *Risk and complexity.* International projects have much greater risk and complexity.

• *Potential benefits.* The benefits of an international project are often spelled out at the start much more than a standard project. This is probably because of the following factors: (1) there is more at stake; (2) it takes more management attention to manage the project.

• *Cost of the project.* While many standard projects can be large and expensive, an international project almost seems to always cost more. There is more transportation, communication, and coordination. Greater complexity contributes to higher cost as well.

How can you employ this chart? Use it to show how international projects are more complex. You can then define alternative versions of the international project that vary in purpose and range or scope. Each alternative can then be charted and compared. This has proven to be very useful in doing trade-offs for an international project.

A summary of differences appears in Fig. 1.2. Some amplifying comments are useful here. Not only are there more organizations involved, but also there are more complex power structures within and between organizational units.

While technology has advanced as we stated earlier, there are often still many legacy systems and individual systems in different locations. The only people who understand and can work or modify these are the staff at each location. This makes work on systems in the international project more complex.

Culture can be considered at both a societal and corporate level. Society level culture factors will be discussed in a later section. The culture of an organization at a specific location can be substantially different from that of the headquarters. Some of the reasons for this are: (1) the location was part of an acquired firm with a different culture; (2) the office reflects the personalities of the higher level managers; (3) training, promotion, and other human resource approaches may have been different.

In a standard project, you can get people focused on the project. Management is right next door so that people feel compelled to support the project. This is not

Attribute	Standard Projects	International Projects
Organizations	Single	Multiple organizations and departments, each with their own self-interest
Systems and technology	Homogeneous	Multiple systems that require local knowledge and support
Society	Single and common culture	Multiple, varied cultures
Company culture	Single	Variations in each area due to local factors and history of the firm in each location
Organization	Can be focused on the project	Many other competing demands for resources
Self-interest	More easily understood	More complex to understand
Regulations	Understood and known	Harder to understand; more subject to interpretation

Figure 1.2 Comparison Summary of Standard and International Projects

the case in an international project. There are many more competing demands on the employees. They have their normal work; they may also have additional local projects.

Self-interest is one of the most powerful factors in projects. People get turned off on a project if they perceive that they will get nothing out of it. This is a prime reason for the failure of many ERP installations. To be successful, an international project must address the local self-interest of the managers and employees at each location.

Regulations and laws are often taken for granted in many countries. The law is the law. However, in much of the world, this is not the case. Laws and regulations are subject to interpretation. Look at China. In one study of the application of twenty laws, it was found that each province of China had interpreted the law differently. Thus, you not only have to be aware of the law or rule as it is written, but also what is really means on the street.

WHY INTERNATIONAL PROJECTS ARE COMPLEX

Let's examine now aspects of complexity. Just talking about complexity is not enough.

• *Lack of control*. While it may appear that you as the project leader have control, in fact you often don't—even with top management endorsement. Each office or organization has its own agenda and overall goals. If the project does not fit within this picture, you don't have much control.

• *Different cultures*. Culture factors impact an international project in many ways. They first impact the setup of the project. They affect the structure of the work. After work gets underway, there are more impacts. Culture impacts projects in an ongoing and pervasive way. This is a key lesson learned.

• *Different time zones*. If you have ever worked on an international project spanning many time zones, communications can be a nightmare. You end up staying awake until the early hours of the morning to talk with people halfway around the world since people's schedules and activities are often structured around the time of day.

• *Different currencies*. Money can be an issue in many ways. In some countries you cannot get money out of the country easily. The currency of the local country may not be valued elsewhere. There can be an underground economy. Inflation may be a factor in a country. Inflation changes the psychology and approach to projects—long-term projects may be shelved in favor of the short-term.

• *Variety of regulations and rules*. Not only does each country have its own rules and regulations, but there can be local laws and interpretation as well. If you ignore this or make some unsubstantiated assumptions, then you are likely to run into major problems that can sink the project.

• *Political upheaval and uncertainty*. Strictly speaking, this is not a cultural issue. However, it deserves mention. Doing a project in a country with a guerrilla insurgency can create, let's say, some challenging problems. We have carried out projects in four countries where there was civil or guerrilla unrest. This changed the project and affected the scope of the work.

• *Visibility of the project to the outside world*. International projects tend to attract wider visibility outside of the organization. This is due to size and scope. It is also due to the fact that more people know about or are involved in the work.

CHARACTERISTICS OF INTERNATIONAL PROJECTS

Culture is an important characteristic of international projects. Here is a list of cultural factors that can impact the success or failure of a project.

• *Management attitude*. Management may take a domineering approach. They feel that they own the operation in a location. That is true, but it is not the way that people work. Management may have left the operation alone up until the time of this project. The project now represents management interference. Locally, there are more factors. Management style in the country may be very paternal and directive. No one questions anything. If the boss in the location does not support the project, you are doomed.

• *Approach toward work*. Even in adjoining countries that speak the same language and have the same religion and racial background, there can be different attitudes toward work. In some countries, work is perceived as something that you have to do, but it is not critical to their life. If you have a country where people live simple lives, they may feel that they do not need to get ahead in the company to earn money for more consumer items.

• *The factor of time*. Different cultures have different attitudes toward time. Until clocks were widespread, people were governed by the sun and darkness. Clocks turn out to be a curse, because they start to regulate our lives. In some countries, there is less time pressure. The people may feel that the work can be done tomorrow if it is not done today. When the project leader tries to get the people working harder, they resist. After all, their everyday, nonproject work does not have this pressure.

• *The value of money*. What do people think about money? Do they want to amass and save it? Or do they just want to get by? This relates to the attitude and approach toward work. Offering money incentives often fails in some countries. It turns people off and they feel insulted.

- *Planning versus doing.* Some cultures have encouraged an analytic frame of mind. This may have been supported by religious attitudes. In such situations, team members may want to spend a lot of time discussing the work rather than doing it—creating an obvious problem for the schedule.
- *Teamwork versus individual effort.* In some countries such as the United States, the emphasis is on individual performance. Teamwork is supported, but when it comes down to it, the pressure is on the individual. This can be very negative because you become overly dependent on a few people. The project can die if they leave with their knowledge. It is easier to carry out international projects in places where teamwork is widely accepted.
- *Religion.* Religion is a factor in any society. It affects how people view life and how they go about their work.
- *The factor of climate and weather.* Work patterns are different in various parts of the world due to climate and weather. Air conditioning has served to equalize the situation, but it is still there.

What is a common element of all of the above factors? They are not controllable in the project. You have to work around and with them. This is a major difference between standard and international projects.

Beyond cultural factors, there are other characteristics of international projects.

- *Management expectations.* Management tends to have exaggerated expectations about the benefits of almost all substantial international projects. These can be based upon vendor promises, experience at other companies, and other factors. This is dangerous since there can be many management-generated changes as the expectations are not met.
- *Management involvement.* Some managers may feel that they have more at stake with the project so that they tend to interfere with the project. They may try to micromanage the project. This will slow things down as no one will want to take initiative.
- *The need for wider employee, customer, and/or supplier participation.* If you want to achieve success in an international project, you must seek out and involve as many affected people as possible.

WHY INTERNATIONAL PROJECTS FAIL

From experience in over 100 international projects and reviewing many more, we have developed a list of factors that contribute to failure. These are discussed in no particular order or importance.

- *Treatment of the international project as a standard project.* This is a common mistake. A manager may have had great success in standard projects.

When faced with an international project, he or she just plunges in and applies the same methods.

• *Excessive management attention*. Management kills off many international projects due to over attention. Micromanagement is a leading cause of project failure.

• *Lack of sensitivity to the local culture*. The typical cause of failure here is the imposition of the same standards and approaches to each location and business unit. This is a sure step on the road to disaster.

• *Failure to stay the course*. When faced with problems in one location, management may give up and move to another location. It is not likely that they will do much better in the next place.

• *Failure to take into account self-interest*. Everyone tends to be concerned with their own interests. This is natural and is true of organizations as well. If you attempt to implement a project for which people perceive that they will receive no benefits, there will be trouble. At best, you will only get lukewarm support and involvement.

• *Overdependence upon technology*. Many people think that the technology can be employed to overcome many problems. It is not just computer and communications technology, it can be construction, engineering, or other technology. Technology can help, but it can also make matters worse.

• *Lack of measurement*. Many international projects are not measured as they are going on. Moreover, results of the project in terms of impact are not measured. This tends to lower morale and lead to problems, because people tend to think of the negative factors since there are no positive measurements.

CRITICAL SUCCESS FACTORS FOR INTERNATIONAL PROJECTS

• *Everyone must win with the project*. This relates to self-interest. You must show at the start and then reinforce it as you go that people have a stake in the success and outcome of the project.

• *Collaborative effort*. If there is one thing that is true of international projects, it is that you have to have widespread involvement and participation in the project. If you involve only a few people, then the others who are not participating may end up resisting the project results. Moreover, experience reveals that involvement leads to commitment and dedication—key factors for success.

• *Measurement, measurement, and more measurement*. You should measure the situation before the project. Measure as the project goes on. Measure the results of the project.

• *Gather lessons learned as you go.* Traditionally, people gather lessons learned at the end of a project. It is too late for international projects. The people are gone—to other work. They have no interest. Therefore, you must work to gather experience as you go.

• *Cultural sensitivity and awareness throughout the project.* It is impossible to know and be aware of all of the cultural factors and their impacts at the start of the project. So you will have to have a great deal of sensitivity toward culture so that you can pick up on new factors and take them into account.

• *Proactive resource allocation.* Recurring problems in international projects are the conflict between people's regular work and the project work. To be successful, you must have a proactive approach to allocate human resources so that work on the project goes on.

• *Project organization and manager and team member selection.* How you structure the project and the people that are selected have always been important in all projects. It is no more true than in international projects. Structure includes how you divide up the project and how you deal with issues.

ORGANIZATION OF THE BOOK

This book is divided up into parts.

• *Part I: Launch your international project.* The chapters in this part will take you step-by-step through developing the international project and getting it going. There are chapters on the project leaders, the team, definition of the project, and establishment of the plan.

• *Part II: Manage your international effort for success.* Once started, you have to manage and track the project. You have to deal with many issues and opportunities. Communications are critical.

• *Part III: Types of global projects.* This part contains three specific situations to which the methods of the first two parts are applied. Three common situations are addressed: widespread software deployment, mergers and acquisitions, and regional construction and distribution.

• *Part IV: Issues in global projects.* There are four chapters here that address commonly encountered problems and issues in the following areas: the project, business and organization, management, and external factors. For each issue, there is an opening discussion. This is followed by guidelines on detection and impact, prevention, and actions that can be taken.

Now move down to the chapter level. Each chapter in Parts I and II contains the following sections.

• *Introduction.* This consists of preliminary remarks and links the chapter material to those that precede and follow.

• *Purpose and Scope*. Because we are dealing with international projects, there are three purposes that are considered: the technical purpose, the business purpose, and the political and cultural purpose. If you concentrate on only one or two of these, you will fail. You have already seen how important scope is. Here the range of what is covered in each chapter is explored.

• *End Products*. This is what you produce and get from the work covered in the chapter. There are not just tangible end products as in standard projects, but also cultural and political end products. After all, we are dealing with the real world.

• *Approach*. Here is where the methods and techniques are. Where possible, these are presented in lists and chart form to make it easy for you to use. Examples are given here as well.

• *Examples*. Several example organizations will be considered here and followed through each chapter in Parts I and II. Part III will contain additional examples. Here are the examples along with a brief description.

— Sambac Energy. This is a joint venture firm between two other energy firms. Each of the two firms has its own culture. The cultures tend to clash. Then there is the third culture—in country. We will be considering a variety of projects here.

— Whitmore Bank. Whitmore is an international bank that is attempting to implement credit card operations in five countries in which it has a limited presence.

• *Lessons Learned*. Lessons learned are guidelines and tips gathered from experience. Note that this is different from the methods in the approach. Lessons learned are additional steps on "how" to use the methods effectively.

• *Exercises*. Specific exercises are given that help you use the materials in the chapter right away.

• *Summary*. This section puts the chapter in overall perspective.

The chapters in Part III deal with specific applications. Their sections are:

• *Introduction*.
• *Purpose and Scope*.
• *End Products*—Major end products for this type of project.
• *Issues*—Specific concerns that arise with these projects.

WHAT YOU WILL GAIN FROM THE BOOK

Let's write down what people and organizations have gotten out of the methods and techniques in this book that have been applied to many organizations and taught through many seminars.

• *International project understanding.* You will gain a better understanding of the complexity and factors that impact international projects. This will make you more successful.

• *Risk reduction.* Reduce the risks and likelihood of project failure through lessons learned and specific tips.

• *Issues management.* Be able to deal with issues more effectively. Key to project management is the capability to address issues. We spend a great deal of time in the book on dealing with problems, issues, and opportunities.

• *Failure and detection of problems.* Address failing projects and detect problems in international projects earlier. This will not only prevent problems down the road, but will lead to short-term benefits as well.

• *More effective communications.* Throughout the book we provide tips and guidelines for better communications with management on all levels as well as employees, customers, and suppliers.

• *Lessons learned.* Over 150 lessons learned in specific sections and throughout the chapters to make you more effective.

• *Down to earth, proven approach.* The methods have been proven and refined through many projects. The approach is jargon and buzzword free.

• *Political and cultural factors.* Specific guidelines are given to address the critical political and cultural factors that you will face.

APPROACH

It's time to get started. Two areas will be examined—learning from the past and measurement.

EXAMINE PAST EFFORTS AT INTERNATIONAL OR COMPLEX PROJECTS

Before starting anything new you should look at the track record of your organization in its past international projects. Otherwise, you may be doomed to repeat the mistakes of the past. Begin by talking to people in headquarters as well as at other locations to find out what projects have been worked on the past. You can give as the reason that you are trying to prevent future problems. You may also indicate that you are looking to find people who have past project experience.

Here are some specific things to look for:

• People who participated in past projects;
• Media relations announcements about the project and results;
• Documentation about the project generated in the project;
• Articles about what resulted from the project.

As you identify sources, you might be able to answer questions such as the following:

- What was the final outcome of the project?
- What happened to the people who led the project?
- How was the project announced at the start and when it ended?
- If the project was killed, why was it killed? What was said publicly?
- Was there any effort to gather experience and lessons learned?
- If people could do the project over again, what would they have done differently?
- How was the project measured and tracked?
- What changes occurred during the project? Why did these come about?
- What were the initial budget and schedule for the project? What were the final figures?
- Were subsequent follow-on projects carried out?

DEVELOP A SCORE CARD FOR INTERNATIONAL PROJECTS

It is clear that you need to be able to sit back from time to time and measure the progress of the international project. You want to do this in an organized manner. Experience shows that a score card can be valuable here. Figure 1.3 contains such a score card. This is a fairly extensive version so you may want to cut it down.

What is being measured by the score card?

- Standard measurements of performance—budget, schedule, effort;
- Team member and employee involvement—joint tasks, collaboration in defining and updating tasks;
- Issue tracking and management.

Issues will be addressed throughout the book. An issue can be a problem or an opportunity. Only substantial issues that impact the project are tracked. For each issue you will analyze and track it using an issues database to be presented later. Data elements include date that the issue was identified, status of the issue (open, closed, tabled), date closed, type of the issue, description, etc. This data can then be used for the issues-related items in the score card.

EXAMPLES

There are two basic example companies used throughout the book—Sambac Energy and Whitmore Bank. In addition, you will see Titan Broadcasting. Titan is a joint venture to implement satellite broadcasting in a region.

Measure	Score	Comment
Budget versus actual		
Planned versus actual schedule		
Number of people from bus. depts. involved in project		
% of business employees involved		
% of milestones achieved		
Tasks identified by team members?		
Tasks updated by team members?		
No. team members that left the project unplanned		
Number of times management contacted you with problems		
Number of requests to change direction of the project		
% of tasks that are joint and not individual		
Total number of issues uncovered to date		
Number of open issues by type		
Number of issues by type		
Total number of open issues		
% of issues unresolved		
Average time to resolve an issue by type		
Average time to resolve an issue		
% of issues not controllable in the project		
% of open issues not controllable in the project		
% of milestones in the future with risk		
Age of oldest outstanding issue		
% of future tasks with risk		
% of tasks with risk		
% of future manpower hours with risk		
% of future manpower hours ahead with risk		
Average time required to reach a decision on issue		

Figure 1.3 International Project Score Card

SAMBAC ENERGY

Sambac Energy was started after World War II as a joint venture between two other large energy firms, Alpha Energy and Beta Energy. These names are picked for simplicity. The examples in the book are combinations of real world companies and situations and do not represent a specific company that exists.

Alpha Energy has a culture that encourages entrepreneurship. Managers are sent out in the field to think for themselves. Beta Energy is very different. Its culture requires decisions to be fed back to headquarters for review. Why and how did two such companies get together? Because of an opportunity to exploit oil and natural gas in developing nations. So there are these two cultures and the culture of the specific country that they operate in. We will be considering various projects that they undertook and their outcomes. Some succeeded and some did not.

One thing to get out of this example is to understand that for years they were not sensitive to culture and they did not, in general, gather lessons learned from their experiences. This led to many project problems and some substantial failures.

WHITMORE BANK

Whitmore Bank is a major international bank that wanted to expand credit card operations into a region of five countries. Whitmore had a presence in these countries in international and some consumer banking, but had not rolled out credit cards in the region. They had extensive credit card experience in their home country and other nations.

Credit card operations are more complex than you might initially think. You have to consider the culture of the country in marketing and selling the credit card product. There are already many banks offering credit cards so that there is intense competition. So why should Whitmore want to expand its credit card operation? First, it makes money. Second, many customers wanted to have credit cards with the bank.

When you receive an application for a credit card, you have to evaluate the application and make a decision on whether to issue the card. In some developed countries there are automated scoring systems and credit bureaus. In the countries in the region only one had such capabilities. This raises the level of complexity.

After the credit card has been issued, then there is customer service. Payments, collections on delinquent accounts, overlimits, charging off cards, cancellation, fraud, and maintenance of the cardholder information also come into play. Cultural factors impact some of these.

LESSONS LEARNED

- Use tables and charts as much as possible. If you start writing up reports and making exotic presentations, you will become consumed with this as people will expect it all of the time. Try to use tables and charts that can reused and updated as you go along in the project.
- Measure the situation before you start the project. Every international project attempts to make some change or addition to infrastructure, systems, processes, etc. In order to see that you are getting the benefits, you should measure the situation before the project gets underway.

EXERCISES

1. Look in the literature for examples of success and failure of international projects.
2. Here is a list of international projects. Try to uncover why these were successes and failures.
   - The Aswan Dam in Egypt;
   - The merger of Chrysler and Daimler-Benz;
   - Mergers of wineries around the world.
3. Use the above examples and others to start building a list of factors that lead to failure or success.
4. Try applying the international score card to a specific project. You will have to make some assumptions and do some thinking since you will obviously not have all of the data.

SUMMARY

This book's title says "international projects." This phrase is used throughout. However, the methods and tools that are presented in each chapter apply to most types of complex projects.

It is tempting to be overwhelmed by the complexity of international projects. Look at the problems, failures, and complexity. However, when all is said and done, international projects are a fact of life. In the future, there will be more, not less of them. Not only that, but we have found that international projects are more fun, interesting, and challenging than standard projects.

Define the Project

INTRODUCTION

Many people want to plunge right in and develop the project plan. This can be fatal for an international project. Instead, you have to define where you are going and how you will get there. Most importantly, you want to get consensus from the parties who will be involved in the project as well as those who will benefit from the project. Without consensus, the project will be subjected to changes in direction and the dreaded *scope creep* where the project direction changes as often as sand dunes change in a desert.

For international projects you have to be concerned about the self-interest and resources of each location or business unit from the start. In one company a project was started only to be stopped cold, because the first regional office that was to be involved was undergoing relocation and reorganization. Yet, management had approved the project knowing this!

PURPOSE AND SCOPE

TECHNICAL PURPOSE

The technical purpose of the work in this chapter is to define the specific elements of the international project in terms of purpose, scope, roles, issues, overall cost, and schedule. By doing this you can determine the technical feasibility of carrying out the project.

Business Purpose

The business purpose of this chapter is to define the international project from a business view. This is often very different from the technical view. Consider the project of installing a system in multiple locations. The technical purpose is rather straightforward. The business purpose is to achieve positive results through change resulting from achieving the technical purpose.

Political Purpose

The political purpose of this chapter is to get management to agree on the project. But this is not just upper management. It is also management at each location or within each business unit. Now sit back and consider the three purposes. You can most easily define the project from a technical view. However, if you achieve the technical objectives, there is nothing to say that either the business or political objectives have been achieved. Furthermore, if you achieve both the technical and business goals, you can still fail because you did not get support for the project.

Scope

At this stage in the international project, everything is included. There are no restrictions since you are trying to define the project. Thus, it is wise to consider many options.

END PRODUCTS

There are a number of end products that you might typically find in any project. These are more complex in international projects because you are projecting the project down to each location or business unit. Here are some specific end products.

* Technical, business, and political purposes of the project from different viewpoints and levels;
* Scope of the project in each location or business unit;
* Roles and responsibilities that headquarters and business units are to play in the project;
* Resource availability in each location to support the project;
* Initial list of issues at the local, regional, and global levels that will have to be addressed;

- Estimated budget that will be required to carry out the project;
- Overall schedule for the international project;
- Estimated benefits at each level and location.

More important than each of these is the end product of political acceptance and commitment to the project. Why do all of this work now? After all, if management wants to do the project, then that is that. Not true. Starting an ill-defined project that impacts multiple locations and business units is just asking for continuing problems and headaches.

APPROACH

MEASURE THE CURRENT SITUATION

When someone proposes to do something, you want to avoid rushing out and taking action until you know what is going on. You want to observe and measure what is going on before the project gets underway. This is useful for several political reasons.

- You understand the current situation or process better so that you can define the project with greater clarity.
- You can help people to understand the problems and limitations with the current situation. You must assume that most people have no desire for change or the new project. They have functioned just fine without it for many years. A fundamental tenet of alcohol and drug rehabilitation is that the person must be aware of and admit that they have a problem before they can be cured. It is the same with the project.
- You can validate that the project is, in fact, needed.

How do you do this? By observation. Now we realize that each international project is unique in detail and that there is a wide range of potential projects. However, it is also true that many projects relate to business processes. In order to provide an example, business processes will be considered here. You observe the business process and note problems that arise in doing the work. You seek to have the employees identify problems and issues with their current work. If you were looking at marketing a new product, you would be looking at the marketing process that is followed currently.

What information do you collect? How do you structure the information? An approach that has worked many times from experience is to employ a score card for the current situation. Figure 2.1 below is a score card for a current business process. You can create a similar score card for many other situations. For example, if you were doing a large construction project, then you might include

Measure	Location 1	Location 2
Number of people directly involved in the process by location or business unit		
Turnover of employees at the location		
Turnover of employees in the process		
Facilities employed by the process		
System used for the process		
Technology infrastructure		
Total volume of work performed per unit of time		
Total cost of the process		
Cost per unit of work		
Average time to perform specific work		
Frequency of work		
Top three reported problems		
Extent of rework		
Exception volume		
Existence of homegrown systems and procedures		
Skill level of employees doing the work		
Policies followed in doing the work		
Quality and completeness of training		
Revenue per transaction		

Figure 2.1 Sample Process Score Card

survey information of similar projects that have taken place in the same location. Note that the score card measures the business and technical aspects of the situation as well as political and cultural factors. Also, consider the columns. There is one for each location or business unit. This is because the situation in each organization or location is specific to that unit. Developing the scores is subjective and should be done in a collaborative way with employees and supervisors in each location.

How can you employ this score card? First, you use it to summarize the problems and issues related to the situation in each location. Second, it is useful in presentations to management. Managers see the score card values and they tend to react. The reaction leads naturally to intense discussion about both the current situation and the future project. It will likely result in some change in thinking among the managers.

This sounds like a lot of work to do before you even get started. It is but it is also essential. You have to understand what is going on now and you must start to build up support for change. Remember that collecting information early is much cheaper and easier than making changes later. It should also be stressed that you are not looking in detail at the situation—just an overview.

There are some other things to do when you are collecting this information. You should collect data on the level of current work, what resources are available to support the new project, and whether current projects are making progress. You will be using this later when you propose the project and enter the fray for fighting for resources.

What is another major reason to measure what is going on?

If you do not measure before the project is started, you have no real way of determining the benefits of the work.

THE PROJECT CONCEPT

With background knowledge of the current situation at each location, you are now ready to create the project concept. The *project concept* consists of the general view of the project. It is developed prior to developing the plan or staffing the project. Elements of the project concept include the following:

- Purpose of the international project from different viewpoints;
- Scope of the international project—what will be included and excluded;
- Roles and responsibilities of departments and business units in the project;
- Availability of resources to support the international project;
- Initial issues that the project is likely to face;
- Budget and schedule for the international project;
- Likely benefits that will accrue when the work is completed.

Why is the project concept important? It gets everyone "reading off of the same page." It provides a forum for arguments and trade-offs as to what to do with the project. Creating the project concept also builds consensus in terms of agreement and commitment. As such, it's really more important than the project plan. The project plan validates the project concept and provides more detail. Now let's move on and develop the elements of the project concept.

DEFINE OBJECTIVES FOR THE INTERNATIONAL PROJECT

As with each chapter, there are technical, business, and political purposes. Each will be considered for a specific example.

Technical Purpose of the Project

Almost all projects have some technical purpose. Examples might relate to IT, engineering, construction, marketing, or distribution. The technical purpose relates to the physical activity of the project. For international projects the technical purpose relates to the implementation of change in one or more locations.

But you are just starting the project. Here the technical purpose is to get a precise definition of what is to be done in the project. This is simple if there was just one department or location. For international projects, you could have variations of the technical purpose in each location or for each business unit. Why? Because change does not go in the same way in different cultures. Let's take an example of a marketing campaign for a new product. Sounds simple enough, eh? In one country the decision to buy the product might be made by females. In another country it might be purchased based on a decision by a male. Because of cultural and society factors, the advertising might have to be substantially different between countries. Even the product name may have to be different.

As was stated in Chapter 1 you want to try to create tables, lists, and charts that support communications. In Fig. 2.2 there is a simple table for the technical purpose for the marketing campaign. Look at the differences. In country B you have access to both sexes and can reach them through television. Thus, the campaign can be shorter. You will know how the product has performed in less time. In country A printed media is more important. It will take longer given that the population tends to adopt new products at a slower pace. For whatever project, you should construct this and the tables presented later.

Why is this politically useful? Here are several reasons.

Specific purpose	General/headquarters	Country A	Country B
Audience	General population	Females	Males and females
Type of advertising	Multimedia	Print	TV, print
Length of campaign	6 months	6 months	3 months

Figure 2.2   Technical Purpose by Area

• Construction of the table requires that you get a good understanding of the environment in each location. This serves to increase your awareness of the area and market.

• By reviewing the table management can then perform trade-offs and may, in fact, change the purpose. The project can be dropped or changed. This is cheap and effective to do at the beginning. It gets much more expensive later on.

Business Purpose of the Project

The business purpose is the true purpose of the project whereas the technical purpose is how you are going to go about achieving it. The business purpose typically reflects a combination of goals. Examples are:

• Increased sales and market share;
• Reduced costs;
• Improved productivity;
• Increased performance in terms of throughput;
• Reduced error rates and improved quality;
• Improved controls.
• Greater business flexibility to respond to changing conditions.

However, as with the technical purpose, you have to project these fuzzy goals down to the level of the location or business unit. Figure 2.3 gives the same example. Now you can start seeing more differences. Country B's marketing has not been going well. It is desired that the new campaign will help straighten out this situation. Management information is necessary for headquarters, but the in-country managers just carry out the campaign. They do not initiate marketing campaigns.

By now you should start to see the complexity of international projects. You are dealing with multiple objectives in multiple dimensions—very tricky.

Specific purpose	General/headquarters	Country A	Country B
Increased overall market share	Increased sales	Increased market penetration	Establishment of market
Cleanup of marketing	OK as is	OK as is	Clean up
Management information	Greater and more accessible information	Not applicable	Not applicable

Figure 2.3 Business Purpose by Area

What if you just defined the overall objectives and did not worry about each country? Then you probably would not get much support from each country. Oh, they might pay lip service to the project, but the project would probably be DOA—dead on arrival—at the remote locations.

Political Purpose of the Project

At the core of most international projects is politics. There are various political agendas. Here are some that we have encountered frequently:

• One or more top managers want to use the project to increase their power or prestige. This occurs sometimes in firms that launch some improvement initiative such as Six Sigma.
• The headquarters feels threatened by a major business unit and so initiates the project to increase the power over and control of the business units.
• The project is started in reaction to what a competitor has done in one or more locations. This is often a panic reaction.
• There may be pressure to do the project from external sources such as investors. Examples of this were efforts by firms in the late 1990s to implement e-business.

These political purposes are not bad. They are not good. You have to define and recognize them. Here is a fundamental rule of international projects.

An international project is shaped by the political objectives for the project.

There are additional overt political goals in addition to these general ones. Some examples are:

• Achieve increased levels of standardization across business units.
• Narrow the focus of business units to their core activities.
• Instill a greater sense of the corporation overall across all locations.

You will also want to create another table similar to the ones for the technical and business purposes. However, you probably will not want to reveal it to many people. You want to use it yourself to be constantly aware of why the project was started.

Once you have developed the objectives, then you can check on whether they align with each other. This is important and something that is not carried out often enough. In the VietNam War, the technical goal related to seizing territory and eliminating enemy soldiers. The political goal was to win the war. However, these were not aligned. The real business and technical goals should have related to the "hearts and minds" of the population.

DETERMINE THE SCOPE OF THE PROJECT

There are two ways to look at the scope of an international project. One is to consider the dimensions of the project overall and in each country or business unit. The second is to consider the impacts that derive from the dimensions. Here is a list of possible dimensions for you to consider.

- Number of locations;
- Number of departments involved in the project;
- Extent of systems and technology;
- Number of processes involved in the project;
- Other projects.

These dimensions reflect what is to be done.

Next, we move to the impact factors. These may include:

- Cost;
- Benefits;
- Risk;
- Elapsed time for the project.

Obviously, if you change the values for the dimensions, you will change the resulting factors. A bigger project can result in more time and cost as well as increased risk.

What you seek to do is to involve management at both the local and headquarters levels in trade-offs regarding scope. There are a number of benefits and reasons for doing this.

- Managers gain a common understanding of the scope at each location or within each business unit.
- You are more likely to prevent future scope creep and project change in direction.

In order to carry out the analysis, you can employ a spider chart. Figure 2.4 is one example. Note that there is no precise number for the values on the lines. They are subjective by intent so that you generate a great deal of discussion.

This example pertains to improving processes. The solid line chart represents a version of the project with a narrower scope. There is little organization change, for example. The dashed line represents a major reengineering effort and has much more risk, cost, and elapsed time. However, it yields only slightly more benefits. You would generally prefer the solid line version of the project.

Now you will want to draw similar charts for some of the locations or business units. By doing this you will better understand the risks and other factors involved in the scope.

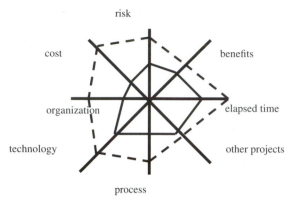

Figure 2.4   Example of a Spider Chart for the Scope of an International Project

It is sometimes helpful to use trigger thoughts or ideas to generate ideas for versions of the scope. Here you could consider some of the following:

• Money is no object for the project. This shows one extreme.
• Time is not a problem. This allows you to consider stretching out the project.
• Adopt a very narrow view of the project in terms of what will change.
• Adopt a comprehensive view of the project in terms of change.

ESTABLISH ROLES, RESPONSIBILITIES, AND RESOURCE AVAILABILITY

Let's suppose that you have narrowed the project down to two versions of the scope. It is useful now to consider what roles each organization will play in a version of the project. In order to define roles and responsibilities, you can employ the table in Fig. 2.5. This table identifies each role in the first column. In the second column you enter the headquarters role. In the last column the role of the location or business unit is placed.

Often, everything will move along smoothly until you present this table. People start to get excited because they start to see the impact of the project on them and their people and other resources. You can use these tables to support the trade-offs in scope.

You are not finished yet. Given the roles and responsibilities, each business unit and headquarters have to define resources needed as well as any issues related to resource availability.

Specific role/responsibility	Headquarters	Remote locations/business units

Figure 2.5   Roles and Responsibilities for an Alternative Version of an International Project

- Land acquisition
- Construction materials
- Consultants
- Contractors
- Facilities work
- Infrastructure work
- Networking and communications
- Hardware
- Software
- Travel-related expenses
- Staffing

Figure 2.6   Examples of Cost Elements

- Reduced labor costs in operations
- Reduced utilities and other facilities costs
- Increased revenue from the same customers
- Increased revenue from new customers
- Reduced errors
- Improved quality
- Improved productivity
- Reduced training costs
- Reduced staffing
- Reduced staff turnover

Figure 2.7   Examples of Benefits

ESTIMATE COSTS, BENEFITS, AND THE SCHEDULE

Of course, you cannot do these estimates with precision. That requires the development of the project plan. Here you will develop estimates based upon past projects for the costs and the schedule. This is another reason for developing lessons learned from experience. To assist in doing the estimates, you should develop lists of potential costs and benefits. Examples are given in Figs. 2.6 and 2.7, respectively.

IDENTIFY POTENTIAL ISSUES FOR THE PROJECT

Go to the table of contents and look at the contents of the last four chapters. Lists of specific issues are given that are covered in these chapters. You will want to start with these and add to them. To help you, consider generating issues in the following categories:

- Organization;
- Management;
- Systems and technology;
- Customers;
- Suppliers and vendors;
- Project work;
- Project staffing and leadership;
- External factors such as laws, regulation, and competition.

Note that there are also negative benefits that you must consider. These are the answers to the following questions.

- What will happen if the project is not carried out?
- How could the resources be utilized otherwise?
- What will happen if the project is deferred?

What is the purpose of generating a list of potential issues? One reason is political. You desire to ensure that management has a realistic idea of what lies ahead. This will dampen expectations.

A second reason is to employ the issues to discuss how to resolve issues. It is absolutely critical that people agree on an approach for resolving issues early before issues start to arise and become pressing. It is difficult, if not impossible, to develop a consistent method for issues management while at the same time solving major issues across the globe.

DETERMINE PROJECT INTERDEPENDENCIES

Projects tend to be interdependent in many potential ways. In this action you will work to identify the other projects that your project concept links to, how they depend upon each other, and what the potential issues and problems are. You can then add these issues to others in the previous section.

Here are some ways two projects can interrelate.

- They share the same resources. This creates resource conflicts.
- They employ the same network or technology. This can create a load and stress on the network and other resources.

- They contradict each other in terms of policies, procedures, or organization.
- The results of one project are necessary for the other project to be successful.
- They compete for the same limited pool of available funds.
- The projects together exact too much stress and load on the employees or management in one or more locations.

Now create a table. Yes, another table. The rows and columns of the table are the projects—both current and new. The table entry is the way in which two projects (for the corresponding row and column) interrelate.

Let's consider an example. Suppose that there are two projects going on in three countries. One is network expansion and upgrading (called A). A second is a project that has been started to upgrade employee skills through training (called B). The third is the project concept for a new human resource system (called C). Figure 2.8 gives the table. Note that the diagonal is always blank since it corresponds to the row and column being the same project. Both B and C require the network and also people resources. The training and upgrading of staff skills will have to be dome again when C is carried out.

This table helps management to understand competing demands among projects.

PRESENT THE PROJECT CONCEPT

Now you have to gain approval and consensus from management for the international project. Let's start with how you go about working with management. In collecting the information on the current situation, you started to create grass

Projects	A	B	C
A	—	Needs resources that will be involved in the training	Potential resource conflict
B	Will use the network	—	Potential resource conflict
C	Needs the new network	Will require more training—overlap possible	—

Figure 2.8   Project Interdependence Table Example

roots support. With the development of the project concept, you can now involve management in trade-offs related to purpose, scope, roles, etc. This gets management involved and moves them toward commitment.

You also will have to present the project concept. Here is an outline to follow. Notice that there is no mention of the technical approach for the project. There is probably little interest, understanding, or time for this.

- Overview of the current situation. Here you highlight some of the issues and problems today.
- Impact if the issues and problems are not solved and the project is not undertaken.
- Benefits and effects of the project after it is completed.
- Costs and schedule of the project.
- Roles and responsibilities.
- Action items.

Does this outline look familiar? It should! It follows the general structure of successful television commercials.

MULTIPLE PROJECTS AND THE PROJECT SLATE

The discussion in this section has focused on single projects. A trade-off approach has been defined to determine the most appropriate project concept for an international project. However, in the real world there are multiple projects that are reviewed and approved at the same time. The same approach can be extended to multiple projects.

The real world is a political world where there are multiple projects, hidden agendas, and trade-offs. It is better to make trade-offs in a proactive way. The project slate is the set of approved projects at a particular point in time.

Here are the steps to follow:

- Step 1: Identify potential projects at both the local and international level.
- Step 2: Undertake to develop project concepts for each of the projects with the most promise.
- Step 3: Collect the roles and resource requirements for the projects.
- Step 4: Prepare a resource analysis table.
- Step 5: Perform trade-offs and select which projects are to go ahead and which of the current projects should be cancelled.

What is a resource analysis table? A format appears in Fig. 2.9. In this figure the locations or business units are listed as rows in the first column. In the second

Locations/business units	Regular work		Current projects		New projects

Figure 2.9   Resource Analysis Table

column comments about nonproject work are entered. The next set of columns is for the major current projects. The third set of columns is for new projects. The entries in the table for these columns are comments about resources and resource requirements.

How do you employ this table? Well, much of life is a "zero-sum" game. That is, there are only so many resources. If you allocate a resource to one project, it is really not available for other projects. The purpose of this table is to actively support trade-offs between projects and regular work with regard to resources.

A fundamental lesson learned for us has been that companies embark on international projects without performing this kind of trade-off analysis. Projects are approved individually without regard for the available resources. You have to look at the available resources and what has already been committed before you can commit to more projects. This is a basic point of the book. This theme will return again and again in almost all chapters. If resources are not proactively considered in approving projects, here are some of the major problems that are likely to occur.

• A new project will be approved. When work begins, each location and business unit will be forced to make on-the-spot trade-offs. What is more important? To finish the current project; to complete other work; or to start another project? From the wording it is clear that the new project loses.

• The new project will begin to cause a ripple effect. Problems in other projects due to resource shortages will start appearing. It is as if starting the new international project is like casting a stone in a lake—the effects emanate out from where the stone hit the water.

That is why you must work to sell the new project to management and employees at the local as well as headquarters levels. That is also why you want to encourage people to review current projects and kill off those that are not making progress or that will not produce substantial benefits.

MANAGEMENT REVIEW AND APPROVAL OF INTERNATIONAL PROJECTS

There are many good project ideas that never get supported. Why? Because people want management to approve everything. What is everything?

- Approval of the project as a good idea.
- Approval of funding for the project.
- Approval of resources for the project.

It is asking a lot to ask someone to approve all of this without further analysis. That is why you should get approval for the idea now and pave the way for more analysis. You can identify the project leaders and develop the plan. This can lead to funding. The third stage is for management then to determine where the resources are going to come from. That is why resource issues are so important. You can approve something and throw money at it. But that does not make the project come true. You have to obtain the resources for the project.

EXAMPLES

SAMBAC ENERGY

At Sambac upper management came from the two owner companies in alternate years. In the previous chapter the differences in culture and style between the two companies was noted. When an entrepreneur manager was in charge, projects were initiated without much preplanning. The local in-country employees and managers had little direction. Projects would get started, but few would finish successfully. Some projects became sidetracked into purposes that were totally different from the original purpose.

When the next manager appeared from the other company, all projects would stop and be subjected to review. Since this manager was used to a more bureaucratic approach, mountains of paperwork had to be generated to start a project. This took so long that many projects were not completed at the end of the year. And the cycle started all over again.

This example points out the need for a structured method for defining projects. However, the method cannot be excessively bureaucratic due to the cultures in many countries where the focus is on the short-term. The approach in this chapter was employed to analyze each project and to select which projects should go ahead.

At Sambac the method for overall project selection and the project slate was also implemented. This resulted in many benefits, including:

• The transition of management from Alpha to Beta and vice versa was made easier since the analysis of the project slate was carried out and made available to each country.

• There was a more active effort to kill off projects. People became aware that just because a project was underway, there was no protection for it from being cancelled if it was not progressing satisfactorily.

WHITMORE BANK

As you recall from Chapter 1, Whitmore wants to deploy credit card operations in a number of countries. This is a very large project involving many elements. To give you an idea of the complexity here is a simplified list of areas.

• Implement a modern data center and systems for credit card.
• Implement authorization networks.
• Establish an organization structure for credit card in each country.
• Identify potential customers.
• Develop marketing campaigns.

This was first considered as one large project. It became impossible for management to cope with. The decision was made to create subprojects that interrelated. How this was set up is a subject of Chapter 5.

E-BUSINESS EXAMPLE

An international construction firm decided to embark on e-business. An initial problem was to define the direction. Where to go—business to consumer, business to business, or intranets? Rather than argue endlessly, several alternative purposes were defined along with relevant specifications of scope. As a result of trade-offs, it was decided that internal intranets along with some business to business offered the best opportunity. Business to consumer was deferred until the consumer market increased.

LESSONS LEARNED

• It is important to review all projects as well as project candidates on a regular basis. In traditional business this was performed once per year. This is no longer sufficient. The world is more dynamic. Management is besieged with new projects all of the time. If the period of time between project reviews is too long, then there is a greater danger of new projects being started one at a time. Therefore, the project review and setting of the project slate should be carried out more often—three to four times per year.

• This book focuses on multiple as well as single projects. Projects tend to interrelate and have interdependencies. That is why an important part of the project analysis is to identify how projects relate to each other.

EXERCISES

1. For a project idea define several technical, business, and political purposes. Then work to see how these align to each other.
2. Take a specific project idea and define both a narrow and wide version of scope. Then develop the spider chart as was shown.

SUMMARY

A basic point in this chapter has been that you cannot consider a single potential international project in a vacuum. It must be seen in the context of other projects and nonproject activities. That is why substantial space and time was devoted to multiple projects and the project slate. While we examine and work on single projects in each chapter, the overriding theme and concern is for the slate of projects.

Chapter 3

Identify the Project Leaders

INTRODUCTION

Catching your breath, you have developed the project concept and have an understanding of the relationship between the international project and other work. You also have identified a number of potential and likely issues that will have to be faced in the project. Management has given a tentative approval to find a project leader, identify team members, structure the project, and develop the plan.

The first action now is to define the management structure for the project. How the project will be organized comes later. Here you will be concerned with the number, type, and roles of project leaders for the work. The second action is then to move ahead to determine who the project leaders should be. Look how different this is than the standard project. In a standard project, you just chose the project leader and got started. It is not that simple. In addition to dealing with coordination across multiple locations or business units, you have to be concerned with politics. If you pick the wrong people, you may cripple the project from the start.

PURPOSE AND SCOPE

TECHNICAL PURPOSE

The technical purposes are to define a workable project management structure and to select qualified project leaders. The two words that should catch your eye are "workable" and "qualified." The project leaders have to be qualified in terms of the project. This does not mean that they are technical or engineering geniuses. That can just get in the way. The project leaders will have to be able to cope with both local and regional or global issues and situations.

BUSINESS PURPOSE

The business purpose is to determine a project management approach that will handle issues and be flexible to deal with situations that arise during the work in the international project. If you create a bureaucratic structure or, at the other extreme, if you ignore setting this up and go by "the seat of your pants," you will run into trouble. You will have to start inventing rules and structure as you go in a reactive mode.

Another business purpose is to obtain project leaders who can handle situations on their own without constant interference and support. Even with modern communications, it is valuable to have project leaders who can think on their feet and resolve problems.

POLITICAL PURPOSE

The political purpose of this chapter is significant. Here are some specific goals:

• Managers have to buy into and accept as well as understand the project management structure. In this way, they will be less likely to undermine it later. This also means that they will have to have a role in its definition.

• The individuals selected to lead the project have to be respected by not only headquarters, but also the people at the locations. Otherwise, the authority of the project leaders will be undermined.

Note that for all of these purposes, there is nothing said about getting the "best" project leaders. After a combined total of over 40 years in project management, we have yet to be able to define the term "best." You can, however, define "acceptable" and "good."

END PRODUCTS

There are three basic end products here. The first is the project management structure. This structure reveals how the project will be controlled and work will be coordinated. It also defines how issues and problems will be addressed. It is insufficient to just define it; people have to understand and support it—not just pay lip service to it.

The second end product is to identify the project leaders at both the overall project level and the detailed levels. The third end product is for the project leaders to work together to understand how they will carry out and support the project management structure. Doesn't do much good to define something if people don't understand the ramifications of what it means.

APPROACH

PROJECT MANAGEMENT FOR INTERNATIONAL PROJECTS

Let's turn to a discussion of managing projects on an international level. There are multiple cultures involved. Knowledge is required at the headquarters and local levels. The project leaders have to have management contacts at both the headquarters and local levels. The project leader role has to be able to be nice and firm. This means that project leadership requires both the good guy and bad guy roles. Some people call these "white hat" and "black hat" roles, respectively.

It is important to have two project leaders for any substantial international project.

It should now be clear why you want to have multiple project leaders—both overall and at the local level. Figure 3.1 gives some of the reasons and benefits for multiple project leaders. Some of you in reading this are likely to say that it is unworkable because there is a lack of accountability. You achieve accountability by enforcing the rule that at any time one person is in charge. The benefits of having multiple project leaders are overwhelming. A benefit that is not listed in the table is that there is a cumulative effect. That is, as you employ the approach,

- Knowledge of the work and projects is widened.
- Junior project leaders advance their skills at a more rapid pace.
- There is more commonality in the approach to project work.

MANAGEMENT STRUCTURE FOR INTERNATIONAL PROJECTS

In this book we will consider a management structure and an administrative structure. The management structure pertains to how the international projects

Factor	Approach	Comment
Accountability	Single point of responsibility at any point in time	Achieves control goals
Skills	Different people have different skills	Take advantage of different experience
Perspective	Multiple project leaders have different perspectives	Catches problems early
Level of abilities	Junior leaders can be paired up with experienced managers	Provides for apprenticeship
Range of knowledge	Wider range of knowledge is available	Goes with skills and perspective
Backup	Multiple leaders provide backup	If the project is important, this is critical
Elapsed time	Multiple project leaders allow you to phase in new leaders	Provides for continuity
Black hat and white hat	Two project leaders can play different roles	If one person did this, they might be viewed as insane
Political contacts	Each person has different contacts	Less likely to burn bridges with one manager
Areas of knowledge	Greater flexibility in having one technically oriented person	Allows you to take advantage of technical people

Figure 3.1 Benefits of Multiple Project Leaders in an International Project

are directed and managed. The administrative structure deals with specific techniques involved in the projects. Examples of administrative structure include project reporting, standardized project files, project communications, project templates, issues management, and lessons learned coordination. These topics will be addressed in the following three chapters.

A two-tiered management oversight approach provides flexibility.

An effective project management structure has proven to be the use of a steering committee. A steering committee is a management committee that oversees substantial projects. In international projects there is often more complexity and organization structure to deal with. It is for these reasons that two levels of steer-

Upper-Level Steering Committee

Members: High-level in-country managers
                Headquarters managers
Mission: Oversee the direction of the project
Specific duties:
- Review and deal with issues that the lower-level committee cannot address
- Provide the basis for appeal in the event of problems
- Approve funding and resources

Lower-Level Steering Committee

Members: Some headquarters managers
                Local, in-country managers are in the majority
                Selected members of the project team
Mission: Oversee the details of the implementation of the project
Specific duties:
- Approve specific resource assignment
- Approve the use of technology in the project
- Address local problems and issues
- Resolve priority issues between the project and other work in country
- Provide continuity between the project team and upper management

Figure 3.2 Activities and Makeup of International Project Steering Committees

ing committees are recommended. One is the traditional steering committee. The second committee, to which the steering committee reports, is the executive committee. Figure 3.2 lists the duties of the steering committees and their members along with the respective missions.

Why have two committees? First, if there is only one committee, there is less flexibility for placing management. Both middle managers and upper level managers have to be on the same committee. Politically, this can cause the upper level managers to bail up and be replaced by subordinates. There is no middle link between upper management and the project team—issues that the team cannot cope with are taken up to the steering committee. If there are two levels, there is the opportunity to sort out issues without going to upper management in the executive committee. Two committees can provide political cover for the project team as well.

The two committees also give project flexibility. If there is one thing that international projects need, it is flexibility. You can organize the lower-level committee by region, country, function, or activity. How you organize it can support your cultural goals in the project. For example, if you want each country to work on its own, then the committees can be established in each country. If you want to instill greater collaboration and cooperation between countries, then you can organize the lower-level committee by functions. Having two levels also allows you to have multiple lower-level steering committees.

EXAMPLE: TITAN BROADCASTING

In one situation the project goal was to implement direct satellite to business broadcasting in a nineteen-country region. The initial plan called for a sequential approach that would have taken three years. It was decided to try to speed this up. The problem was how to organize the project so that this could be accomplished. The two-tiered committee structure was established. There was one high-level executive committee. In the lower-level committee, it was decided to establish several committees based on function. The functions included government relations (getting permits, etc.); construction; television and signal transmission; and programming (what would be shown). These committees were established across the region. Since having 19 members for each committee is unwieldy, the approach was to identify one person to represent 3–4 countries. This turned out to be successful. The structure encouraged parallel effort. The overall project team acted to coordinate the implementation across all of the functions. Had the sequential approach been adopted, the first step would have been government approvals. After this, construction would have begun. Then television and programming would have kicked in. By establishing the committees in parallel, the project pace was accelerated.

How does the management structure work? There are both informal and formal channels. Informally, you seek to have project leaders establish direct informal contacts with members of both committees. Formally, the steering committee for the project deals with more tactical issues and problems. They approve how things are to be done and more detailed results and benefits. The executive committee, by way of contrast, meets less often and deals with reviewing and approving what is to be done as well as overall results.

WHAT TO LOOK FOR IN A PROJECT LEADER

In order to understand what you need in an international project leader, you must first understand some of the situations and barriers that such a person will face. Here are some of the pressures, duties, and other factors that we have gathered from project leaders in over 45 major projects:

- Time zone differences create havoc in dealing with problems.
- When you are traveling, it is difficult to stay in touch.
- There are many family pressures when you are working on an international project.
- Even when people speak the same language, the meanings are very different.

• People in the country prepare too well for your visit so that it is difficult to get at the truth of the work.

• After you leave a country, you find out about all of the hidden issues.

• It is difficult to deal with the politics at headquarters and the individual political situation in each location.

• Management in a location pays lip service to the project, but does not give it the right or even adequate resources.

• It is difficult to coordinate the work of the team, consultants, and local management.

• It is difficult to track issues and problems to see that they are handled when there are so many things going on at one time.

As you can see from the list, identifying one person as a project leader would lead you to select Superman or Superwoman. Given you have to deal with real people with their limitations and assets, you must center your attention on the most important attributes. Let's try to identify some of the most important general attributes and then move down to the details.

• *Problem-solving ability.* From our experience, this one has to rank very high. Managing even small international projects often means dealing with problems, issues, and opportunities. But there is more here than you might think. It includes the ability to sense and detect problems, know when to leave problems alone, know how to do research and investigate problems, and know how to get problems solved with the appropriate actions and decisions.

• *Ability to cope in multiple cultures.* You might think that this refers to the country culture. That is only one of the cultures. There is also the company culture in the country. Then there is the culture in a specific department—in part generated by the personality of the department manager and what the department does. Can you as a project manager know about all of these cultures as you manage the project? Of course not. However, you must be sensitive to the various cultures that are present. Be ready to learn and listen to what people say.

• *Tenacity and the capability of pursuing issues, etc.* Although this relates to problem solving, the tenacity is required in international projects, because it is often the case that an issue is not fully understood. There is often much ambiguity in what is a problem. It is a matter of culture and interpretation. You have to get behind what is being said, how it is being said, and the situation in which it is being said. In some projects, it took us over a month to run an issue to ground and to fully understand it. The final interpretation was much different than what was expected at the start. What is stated as a problem in one location may be really something very different due to what you learn in another location.

• *Ability to communicate.* It would be nice to be functional in many languages. And it is too bad that many people know only one language. What is meant here is the ability to get your sentences and thoughts across in a clear and unambiguous way. It is also the ability to listen to what people are telling you. We have found that these qualities can go a long way even if you do not speak a foreign language. In terms of picking up foreign terms, it is probably easier in projects to work on the written, rather than the spoken word. You find that in most industries a base of about 50–100 words will keep recurring in projects.

• *A sense of humor.* It is extremely important to be able to laugh and enjoy a project—even when the times are difficult. Both of us have found a sense of humor to be very useful politically as well. You have to be able to step out of the project and situation and look at things from the big picture view. This should help you see something funny about it.

• *Familiarity and knowledge of the business.* Here a knowledge of the basic business processes and how things get done is useful. In-depth knowledge about a specific department or function can actually impede your work since it may give you a bias.

• *Prior experience in projects.* It is not necessary to have headed up a large number of projects previously. However, you should have worked in projects and participated in project activity. Hopefully, you were in projects that were not successful so you have an idea of what can go wrong.

TYPICAL DUTIES FOR AN INTERNATIONAL PROJECT LEADER

Since there are an infinite number and type of international projects, there is not one detailed list. However, from observing and participating in many projects, you can identify some of the key duties.

• *Definition of the project.* In many international projects, the project leaders are named before the project is really underway. The project leaders would then work to define the project concept elements discussed in the preceding chapter. Remember that the political purpose here is to get consensus on the project at different levels—local and headquarters. Defining the project is a good test of a project leader since you are meeting people for the first time and you are dealing with a situation and project that has not yet been defined in detail. Dealing with ambiguity and politics are important here. Communications is a must.

• *Project organization.* Here you are identifying team members, organizing the project, getting approvals, and kicking off the work. This tests the project leaders' analytical ability to assess people's skills and fit with the project. It tests the organizing ability to deal with getting the plan put together and work started.

• *Dealing with the routine work.* This includes the administrative work in the project. Communicating with management is key here. In addition, being able to get behind what people are saying about their work to learn the true status of the project is important. Experience has shown this to be a source of failure in that the project leaders were not able to identify problems early enough so that the problems blew up.

• *Addressing issues and crises.* Almost every international project has many issues and opportunities arise. There are also crises. What is a crisis? A crisis occurs when a group of issues become dominant factors in the project at the same time. For example, several key people leave the team at the same time that management wants to have the schedule of the project moved up.

• *Doing real work in the project.* A project leader in an international project must lead by example. That is, he or she must demonstrate to the team that he/she can get in there and do work on the project with the best of them. That is why the term "project leader" is employed much more than "project manager."

• *Administrative coordination.* People working on an international team often encounter problems that the average project never faces. While the project leader is not responsible, the leader ends up doing a lot of support and coordination. Here are some things that can occur:

— A team member does not have a valid passport.
— A team member requires a visa for travel in two days; you have been told by the travel people that it takes three days to get a business visa.
— Team members run out of money while traveling. Or they become maxed out on their credit cards.
— A team member is on an extended stay in a foreign country. His travel reimbursements are not being processed fast enough.
— Civil unrest breaks out in a city and you have to extract some of the team members.
— A team member has to get a series of shots and inoculations prior to a trip, but there is not enough time.
— A team member becomes ill on a trip.

This sounds like the project leader is playing the role of a mother hen to the team. Well, it is true. Who else is the team member going to turn to for support? Here is also a political lesson learned. If you help your team members in these things, they will be very grateful and give you and the project that extra effort that can make the difference.

A key trait that cross all of these duties is the sensitivity to the people in the project and interfacing to the project team. The project leader must show a great deal of sensitivity because of the following factors. These are important lessons learned for any project leader:

• The people on the team typically have many other duties to perform. Their pay and rating is tied to these duties and not to your project.

• Many of the people have not worked on a project like yours or even any project. They are unsure of what to do.

• Everyone is afraid of making mistakes and screwing up. So many people tend to remain silent and avoid volunteering. Don't make the mistake of assuming silence to mean understanding.

• The culture in the country and organization does not encourage initiative or creativity. Do not assume that people lack creativity. It is your challenge to find ways to open the people's abilities up. This has been one of our greatest satisfactions in managing international projects. People themselves grow and benefit through the project. That makes all of the travel, hotels, airports, and hard work worthwhile.

Duties evolve over time in a project. At the start, the challenge is to organize the project and get it correctly started. Then the day-to-day management of issues and work goes on. As the project progresses, there will typically be more outside pressures that the project leader must cope with. Here are some of the factors:

• People are taken from the project due to being needed elsewhere. Most often, this is for nonproject work such as year-end closing, etc.

• Management wants the project sped up and finished. This is normal and should have been expected on day one when the project started.

• Project issues tend to recur and combine later in the project so that there tend to be more crises at the back end of the project.

How does managing a small international project differ from managing a large project? One difference is that the larger project tends to last longer. This entails more risk. A second difference is that more people are involved—which means more coordination. A third difference means that there are more potential political problems and more management oversight to cope with. However, when all is said and done, the basic duties are the same.

What is a good mix of time across major activities? Of course, this varies by the project and the time or phase of the project. However, here is a general percentage list that has proven useful as a target:

• Dealing with issues and opportunities—40–50%
• Communicating with management, team, and others—30–40%
• Doing work in the project—10–15%
• Administrative work in the project—10–20%

Notice that the emphasis is on the issues and communications. These are much more important than administrative work in an international project. In traditional project management, administrative work can consume up to 70% of the time.

WHAT TO AVOID IN A PROJECT LEADER

There are some attributes to avoid in a project leader. Here are a few from experience:

- The project leader who loves the administrative side of the project work. This person almost avoids doing real work in the project. This can really turn people off.
- Not listening to people and jumping to conclusions and findings. This can be very dangerous politically in a project and may then later cause more effort to be spent in undoing the negative impacts.
- Being domineering. This is one that we have seen a great deal. The person arrives from headquarters to the company that was just acquired. He has the attitude that "he is there to straighten these people out." That is about the worst and very common problem that project leaders have.
- Trying to impose methods or tools used in one location in another without adequate analysis. This is a major problem in that people often think that since their methods have worked elsewhere, they will work someplace entirely different. Not true. Most methods and how tools are used have to be adapted to the specific setting.
- Focusing on areas where the person is comfortable rather than on areas of risk and issues where there are problems and where the project leader is really needed.

PROJECT LEADER SELECTION

How do you evaluate and select people for project leadership? Putting it another way, you have been given a stack of resumes of people who want to manage the project. What do you do? Evaluation starts with defining the approach to interview and assess the candidates. Here are some guidelines for international projects:

- Ask them about the issues and problems they addressed in the past. How did they handle them? This is very important since you are testing their problem solving ability.
- Ask about political problems. Find out how they identified and dealt with political factors. This reveals their sensitivity and awareness of political factors.

- Ask what key things they learned from their past work and how they put it to use. This helps test their ability to learn and improve. This also gives you an idea of what was learned from project failure and success.
- Pose several situations from your own projects. You might include some of the things we have mentioned earlier in this chapter. See how they respond. How quick are they on their feet in dealing with issues?
- If you are seeking some specific area of skills such as finance or engineering, then rather than ask about general experience, you should pose a situation in that field and see how they respond.

Experience over the years has shown that this approach has gotten to the person's strengths and weaknesses far better than asking about items on their resumes.

How do you evaluate and select a project leader after doing the evaluation? Follow a two-pronged approach. For each candidate rate their suitability in terms of the criteria that was mentioned in the previous sections. This gives you a rating of their strengths.

Now turn it around. Go for the weaknesses and risk. For each candidate identify three areas where they are weak and where the project would be at risk. This gives you the negative side of the coin. Many times this is more important than the strengths.

For multiple project leaders, you can probe and consider more criteria related to the specific business or technical functions, experience in the country, etc. Again, this reveals the benefit of going with two project leaders.

An even more proactive step is to seek out people who would be good project leader candidates. Often, these people have not even thought of being project leaders. What do you probe for to see if these people are suitable and interested? Here are some questions:

- Can they work with limited supervision? This relates to initiative.
- Can they be extracted from their current work? This is a good test since it considers the ability of the person to turn over work and whether they are willing to make a major change.

HOW TO SUCCEED AS A PROJECT LEADER

You have already seen some of the key success factors in the list of what to look for in a project leader. Let's expand on success. Success means building up a pattern of dealing with issues. People tend to have more confidence in you since you have dealt with many issues before.

Try to read up on the culture and history of the country. Learn what political and economic issues are hot in the country ahead of time. You will not want to discuss these in-depth because you will likely not have sufficient accurate knowledge, but you will be showing sensitivity. In one country that had been through a long military rule, we showed sympathy for the need for stability.

By plunging in and doing work in the project wherever you are geographically, people tend to respect you more. They see you getting your hands dirty. Related to this you have to socialize with the team members and managers in each country. You should dress in the attire appropriate to that office after you have been there for a day or two. Politically, it is useful to show up in formal attire the first day and then to dress as a local on the second day. This shows respect for the working culture.

Eat and drink what the local people consume. Do not be overly picky—you risk raising resentment. Socialize with them when they visit your home office. Try to remember birthdays and anniversaries. Send paper cards and letters—not just e-mail—it means a lot more and shows that you went to greater effort and expense.

Success also must be achieved in dealing with managers. Follow the same guidelines as for the team in the country. In addition, try to communicate with upper-level managers informally on a regular basis. When you visit a country go to the manager of the office several times—not just at the start and the end. Find out what other projects and work are going on. This is useful for several reasons. First, you are getting a better understanding of what you are competing with in terms of your project. Second, you can probably help in any resource allocation issue if you better understand what is going on in addition to the project.

HOW TO FAIL AS A PROJECT LEADER

Failure can take many forms. The project could succeed, but you failed as a leader. Both you and the project failed. There are many variations in between. In international projects, there is often more turnover of project leaders due to problems. In many international projects, there is often no alternative but to finish the project—with different leadership.

Here is a list from observations of how some project leaders failed:

• The project leader was insensitive to local needs and demands on the staff.
• The project leader took the view of corporate and tried to boss the local people around.
• The leader assumed that he/she had more authority than he/she really had. Overstepping authority bounds is a frequent cause of failure as a project leader.
• Not being sensitive to issues and not dealing with issues on a timely basis. As a result, the issues grow and become more severe over time.

• Being inflexible in terms of the project when the scope, needs, and requirements change.
• Being inflexible in terms of changes at the local level. This can be due to economic or political factors. Or it can be success where a plant must gear up to do more production.

THE SCORE CARD FOR THE PROJECT LEADER

The use of score cards has always been a good idea for regular measurement. Later in the book you will see score cards for a project, for department participation, and for consultants and contractors. Figure 3.3 contains a score card for the project leader. You should evaluate yourself on a regular basis. Also, use this list as a starting point. As you review the list, you can see that some of the factors are subjective. This is by intent since project management is not a science; rather, it deals with the world of politics and personalities.

How often should a project leader be measured? Certainly, not just at the end of the project. If you have a year-long project, then three measurements would be useful. This would give the opportunity to make some changes and improvements when the project is still going on.

MANAGING MULTIPLE PROJECTS

If the discussion of project leadership were to stop here, this would traditionally be in line with other books. However, international projects really benefit

• Number of times that management found out about an issue before being notified by the project leader.
• Focus of project meetings and number of meetings. Here the effort is to measure not only if too much time is being spent on meetings, but if the meetings deal with issues and lessons learned, or status.
• Perceived morale of the team. Here you would talk informally with some of the team members.
• Number of issues and type of issues that remain outstanding and unresolved.
• Major issues that were solved.
• Milestones achieved.
• How the project leader was able to deal with change.
• Extent and quality of communications as perceived by the local management.
• Turnover of the project team members.
• Current state of the project.
• How the project coped with changes in direction and scope.
• Allocation of manager's time.

Figure 3.3 Score Card for a Project Leader

from gathering lessons learned and from building project management capabilities over time. Cumulative effect and benefits are the keys to long-term success in international projects. Your goals for managing international projects extend beyond a specific project and include the following:

• Make project plans more accurate and estimation better through improved project templates. Projects are reviewed during and after the work to improve the project templates.
• Lessons learned are gathered during and after the projects and associated with the project templates. The lessons learned are then applied to work in new projects, generating more experience.
• Experience in dealing with issues grows and people become more aware of what methods work and fail in dealing with issues. The awareness that the same issues recur again and again in international projects grows.

Some would argue that this experience is not really that relevant since each international project is unique. Take construction. Each building project is unique to the situation. The same is true with mergers and acquisitions. Yet, look at the real world. The details are different each time, but the general structure of types of projects is the same. Thus, if you were going to deploy a new purchasing process in four countries, each country could use the same project template, but the detailed plans would be different. Moreover, after you finished in one country with one project, you could learn from this effort to benefit you in the second. The same would be true for the third and fourth. This is true even if the efforts were undertaken in parallel.

The same is true with issues and lessons learned. The same 400–500 issues have been found to recur again and again in projects. Lessons learned gathered about dealing with cultural or political issues tend to remain valid in different situations.

THE PROJECT OFFICE AND THE ROLE OF PROJECT COORDINATOR

If keeping experience is a good idea, then the problem becomes one of how best to gather, retain, and organize the information. One method is to employ a project office. A project office is a centralized group in an organization that is concerned with projects across the corporation—not just the international projects. However, project offices sometimes fail because they become too bureaucratic. They also fail because the people in the project office are only schedulers and have not managed a real world project.

Is there another approach that can work better? Experience shows that the use of a project coordination role is very useful. To be effective the position of project coordinator should rotate among different organizations and people. In this way, it will have less of a chance of becoming bureaucratic. What is the role of project coordination?

• *Analysis of multiple projects.* The project coordinator rolls up the information for multiple projects and presents it to management.

• *Initial analysis of issues and questions posed by management.* A central lead is needed to follow up on issues and problems that are defined by management and have to be coordinated across multiple projects.

• *Organizing the project files and project history.* This seems like a mundane and routine job, but it is significant. Project history tends to get lost in the rush of other work. Here the project coordinator oversees a library of completed projects for future reference.

• *Oversight of the lessons learned and issues databases.* These databases have been defined and will be addressed in more detail later. Obviously, for any database there must be someone who oversees the quality, completeness, and accuracy of the information.

• *Identification of new, potential project leaders.* The project coordinator can help to identify, evaluate, and recommend candidates for project leaders for international projects.

• *Support and mentoring of project leaders in the field.* Project leaders are often on their own. Even with having two project leaders per project, there are times when some outside help and guidance can be useful. That is the purpose of this role.

EXAMPLES

SAMBAC ENERGY

Sambac attempted to do project leader rotation for many years. That is, in one year a manager from Alpha would arrive to run the office and projects. The following year someone from Beta would come to manage. As was discussed in the first chapter, the two companies operate with very different cultures. In one there is encouragement to be entrepreneurial. In the other, the organization is hierarchical. Thus, one manager would tend to make decisions and take action. In the following year, the entire pattern would change and decisions would go back to headquarters for analysis.

This created many problems with projects as well as with the local employees. Many projects extended beyond one year. The original estimates of time and budget would have to be thrown out of the window due to the change of management and a different management style. Projects were not the only things in turmoil. The local managers and staff would often receive contradictory instructions from the new manager.

There was also no overlap of managers. In some cases, the manager who had been there would leave before the new manager arrived. In other cases, the overlap was minimal. With all of this it is in a way a miracle that anything got done. The salvation was that much of the work was daily production work that went on in the same manner. That kept the money rolling in.

As time went by, the nature and seriousness of the problems began to be understood by both firms. However, there was no real incentive to address the issue. Finally, since the two companies could not deal with it at headquarters, they assigned someone to go out and address the issue locally.

The first recommendation was to implement local management as senior leaders under the expatriate manager. This gave more stability to the organization and more local accountability for the projects. The effects and benefits were almost immediate. With more stable project environments, projects began to be completed at a higher rate. Both schedules and budgets were met more often.

With this success, the next step was to define the role of the expatriate manager in more detail. There were many larger potential projects that spanned several years that were promising, but had not been given attention due to the management situation. It was recommended that the expatriate managers focus on these longer-term projects. Again, this was successful.

A final recommendation was to address the problem of lack of overlap. The recommendation here was to have a 3-month overlap so that the new manager could get up to speed on the work. Another benefit was to have shared management over the large projects. Today, this has been extended further. There are now two managers at all times. They overlap each other by 6 months (a staggered 6 months).

WHITMORE BANK

The initial idea of project management was to appoint one manager from the most technologically advanced country in the region. This was done and seemed to work. After all, this approach reflected the style and approach of management of Whitmore Bank to ensure that there was accountability. However, it soon became clear that there were problems. First, the manager was insensitive culturally to people from the other countries. It turned out that he had traveled very little to these other countries. He also had a domineering personality. Second, the plan and direction came entirely from his office. People at the local level were given no opportunity to give input into the plan. They felt cut out of the loop.

The problems grew worse because the manager was not tracking the work closely. People would generally tell him what he wanted to hear. Needless to say, issues started to grow. The good team members were taken off of the project in different countries since local management saw the effort as a failure. They figured that once headquarters saw the failure, they would replace him and work could really get going. This turned out to be true. Unfortunately, over nine months was wasted in finding this out. The nine months translated into millions of dollars in lost revenue. However, the costs were still there.

What are some of the lessons learned from this example?

- You cannot assume everything is fine even though you hear no complaints. Management at headquarters was overtrusting of the assigned manager and did not verify status of the project.
- Be careful in assigning one local manager to oversee a regional project. Just the same as for assigning someone from headquarters.
- Force the manager to report on issues and problems from the start of the project on an ongoing basis. This gives the basis for tracking work.

Instead of just replacing the manager, the decision was made to institute the two-level steering committee approach presented earlier in this chapter. The executive steering committee included managers from headquarters as well as from each country. The working level steering committees were organized by function across the region. There was a big debate as to whether they should be organized by country. This was rejected (and rightly so) because it would just support more isolation between the offices in the different countries. Steering committees were established for marketing, sales, application processing, payments, servicing, collections, and accounting.

LESSONS LEARNED

- Do not approach international projects in the same way as standard, one-location projects. Project leaders have to become aware of the differences and unique issues involved in international projects. The project coordinator can help in bringing new project leaders up to speed.
- Consider pairing up a junior and senior project leader so that they can share information and skills. What is in it for the senior project leader? One thing is the ability to offload some of the routine work. Another is to have someone to share problems and issues with.
- Have project leaders for international projects get together periodically to share information and notes regarding their projects. Before meeting, their issues and lessons learned could be shared to serve as a basis for the dialogue.
- Collect focused lessons learned related to specific locations, methods, tools, technologies, and types of projects. This can be more valuable.

• Ensure that no project leader is assigned to one location for too long. Rotation is important as the independence of the person is jeopardized if they stay in one place too long.

EXERCISES

1. Look around at several project leaders and try to use the score card for project leaders presented in this chapter. This will help you focus on measurement.

2. Read in the news about some current international projects. Make a list of issues mentioned in the article. Follow the projects over time using the Web. See what happened to the issues.

3. Look at some of the major leaders of firms that do business internationally. Research what their previous experience was. How much time did they spend acting as project leaders?

SUMMARY

Project leadership is different in several ways for international projects. First, there are additional pressures and constraints that are not as severe in single-location projects. Second, political and cultural factors have a major impact. Third, the visibility of the project to management is more pronounced than for regular projects. However, even with this the major qualities of project leaders remain much the same—the ability to identify and solve problems and the capability to communicate.

Chapter 4

Nail Down the Project Organization and Team

INTRODUCTION

In a standard project, the project team consists of individuals with specific skills and/or experience, and those who have specialized business or technical knowledge. It is not as simple as this in international projects. Team members are sometimes assigned to projects for political reasons. There are a number of other differences, including:

- *Collaboration.* There must be more cooperation and collaboration in international projects as many of the tasks are replicated or adapted from one country or location to another.
- *Parallelism.* There are more opportunities for parallel effort since work can be going on simultaneously in multiple locations at one time.
- *Changing requirements.* International projects tend to require different skills at different phases or parts of the project. This leads to more team turnover. Turnover also occurs due to management changes in direction.
- *Conflicts with normal work.* Most international team members are not dedicated to the project. In fact, in the past 20 years, we have had only one project with fully dedicated resources. People have to do major parts of their regular job in addition to work on the project.
- *Semiautonomous work.* In a standard project in one location, the project leader can oversee the detailed work of the team members. This is not practical or possible in international projects. Even with e-mail and the telephone, you are only marginally in touch.

A suitable method for team management must reflect these realities for international projects. Managing an international project in the traditional manner can lead to many problems that will be discussed in this chapter.

PURPOSE AND SCOPE

TECHNICAL PURPOSE

The technical goal is to assemble and organize a team that will produce success for the international project. This sounds really good. Underneath this general purpose are several more specific objectives, including:

- There must be a smooth transition of personnel and work in the project.
- The project must be organized so that the team is stable and that people are not pulled off of the project for other work.
- Work must be done in the project in such a way that minimal reviews are required. In an international project, you must have reviews, but these must be selective given the effort, time, and expense.
- There must be a high degree of communications among the team members and with the project leaders. Otherwise, issues and questions might linger for weeks without people being aware of this.

BUSINESS PURPOSE

Start at the local level of the team. One business goal is that the team covers the areas of the project adequately in terms of skills and experience. Another business goal is that they work in a collaborative way and do substantial joint work in the project. A third purpose is that there be something in it for them. That is, they will benefit from doing work in the project in terms of their self-interest.

At the level of the specific country location, the goal is the project does not disrupt the normal work of the departments. This factor is often ignored in international projects where the project leaders assume that since management of the organization overall wants the project, it is *automatic* that each location should devote its best resources and efforts to the project. Not really true. This was not true in ancient Roman times and certainly not true today. Each location has its own business goals—the attainment of which requires resources.

Now move up to the level of the organization overall. The business objective is to ensure that the benefits of the project are achieved within the limits of the budget and schedule. In support of this another related goal is that the project will support greater sharing of knowledge and information as well as cooperation across the organization.

POLITICAL PURPOSE

The team must be aware of the politics involved in the various locations in which the work in the international project is being performed. Politics are at work at headquarters, locally, and between locations. You almost need a roadmap to see through the "Byzantine world" of some organizations. So then, what is the political purpose? The political purpose is to ensure that there are minimal political problems that affect the performance of the team and the work of the project. More positively, the goal is to ensure that people understand how the project will benefit them as well as the organization at large.

SCOPE

Normally, you would expect the scope to be restricted to the team members— their selection, their work, their management, and their collaboration. However, in modern international projects, this is not sufficient to guarantee success. You have to include the following factors in the scope:

• Local offices, activities, and management. As was stated earlier, this cannot be ignored.
• Long-term goals and aspirations of the team members. You really have to think about how the work in the project can help the individual team members.
• Working relationships between headquarters and the local offices. The hope is that the work in the project will facilitate better relationships between people at headquarters and the local offices.

END PRODUCTS

The end products of managing the project team consist of the following:

• The project obtains for team membership people who are qualified and supportive of the project.
• The team members can effectively work in the project and do their normal work.
• The team members collaborate and work together effectively—paving the way for an improved culture after the project is completed.

APPROACH

As you saw from the purposes and the scope, the range of things to be considered goes beyond just getting people on the team. In addition, international projects have more risk and potential problems than many one-location projects. These factors point to the need for taking a different approach. You cannot just go out and get team members. You have to first think about where the areas of risk are in the project. Then you can begin to address how to organize the project using the knowledge of where the risk is. After this you can start lining up team members and do work.

IDENTIFY AREAS OF PROJECT RISK

There are chapters in the last part of the book that deal with handling specific risks that you might encounter across an international project. Here we will concentrate on risks that you are likely to meet up with at the start. Some of these, hopefully, will already have been addressed in the work of the project concept addressed in Chapters 1 and 2. Before we begin, the term "risk" should be discussed. Risk is a rather fuzzy concept. It is slightly different to each person. There is a need for a common definition. Throughout the book and for the past two decades, we have used the following definition:

A part of the project such as a task, subproject, or milestone has risk if there is one or more significant issue related to the part of the project.

This definition makes risk more precise. Now earlier in Chapter 2 you defined the project concept, which included identifying potential issues associated with the project. You also defined the general areas of the project. It is now time to associate these. You can use the table in Fig. 4.1. In this figure the first column lists the areas of the project. Some sample areas are given as an example. Then the second column indicates the issues that could arise for that part of the project. The third column contains any comments.

Let's now consider some of the typical issues that you are probably going to encounter.

• Get local management buy-in and support. Almost all local managers will tell you that they will support the project. Talk is cheap, so they say. The real test is whether they are willing to assign resources to the project and participate in managerial work in the project.

• Identify and obtain team members for the project.

Area of the project	Issues	Comments
Starting the project	Getting local management support; lining up local employees	
Project reporting	How to get efficient reporting	
Issues management	How to get issues resolved in a timely and complete manner	
Milestone review	Which milestones to review	
Areas of work in the project		

Figure 4.1 Association of Issues with Areas of the International Project

• Build teamwork and collaboration within the team. This is easier said than done. Many of the problems in international projects stem from talking teamwork, but then not establishing an approach in the team to ensure that collaboration is achieved.

Specific project areas may have risk. This depends on the specific project, but a general area of risk is where two locations have to work together in integrating their work. Examples can be substructures in engineering projects, software programs, business processes, etc.

DEFINE TEAM MEMBER REQUIREMENTS FOR SUCCESS

Once you have identified the areas of risk and associated areas of the project, you are ready to organize the project. In an international project there are different types of team members, including:

• Team members who are key to the project in terms of being required throughout the project and who have to interact with other locations, including headquarters. An example might be a design engineer. These individuals will be called **critical team members**.

• Team members who do work in the project locally that only affects the local part of the project. An example might be someone who performs facilities work to support the project. These people will be referred to as **locally focused team members**. They have limited interaction with headquarters or other locations. Some of these people may be at headquarters as well as local offices.

• Individuals who perform very limited, but significant tasks in the project and then have no other role in the project. These will be called **cameo members**. They walk in and walk out—like a movie.

Note that no distinction was made between employees and contractors. This is by intent. In a team you generally do not distinguish between these in terms of work. Of course, managing contractors or consultants is a major topic in international projects. So there is an entire chapter devoted to this (Chapter 8).

You can now return to the table in Fig. 4.1 and create a new table. In this table you will list the areas of the project in the first column, borrowing from Fig. 4.1. In the second column you will indicate the type of team members required for that part of the project. In the third column you will list specific needs and skill requirements for the personnel in this area. How will you use this? For one thing it will help you when you go to managers and make requests for people for the team. A second use is when you interview the potential team members to determine their fit with the project. The structure of this table is given in Fig. 4.2.

You can also create a table of areas of the project versus skill requirements (see Fig. 4.3). Here the table entry can be an "X" or blank, or you can put in specific requirements. This table is useful when you go to management to indicate the project structure and the types of people you need.

There is a strong political lesson learned here with these two tables. In order to be credible to managers when you start an international project, you must show them that you are organized. This is not just a good project plan and concept; it is also that you are on top of what you require in terms of people. There is also

Project areas	Type of people needed	Specific requirements

Figure 4.2   Types of Team Members Needed by Project Area

Skill areas

Project area			

Figure 4.3   Areas of the Project versus Skills Needed

a business need for preparing these tables—planning the staging of staff. You neither want nor need all of the team members on day 1 of the project. Some people will be entering the project at later stages. So you must have a plan for when these people are needed to be able to arrange for staffing.

ATTRIBUTES OF TEAM MEMBERS

It is not just technical or business knowledge and experience that counts. There are a number of other important attributes for the team that are especially important to international projects. You will want to use this list when you prepare and conduct interviews of potential team members.

Some key attributes for international team members are listed below. To be useful, interview guidelines for each attribute have been included.

• *Experience in terms of projects similar to your project.* This is obviously important. How do you test for this? You can ask for experience, but you are likely to get general words. A better approach is to ask what issues they encountered in their past projects. Also, ask what lessons learned did they get out of the previous project.

• *Previous experience in international projects.* This is similar to the first one. However, you want to probe into their role in the international project. You can make inferences from what they indicate as issues and lessons learned. You are trying to ascertain if they performed critical work or locally focused work. If they did good local work, this is not a sure sign of success in moving up to a critical role in the project.

• *Ability to work with other people on tasks and work.* You will want to test this several ways. You want to ask them what problems they encountered when they worked with other people. If they indicate that there were no problems, then you can probably infer that they did not work much with others. Working with people in foreign countries is never smooth. There should be issues. Another test will occur early in the project.

• *Ability to solve problems and work within the organization.* Problem solving is a critical skill in international projects because there will not always be help immediately at hand. Some critical team members will have to make judgment calls on the spot. Take the issues from the past four chapters and extract two or three of these. Ask them if they have encountered them and what they would do if they were faced with them.

• *Sensitivity to issues and potential problems.* Some people focus entirely on the work. Problems and issues may arise, but they do not give them much attention. Here you can pose specific situations and ask them how they would respond.

- *Availability from their other work to perform tasks on the project.* For almost all projects in the late twentieth and the current century, people are spread among many different types of work. They must juggle their time between work on your project with work on other projects as well as nonproject work. You must assume that there will be conflicts—even if they indicate that this is not the case. Pose the conflict issue directly. Give them the following situation and see what they do. They are doing work on your project and one of their managers comes to them and asks them to do something else immediately. What would they do?

- *Communication skills.* The ability to get along and communicate with managers and other employees is critical. There are several ways to get at communication skills. You can ask about issues and problems that they have had. You can also pose a situation and see how they would respond. Also, ask them how they would organize communications in the team. How would they find out about status of the project, for example?

- *Ambition and energy.* This is a hard one to evaluate. You can try and assess the volume and nature of work that they have performed. Here is a method we have used effectively. Have them take their resume and with their knowledge of the project, have them prepare an updated resume that reflects the experience at the end of the project assuming that it is completed. This will work in any country or culture and reveals self-interest. If the resumes are the same, then their expectations for themselves in the project are very low. Not a good sign. Another technique is to pose a situation in which they must complete a great deal of work in a short amount of time. Find out how they respond.

- *Knowledge of the organization's business processes.* Typically, your project will involve some business processes in the organization. Ask them how the current process works. Have them identify problems and issues with the current process.

- *Knowledge of the methods and tools that will be employed in the project.* In the project concept you defined some of the major methods and tools that will be employed. Many people will list the various tools or methods they are familiar with on their resumes. But resumes are just paper. You need to test their knowledge of the specific method or tool. Ask them how they employed the method or tool. What are some of the problems with the method or tool? What are gaps where the method or tool fails?

- *Ability to cope with different cultures.* This links to their work with other team members in doing tasks together. Move away from projects and work and ask about their hobbies. Do they like to travel? Where have they gone? What type of foods do they like? If they don't like to travel and prefer a fairly regimented life, then this could be a problem.

• *Ability and willingness to travel for an extended period of time.* Many people will indicate that they don't mind traveling. But when the rubber meets the road, there are problems. So you need to probe about what they do off the job. How old are their children? Does any family member have some specific need or problem? Then pose the situation of a month-long trip to some location halfway around the world. How would they communicate with their family? Getting this answer will tell you a great deal about whether they have thought this through. They may think that they can reduce the travel once they are on the team.

• *Multilingual capability or at least the ability to work hard at understanding and getting ideas across.* This relates to travel, culture, and communications. Are they willing to learn about other cultures and languages? What would they do to gather information? How could they use the web?

Of course, it depends on the type of team member and their role as to what you emphasize. For the critical team member type you will want to use all of these. You will likely value problem solving, communicating, collaboration, and related skills as important or more important than specific technical knowledge. For the locally focused team members you will focus more on their business and technical knowledge and skills. However, the ability to get along with others is still important. For the cameo member you will focus on their capabilities along with being able to deal with issues and work within the scope of defined tasks.

IDENTIFY AND SELECT TEAM MEMBERS

You have identified requirements for team members. Now the job is to actually find the team members. Questions for interviewing specific individuals are found in the next section. A common approach is to start at headquarters and find the team members there and then to move out to regional and local locations. This is not a good idea. It reinforces the mentality of the centralized project that cares little about what goes on in the local offices—where the money is really made.

So let's step back and look for a better strategy. You know what you want. At headquarters getting people will be relatively easy from a political point of view. The risk is in the local offices. So that is where you should focus your efforts first. You should line up the people who are needed for local work. This is what was termed locally focused team members earlier. Why is this a good place to start? Here are some reasons.

• You need to build rapport with the local managers so that they are aware and supportive of the project.

- Getting the local managers to commit their people to locally focused work is a good political test of their commitment and involvement. Locally focused work tends to take less effort than that of a critical team member who will have to spend more time away from their current work.

You now travel some thousands of miles through a smelly airplane and airport and arrive at the office. You go to sleep and go to the local office the next day. You arrive at the office. The manager is expecting you. He or she expresses happiness to see you and to be involved in the project. This may really be insincere. The person may really be thinking "What can I do to get this person out of here as soon as possible?" You should assume that this is the attitude. Immediately, you should indicate that you are aware of their many activities going on and that you don't want to place a burden on them with the project. Do not under any circumstances stress that this is a corporate project and that they must cooperate. There will be verbal agreement and then you will later be knifed in the back. After you have covered the sensitivities, indicate that they know that there are many corporate projects and that here is another one. Then go into the benefits for them in terms of what was discussed in Chapter 2. Indicate that you want the project to proceed with as least pain on them as possible. Also, indicate that they could assign people who are not firing on all cylinders. As an aside, we have other phrases—these are: "not the sharpest knife in the drawer" or the "wheel is turning but the hamster is dead." Basically, you are appealing to their self-interest. To minimize the pain on them, they need to assign someone who can do the work and who is not incompetent.

After this discussion you can move on to the core team or critical team members if they are potentially to come from this location. You should state that it is in their interest to name someone who can participate to avoid potential problems later. Also, by using their own people they will have more say in the project later. This is politically useful point to bring out.

In the previous section some of the items to cover with potential team members were listed. For a new team member who has been brought on board the project, you want to discuss the following items:

- Your expectations of them;
- Their expectations of the project and benefits to them;
- Time conflicts and other problems that arise during the project;
- Turnover of their current work to others so that they can spend time on the project.

Now let's return to headquarters. Often, it is not hard to find people to take on the project. How is it that headquarters offices have many people available on call? We don't know, but you are taking advantage of this by going to the region first. Now let's suppose after explaining the purpose of the project and work that you run into resistance. A manager, for example, states that he or she "has no one available." Now you can state that the local offices have made people available and that management is behind the project. There is just no place to hide. They must give you decent people soon—or else!! Don't you see the strategy? You are using the support of the local offices from afar and that of management from above to put pressure on these middle level headquarters managers.

There is one issue that comes up frequently. That is that a manager assigns someone who is not appropriate to the project, but who is not being used effectively in the department. What do you do? Here are some ideas. First, indicate that the needs that you are stating now are temporary and that there will be future needs. This leaves the door open for future requirements and changes. Next, evaluate the person right away. Assess whether they are suitable or whether they are a "turkey." If they are the latter, then you can go to the manager and indicate that you know that they are not really the right person for the project, but that you will make the best of the situation. In return, you indicate that they may be returned from the project for others. Also, indicate that they owe you—big time. What do you want? Help in resolving political and other issues. In other words, you can leverage a weakness into a strength!!

BUILD A TEAM MENTALITY

Team building begins with the kickoff meeting for the project. In an international project it is important that all of the critical team members attend the meeting in person. If the budget is tight, then you can resort to videoconferencing. In the first meeting it is important to instill a common sense of purpose and goal. You also want to address some of the potential problems that will arise. Figure 4.4 gives a checklist along with comments.

We take teamwork and a team mentality very seriously—not just pay lip service to it. Here are six proven ways to instill a greater degree of teamwork and a team consciousness. Throughout the book other opportunities for collaboration will be given.

The first place to build the team approach is in the planning of the work. In the next chapter, a collaborative approach will be taken in creating the detailed schedule or work plan. Here there are six specific actions you can take to implement teamwork. Do these things early in the project and keep them going. You will build a successful pattern of collaboration that will last beyond the project end date.

In terms of the work itself in an international project, it is useful to assign 40% of the tasks to be jointly shared among two team members. Of course, you always must have one in charge of each task. However, assigning the tasks to two people

Topic	Comments
Management support of the project	Appearance by manager who will explain what will happen with the results of the project after completion
Objectives of the project	Cover business and technical objectives at both headquarters and local levels
Project management approach	Collaboration; participation; etc.
Roles in the project	What each person's role is and how people will interact
Methods and tools	Cover a list of accepted methods and tools
Challenges	Cover at least 3–4 of the issues discussed including time conflict with regular work
Coordination	How this will work across countries and time zones
Culture and language	Recognition of the importance of these factors and how they will be addressed
Milestones and high-level tasks	Discuss milestone evaluation as well

Figure 4.4   Topics to Cover in the Kickoff Meeting for the International Project

reinforces that when you want teamwork, you support your statement. Remember that actions in project management are more important often than words. If possible, assign tasks to one person at one location and one at another. Let them work through the communications.

Taking task assignments further, you should rotate team members among tasks so that different team members work with each other through the project. This is obviously not possible in a short project, but can be done in a project of six months or longer.

A fourth area for team building is in addressing issues. While team members cannot solve all or even many issues, they can participate by sharing their views on specific problems or opportunities.

Lessons learned is a fifth activity for teamwork. In this book the approach is collaborative. In international projects you have to create opportunities for team building. One such is the sharing of lessons learned across the project.

Finally, a sixth opportunity for teamwork is in presentations. Team members who worked on the same tasks can make presentations together.

How can you determine if you are succeeding in building a team mentality? Here are some questions to answer:

• Sit down where the team members take breaks. Are the team members talking about their tasks and work together? If so, this is a good sign—even if they are talking about problems.

• Watch the body language and how team members interact with each other. Are they showing each other respect? Does their conversation reflect previous communications?

There is a major reason to instilling team work beyond quality of work in the international project. It is drive and desire to see the project work through. This will help you and the project when diversions and other opportunities arise. The team member will be more likely to remain in the project since they have a sense of belonging.

REPLACE TEAM MEMBERS

In a project of any duration team members come and go. This is natural. You cannot afford to plan for the transition of the team members. Let's divide this discussion into two parts—the departing team member and the new team member.

Assume that all team members will be leaving. This means that you must make an effort as a manager to ensure that there is a capture of information and knowledge from the departing team member to the rest of the team. If you have organized many of the tasks as joint, this is less of a burden since there is some degree of backup. Have team members present their work in team meetings on a regular basis. Since this becomes routine, it is nonthreatening to the people. They don't feel singled out for attention.

Another guideline is to state to the team that some of them will likely be pulled from the project for other work. Indicate that you expect and anticipate this. Also, indicate that you expect them to keep the project leaders apprised of potential developments that would take them from the project. Keep an early warning system by staying in touch with the team members.

Now let's assume that a team member is leaving within two weeks and that they have been working mainly alone. What steps should you take?

• Review the current work assignments for the individual and determine the status of the work.

• Talk with the departing team member about their work. Ask them about issues in their work. Discuss these issues openly. Look for loose ends. Solicit ideas for people that they think might be useful to the project.

• Move to assign other team members to work with them to get overlap. Oversee directly the early meetings in the transition. Have them develop a small checklist of things to do in the transition.

- If possible, have the remaining team members do some of the work of the departing team member. This will validate that there has been a transfer of knowledge.
- For the departing team member volunteer to help them. Get out the resume that was current at the start of the project and the one they developed for the end of the project. Review this with them. Always volunteer to write an evaluation letter for their personnel file. This is true even for cameo members.

Taking these steps will provide a number of benefits. First, you show that you care about the well being of the team members. This will help with the remaining members of the team. Second, you show that you have an organized approach for dealing with transition.

Now let's turn to the problem of getting someone to replace the departing team member. Here you want to follow an organized approach. Here are some useful steps.

- Step 1: Review the project plan and the work to date.
- Step 2: Identify the open issues and problem areas that you have. Also, review and update the tables related to skills that you developed earlier in this chapter. These two actions will help to give you a better idea of what type of person you need. In general, you don't want to replace someone with someone who is like the departing person.
- Step 3: Create a small list of characteristics and experience that you think would be most suitable for the project.

After you have carried out these two steps, you have a better idea of what would be most useful to assist the project. Next, you will have to approach either headquarters or local managers to get a new team member. Don't present the situation as a problem. Instead, present it as an opportunity to involve more people in the project. Also, indicate that you support their reassignment since there is other important work to be done. Point out the areas where the project could most use additional help. Show them the list from Step 3 above. Don't insist on getting a specific person unless there is one person who is absolutely critical. Instead, make suggestions of other people.

Now let's assume that you have a new team member that has been assigned to the project. Pursue these actions:

- Interview them as was done earlier in this chapter.
- Bring them up-to-date on the project by presenting the original goal and scope of the project. Be open about what issues have been encountered and solved. Point out to them the open issues and areas of the project that have risk.

• Present their area of the project to them. Show them the tasks that were originally created by the departing team member. Send them away to think about the tasks and to develop their own task list.

• Introduce them to team members with whom they will be sharing tasks.

• Follow the guideline related to creating a revised and updated resume for the end of the project.

This last action is important because it gets them involved in the project. Your objective is to severalfold. First, you want to obtain an assessment that this is the right person for the work. Second, you want to get them involved and committed to the project.

After reviewing their plan for their work, have them introduced to the project team in a project meeting. Get them to discuss their background and lessons learned from past projects. Next, assign some of their tasks jointly. This has several benefits. First, it gets collaboration going right away for them. Second, the current team members will probably get back to you on what they think of their skills—not bad information to have.

MANAGE TEAM MEMBERS

Now you have the team on board. You have established joint tasks. Everything should be fine, right? Wrong. There are many operational problems that can be encountered. Let's start with the day-to-day operations. You should gather status from the team members in person. Don't use e-mail. That just masks what is really going on. If the team member is remote, then you should use the telephone. Use voice mail where you can pick up their tone of voice.

How do you really determine what is going on? Do not ask for status. Instead, ask how things are going. Look at their facial expressions and listen to their voice. That will tell a lot about what is really true. Then ask about what problems they are having. Ask what else they are working on. Express sympathy for them being split between their other work and that of the project. These steps will help to draw the team member out. Probe then for detail. Discuss the detail for some time. This will give you a better understanding of what they are doing as well as showing sympathy for their work. Then start to probe issues. What is getting in their way? What do they need?

Listen for statements related to work and personal problems. For work problems log these mentally so that you can later take them up with their managers. For personal problems, ask them how you can help. Let's take an example. Suppose that they state they are under a lot of stress from work. After asking more questions, you find that the reason is that they are needed at home more.

Now you can zoom in on this issue and see what you can do to ease the problem. Give them a day off. Have them work at home for three days.

EXAMPLES

SAMBAC ENERGY

Sambac attempted to regiment employees in remote locations to a common culture. Guess what? It did not work. So when the project arose, there was a feeling that a common culture could not be assumed. Therefore, the approach of addressing local needs was taken as defined in this chapter.

WHITMORE BANK

The bank had many common business processes across the entire bank. The problem was that the bank management did not recognize the culture of each country and location. In order to give the project a sense of reality, management was given some examples of cultural problems. Some of these then became part of the project. Local support of management was gained.

LESSONS LEARNED

• Do not attempt to get the absolute best people for the project. There are a number of problems with the "best" people. First, "best" is hard to define. Second, these individuals tend to be difficult to get along with—making the work of the rest of the team more difficult. Third, it is often difficult for someone else to pick up their work if they leave the project. A fourth factor is that they are often in high demand. Thus, it is likely that they will be pulled from your project. However, and a fifth problem, management expectations were likely raised when they were assigned to your project. These expectations have not been diminished because they are no longer on your team.

• If you need the best people, then only have them for specific tasks. They are part-time team members who do a specific task or set of tasks and then leave. Overall, you want team members who are junior and who have energy and enthusiasm to get ahead. These people tend to be benefited by the project.

• In every department there are "king bees" and "queen bees" who have extensive business rule knowledge and experience. These individuals wield massive informal power in the department. People in the departments come up to them frequently to ask for assistance and to show their respect. Traditional project management would have you put these people on your team. Avoid it! These people have a vested interest in the status quo. Change to them threatens their power. Moreover, these people will try to take over your project. Hold on, it gets worse. Their absence from the department creates a crisis since they hold in their heads the keys for handling exceptions and coping with workarounds.

EXERCISES

1. Look at a past project in your organization that experienced some problems. Try to find out if some of these problems related to the lack of collaboration and teamwork in the project. This will be useful as an example to employ later in projects. Do the same for projects that were successful.

2. Go to the Web and magazines and see if you can find examples of international projects that succeeded or failed. Gather lessons learned by trying to read between the lines as to what was successful in terms of joint work among firms.

SUMMARY

There have been several critical themes of this chapter. The first is planning. You must plan ahead for what resources and skills are needed. A second theme has been politics. You are not likely to often get the best people; they are often too busy on other important work. Make up for the best when you can with people who are energetic and ambitious. Also, employ the third theme—that of collaboration. You must instill in the team how important you feel a collaborative approach is and why they must work together if the project is to succeed.

Chapter 5

Develop the Project Plan

INTRODUCTION

You may be expecting some standard stuff on defining tasks and milestones and then reviewing the project plan. This approach has many problems when applied to international projects. First, you want to use the development of the project plan as a way to build collaboration among the team members. Second, how you establish the project often is a key indicator of success or failure. As an example, suppose that you organize the project with a subproject for each country. That organization almost ensures that there will be minimal communications between the locations—leading to many problems and even the downfall of the project. So the bottom line—this chapter is very important if you want to start the project off right.

What is included in the project plan? Start with the summary, high-level and detailed tasks. A **task** here a piece of work. Then add the milestones. A **milestone** is an end product. You will be producing a **baseline schedule** that will serve as a benchmark to measure your progress as you go. The plan identifies the resources to be applied in the international project. From this information you can then develop the costs and budget for the project.

PURPOSE AND SCOPE

TECHNICAL PURPOSE

The technical purpose is to establish an accurate and flexible plan that will achieve the goals of the project. Now look back at this sentence again. Notice that there is one word missing. This is "complete." In international projects, you will never have a complete, detailed plan at the start. Too much changes during the project. You can strive for a comprehensive plan that covers everything at a high level.

The word "accurate" is understandable. "Flexible" is not used as much when talking about a project plan. Yet, for international projects you must be able to respond to many different situations. You have to structure the plan so that **it can be changed at the detail level while the summary, higher level remains unchanged except for dates**.

BUSINESS PURPOSE

One business goal is to organize the project in such a way that it is reasonable in terms of coordination effort. A second business objective is that the plan can be understood and agreed to by managers at headquarters and the local offices— it doesn't do much good to have a plan that people pay lip service to, but don't really understand.

POLITICAL PURPOSE

A major political purpose is to ensure that the plan highlights areas of issues and risk. It is political dynamite to bury the risk and issues in the detailed tasks deep within some part of the plan. People don't pay much attention to them then.

Another major political goal is to have the project planning start to build collaboration and commitment among the team members. They must participate in project planning to buy into the work.

END PRODUCTS

The major end project is that management at both headquarters and the local level as well as the team support and understand the plan. They believe that if the plan is carried out, the project results will be what they want.

There is a second end product related to culture. Through the organization and construction of the project plan, there is a spirit of communications, collaboration, and information sharing that will be better at the end of the project than at the beginning. For a number of our international projects, this was the most lasting benefit. This is so important that we emphasize it here again.

**Through the project, you have a chance to build a new culture
that is positive and focuses on information sharing,
communications, and collaboration.**

Now you also have the end products of the plan and budget.

APPROACH

SET UP THE PROJECT FILE

This seems like a dumb place to start. However, the project file is the critical
repository of the project. Lessons learned, issues, experience, etc., are all in the
project file. You should establish a standard set of tabs or headings for all project
files. This standardization will facilitate communications, help less experienced
project leaders, and provide guidance for future projects. One of us has a room
filled with project files going back over 35 years. We still go back and pull information out of long dead projects.

You can first divide the project file into management and technical. In the
management section you have:

- Budget and actual data;
- Schedules and plans;
- Memoranda and notes on the project;
- Staffing on the project;
- Issues.

In the technical part, you have the following:

- Technical end products from the project;
- Milestone reviews;
- Lessons learned from the project.

If you establish the project file early, then it provides both structure and
flexibility for whatever may happen.

EMPLOY PROJECT TEMPLATES

Many people begin project planning with a blank piece of paper. This is not
a good idea. The traditional approach was to use a work breakdown structure or
WBS. A **work breakdown structure** is a detailed list of all applicable tasks. It
was thought years ago that this was useful because people could just pick and

choose among the tasks. However, over time a number of problems have surfaced with this approach. First, there is the problem of what tasks mean. In an international project with different cultures and languages, this can be a major problem—leading to misunderstanding and confusion. Second, the WBS is too rigid. What if you have tasks that are not in the WBS? Do you force fit them into some general category? A third problem is that no one on the team, including the project leaders, had involvement in the WBS—they did not buy into this.

Instead of a WBS, develop high-level tasks for each type of international project that you do. In Part III there are examples of international projects and these high-level tasks are given. How many tasks are to be defined? Maybe as few as 20–30 up to several hundred. The high-level tasks serve as the umbrella for the project. Detailed tasks will fit under these high-level, summary tasks. The high-level tasks are the start of the project template. A **project template** consists of the following:

- High-level tasks;
- General resources assigned to the tasks;
- Tail-to-head dependencies among tasks;
- All durations and dates, left unfilled.

A general resource is the name of the role that would typically undertake the task. An example might be construction foreman or systems engineer. Tail-to-head dependencies are the simplest and will cause the least problems.

There are two additional "rules of thumb" for using templates. **One is that all projects must use the same customization form of the project management software.** Almost all useful project management software can be customized. If people use different forms of customization, then you cannot put the schedules together to do analysis.

The second rule is that all project plans and templates must use the same resource pool. A resource pool is a project plan in which there are no tasks—only resources. There are general resources for the template and specific resources for the individual projects. If all of the project plans use the same resource pool, then you can combine the projects for analysis.

When you fill out the project plan from the template, you first create detailed tasks under the template tasks. Then you replace the general resources with the specific people or organizations doing the work. You can also add dependencies and, finally, the dates and durations of the tasks to produce the plan.

There are a number of advantages of using project templates, including:

- It is easier for the team to understand and support these.
- The template can be improved as the project goes on and after the project is over. As such, the body of templates constitute cumulative improvement through experience.

- Management can understand templates easier than the detailed tasks.
- Changes in the project can be made in the detail, leaving the high-level tasks unchanged except for the dates and durations.

How do you develop templates?

- Take several schedules from current and past projects;
- Extract the high-level tasks and milestones;
- Have various project leaders and team members review and refine the tasks and milestones.

This produces the first version of the template. Note that in the third step there is discussion and collaboration to gain a common understanding of the tasks.

There is an overall roadmap here. It is shown in Fig. 5.1. This diagram reveals how templates, project plans, lessons learned, and issues tie together. Each of the arrows is labeled so that the following explanation helps you to see the overall picture.

- Each international project plan is generated from a template (arrow 1).

- As you gain experience from the project, the template can be updated for future use (arrow 2).
- Any task that has risk has one or more issues behind it (arrow 3).
- Each issue that is identified can be associated with one or more tasks (arrow 4).
- Template tasks refer to the appropriate lessons learned that help you carry out the task (arrow 5).
- Each lesson learned would be difficult to find or use if it did not refer to some tasks in the templates (arrow 6).

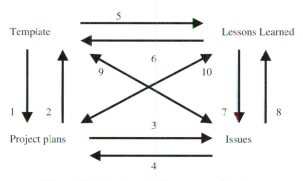

Figure 5.1   Roadmap for Templates and Projects

- You employ lessons learned to help in resolving issues (arrow 7).
- From dealing with issues you gather more experience so that you can improve on the lessons learned (arrow 8).
- Certain issues commonly arise in international projects so that they can be associated with the tasks in the template (arrow 9).
- Lessons learned can be useful in resolving issues and doing work in the project; the lessons learned can also be updated (arrow 10).

In these comments there is a basic definition of risk in terms of the project plan. A task has **risk** or is risky if there is one or more associated significant issues with that task.

Note that without the cross reference of lessons learned with the tasks, it would be difficult, if not impossible, to uncover which lessons learned to use. The same applies to issues. Also, as time goes on and you gain more experience in international projects, you will likely experience the benefits given in Fig. 5.2.

Many international projects involve consultants and contractors. It is important that the issues, templates, and project plans be shared with outside firms. Otherwise, a vendor may continue to use their own plan. Then you will spend literally hours with the vendor manager in reconciling your and their versions of the plans and interpretations of issues.

Benefit	Comment
The effort to build the plan is reduced.	Because the templates become more detailed.
The same issues will tend to recur so that there is a greater awareness of issues. It will then take less time to deal with the issues.	This is because of a common issues database.
Lessons learned will actually be useful.	In many projects, experience is captured at the end of the project. However, there is often no repository for these. So they are never used and the effort is largely wasted.
Lessons learned can be shared across projects.	This is very important for many international projects. It is possible since there is a common lessons learned database.
Lessons learned are relevant.	The lessons learned are related to both tasks and issues.

Figure 5.2   Benefits of a Structured Approach for International Projects

Split Up the Overall International Project

You could just create a giant template for international projects. However, this has many disadvantages. First, it will lead to many more templates. Second, this approach does not reflect the reality that many international projects contain common subprojects. For example, consider a project to merge with a recently acquired firm. There are three manufacturing facilities and two administrative offices. Now you could create five different plans. On the other hand, you could create two overall templates for the merging—manufacturing and administration. Now within each of the five locations, there are common functions such as general accounting, payroll, etc. It is rather stupid to include these individually. It is more useful to create smaller templates for general accounting, payroll, etc. Then the overall template is really composed of smaller templates. This is a basic guideline which we restate.

In order to get economies of scale of effort in project management, you should create smaller templates for specific activities in the project. The overall template and schedule is then a combination of the parts.

This is a modular approach and allows you to improve the individual templates as you go. It also provides more flexibility.

How do you break up an international project into parts? As was stated before, this is one place that many projects go wrong. Here are four actions to take:

- Action 1: Identify and review the major areas of risk.
- Action 2: Create a separate subproject for each area that has risk. This puts the focus on risk.
- Action 3: Review the business and political purposes of the project.
- Action 4: For the parts of the project that remain after Action 2, organize these so as to achieve the business and political purposes.

Remember the following. Many projects can be technical successes, but turn out to be business and/or political failures. They then fail overall. Hence, the emphasis on the business and political goals. Next, by organizing the project around the dual themes of minimizing risk and political/business objectives you work to achieve both. You orient the team and management toward these goals as well.

The areas of risk depend upon the type of international project that you are undertaking. However, the business and political goals are often more common and include:

• There is a need to build relationships among staff and management at different locations so that there will be increased communications and collaboration after the project is concluded. Organizing the project across locations provides support to achieve this goal.

• Instill a more standardized way of thinking across the organization. Look at recent failures in international finance and banking. Many of the problems were due to compartmentalization. People had become isolated in their jobs—making fraud and deception easier to carry out. Standardization and awareness are promoted by a cross location project organization.

Let's take an example. Whitmore Bank wanted to deploy a new banking family of products in a region of five countries. In their first attempt they based the project in the most technologically advanced country. The project leaders came from here along with the key team members. They were insensitive to the needs of the other locations. They ran into a brick wall. The project failed.

The project had the following major parts:

• Marketing for the products;
• Sales for the products;
• IT work for the products;
• Organization setup to support the products—four groups were needed;
• Management controls and measurement of the performance of the products.

Of these the IT and management control parts of the project were the most risky. There were many detailed issues in the systems area as well as in government regulation and controls. Using the approach in this chapter, these were extracted and set up as separate subprojects.

This left three areas to be considered. After extensive discussions it was realized that there would be an ongoing need for collaboration and information sharing across the region after the project was completed. Therefore, each of these areas was organized across the region with two project leaders from different countries in charge of each part of the project.

This second approach was very successful. It became easier for Whitmore to move people around the region. There was greater uniformity and predictability of service for customers. Profitability goals were reached ahead of schedule.

Why don't all or more international projects follow the above approach? Well, there are cultural and political barriers. First, project leaders may not want to force people in different locations to work together due to distance, culture, and other factors. They feel that this increases risk. Actually, it reduces risk.

What about time zones and culture? You are going to assign joint tasks between people in different locations within each subproject. Then you want the individuals to work out how they will deal with time and culture. The project leaders can help, but you want the people to gain experience and lessons learned from doing it for themselves.

Another reason is that many times the project is organized along the same lines as the organization. This often reflects faulty logic since you tend to have greater success using a matrix approach by going across locations.

CREATE THE ISSUES AND LESSONS LEARNED DATABASES

Keys to the diagram in Fig. 5.1 are issues and lessons learned. You do not have time to establish databases for issues and lessons learned for each international project. Moreover, the same issues and lessons learned will recur many times. Therefore, you want to have a common issues database and a common lessons learned database.

What is the structure of these databases? Experience from past international projects has revealed the benefit of having three linked databases for each of the issues and lessons learned. For issues the databases are:

• General issues database. This is a common database for all projects.
• Issues applied to a specific project. This consists of the information for the issue as it applies to a specific project.
• Actions on the specific issue. This database records the actions and results of steps taken for a specific issue.

The data elements for these databases are given in Fig. 5.3.

Turning now to the lessons learned, the three databases are as follows:

• General lessons learned database. This database contains the general guidelines for applying and using the lessons learned.
• Cross reference of lessons learned to projects and templates.
• Update database to record experience in applying specific lessons learned.

Data elements for these are given in Fig. 5.4. These databases can be established using a standard database management system such as Microsoft Access or groupware such as Lotus Notes. You might want to start out by using a spreadsheet first and then migrate to a database later.

All of the databases are resident on the computer network in the organization so anyone can access the information on a read-only basis. Write access is controlled and restricted to project leaders or a central coordinator (discussed later in this chapter).

A. General Issues Database

- Identify of issue
- Title of issue
- Type of issue
- Importance of the issue
- Description of issue
- General tasks to which the issue applies
- Date the issue was created
- Person who created the issue
- Who is impacted by the issue
- Who generally handles this issue
- Related issues
- Related lessons learned
- General impact of the issue on the project if not solved
- Symptoms of the issue
- General approach to solving the issue
- Potential actions to resolve the issue
- Benefits of the solution
- Comments on the issue

B. Project-Specific Database

- Identifier of the issue
- Project identifier
- Task(s) identifier(s)
- Status of issue
- Date created for project
- Whom issue is assigned to
- Specific impact of the issue
- Decisions made regarding the issue
- Actions taken regarding the issue
- Outcomes from the decisions and actions
- Date resolved
- Comments

C. Actions Related to Specific Issues and Projects

- Identifier of issue
- Project identifier
- Task(s) identifier(s)
- Date of action
- Who took action
- Action taken
- Result achieved
- Comments

Figure 5.3 Data Elements for the Issues Databases

A. General Lesson Learned Database

- Lesson learned identifier
- Title of lesson learned
- Date created
- Type
- Status
- Who created the lesson learned
- Situations to which the lesson learned applies
- Guidelines
- Expected outcomes
- Benefits
- Related issues
- Comments

B. Cross Reference to Specific Tasks

- Lesson learned identifier
- Project identifier
- Task identifier

C. Update Database for Lessons Learned

- Lesson learned identifier
- Date of experience
- Who is recording the experience
- Situation to which the lesson learned was applied
- Result achieved
- Recommendation on lesson learned
- Comments

Figure 5.4   Data Elements for Lessons Learned Databases

DEFINE TASKS AND MILESTONES

With the above comments as background, let's consider how to develop the detailed project plan. The sequence of actions is as follows:

- Action 1: Review the template and breakdown of the project into subprojects with the team; assign areas of the template to pairs of team members.
- Action 2: Create a general list of issues using the ones from Part IV. Use this as a checklist for the team. Have them add more issues as appropriate. This gives you the initial list of issues for the project.
- Action 3: Each pair of team members works to define detailed tasks for the next 3–4 months.
- Action 4: Review the detailed tasks with the team members. In doing so, you will identify additional issues that can be added or referenced using the

issues database. This action will ensure that there is a common understanding of what is to be done.

• Action 5: Arrange for presentations of the tasks to other team members. This will widen the understanding of what is to be done and gain additional input.

• Action 6: Each pair of team members will now assign specific resources and dependencies. These are reviewed by the project leaders.

• Action 7: Each pair of team members will develop the estimated durations and dates for the work. This is now reviewed by the project leaders.

As you can see, this approach is collaborative and leads to a better understanding of what is to be done. Later, the team members will update their own tasks. This gives the individual team member a role in project management and also ensures that the project leaders are not driven down to the level of clerks who just update the plans.

What is the appropriate level of detail for an international project? **Experience indicates that you want detailed tasks at the bottom to be 1–2 weeks in duration.** There is a trade-off here. If you go for more detail, the project plan takes more effort to update and maintain. It becomes unwieldy. We know of one international project where the project leader was not experienced. He created detailed tasks down to 1 or 2 days. It drove the project team nuts! It was so unworkable that within one month the plan had to be scrapped and the effort started over. If the team cannot reasonably update the tasks in a short amount of time, then the team members will perceive that using project management is getting in the way of the work. Credibility of the method and the project leaders drops. There is another benefit to this range. If team members are able to leave the project team, there is less potential damage since the tasks are of reasonable duration.

What about milestones? International projects are often far flung and spread out. It will be difficult to get status later if there are fewer milestones. So we recommend that you have more, rather than fewer, milestones.

It can happen that your project is interdependent with other projects that are going on in one or more locations. How do you address this situation? You could just put in the major milestones of the dependent project and then track these. Often, this is not effective. If the other projects are set up in templates, then you can combine the projects to do analysis of slippage. This is feasible if there is open information on the projects and they are on the network.

Another action is to establish a new subproject that addresses the interface between your project and another project. This "interface project" provides a focus for joint management between the two sets of project leaders. It also draws attention to the risk and importance of the interface. This is preferable to burying the interface in some detailed tasks that are not visible. It also makes the two sets of project leaders more jointly responsible; they are forced to work together on issues that affect both projects.

DEAL WITH ESTIMATION, CONTINGENCIES, AND UNCERTAINTY

Here is a series of guidelines for developing the schedule and plan:

• If you cannot estimate a task, what do you do? Break up the task into smaller parts. Isolate the part you cannot estimate. Ask why you cannot estimate it. This will surface one or more issues. This is positive because it gets more issues out on the table earlier. Having identified the issue behind the task, you can now deal with it and then develop an estimate.

• Only develop detailed tasks for 3–4 months in the future. Beyond this, stick to the template level. This will save you more time. For template level tasks later you can temporarily break up tasks to do estimation.

• As the plan is updated, the team members will define additional detailed tasks so that there are detailed tasks for 3–4 months in the future at all times (see Fig. 5.5).

How do you deal with contingencies? A commonly used approach is to pad the time for the work. However, if everyone does this, the project will not finish for years. What is the underlying purpose of contingency planning? To make management and the team aware of potential problems and impacts. We have found that a better approach is to define contingency tasks. These are added at the bottom of the project plan. They are not linked to any tasks in the plan. To show the impact of the contingency, you merely link the appropriate contingency tasks into the plan. Panic ensues as managers see the slippage—very good!

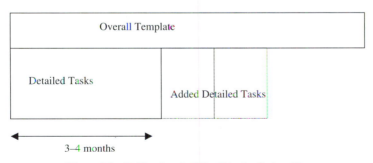

Figure 5.5   Rolling Level of Detail in the Project Plan

What is a major contingency for international projects? The team members must be drawn off the project for other work. Here is another guideline. **Have each team member create their own plan that indicates what other work they will doing.** You should review this with them and discuss the possible demands. This is much more precise that just yakking about their other work in general terms. Later in the project, they can update this and indicate to you what is going on. This will prevent many unpleasant surprises later. Moreover, if a team member has a number of real conflicts, you can consider if this person should be replaced on the team. This is a much better idea at the start of the project than in the middle in a panic situation.

Now suppose you have developed the plan and have a list of issues. How do you test if these are both complete? First, go through the list of tasks and ask if any of these have risk. If they do, then do you have the associated issues identified? If not, then you can add more issues and link these to the tasks. Second, go down the list of issues. Ask if these apply to the international project. If one does, then go down the list of tasks to see if the appropriate tasks are present. If not, you can add tasks. The end result is that you have verified both the issues and the tasks. Another step to take is to review the milestones and label the ones that involve major issues. These issues are related to the tasks that produce or lead to the end product.

PERFORM COST ESTIMATION

Cost estimation is often difficult in standard projects. It is more complex and difficult in international projects. One problem is that there is often no way to link the actual costs in the project to the project plan. Another problem is that budget estimation is performed individually based on the single project leader.

The overall project management approach in this chapter provides for an improvement in this situation.

• There are two project leaders involved so that there is a wider perspective of what is to be estimated.

• There are project templates for each type of project. As time goes on and experience grows, the template can grow in size. Lower-level tasks can be added.

• Estimated durations can be given for some tasks that are performed in the plans that follow a specific template.

• Issues are associated with tasks in the templates.

• Budgeted and actual costs for projects can be inserted in fields in the project plan, thereby facilitating analysis.

• By type of project, the costs (budgeted and actual) can be associated with tasks in the project templates.

Cost estimation is improved since the costs can be linked to the template.

The method is then to associate a new project with a template. Then the project leaders review the template to refine the tasks. They can review the issues associated with the tasks in the template and make adjustments. The project leaders can now perform improved estimation using this additional information.

There is an additional benefit of this approach. When management poses questions, asks for budget cuts or budget increases to reduce schedules, the project leaders can use a copy of the template file to perform "what if" analysis. This is more credible to management since it is based on more concrete data than just raw experience of one person.

PERFORM RESOURCE USAGE ANALYSIS

You might be tempted to use the project management software to do automated resource leveling. **We recommend that you never, ever use automated resource leveling.** One reason is that you want to indicate the resource conflicts and overcommitments by the team and others to them and to management. You will then gain their participation in determining what actions can be taken to manually resolve the resource conflict. If they participate in this analysis, they tend to understand and commit to the changes.

SET THE BASELINE SCHEDULE

The baseline schedule is set in most project management software by copying the start and end dates to baseline or planned start and end dates. For international projects these are done separately for each subproject. Now suppose that you have developed the plan using the method (or any method) and you find that the final date for project completion is not acceptable. This must happen almost 100% of the time, don't you think?

What do you do then? The often tried approach is to look at the critical path. The **critical path** is the path in the project from beginning to end that is the longest path in the project such that if any task in this path is delayed, the project is delayed. It sounds nice and simple, doesn't it? Why doesn't this approach work? Because of issues and risk. Who is to say that the tasks that have risk and issues are on the critical path?

Most of the time the tasks with issues and risk are not on the critical path.

Instead, they linger in the middle, vague zone of tasks. Management pays attention to the tasks in the critical path and ignores the tasks with risk unless they are on the critical path. They try to shorten tasks that have no risk. How can you do this? You cannot. If a task takes 10 days and has no issues, then it will take 10 days unless you make significant changes to the task!

What else can you do? Here is a series of actions you can take to shorten the schedule. It is the combination of the steps that add up to results.

• Divide up tasks in the schedule (including the critical path tasks) to make the work performed more in parallel.

• Consider paths in the project that contain tasks with significant issues. Here is where management and team attention can be employed with advantage. Why? You can examine the tasks that have issues and try to address the issues. By resolving or simplifying the issues, you can develop better and likely shorter durations for the tasks.

• Review carefully dependencies among subprojects and major summary tasks. Can more parallel effort be done here?

How do you use these actions? Bottom up. You begin with the subprojects that have the most risk and issues. Then you progressively analyze and review other subprojects. Since you can link the subprojects together in the project management software, you can always get an overall view of the effects of the changes that you have made.

This approach was employed in a large-scale deployment of satellite television in a major global region. Originally, the plan called for the rollout to be done in 17 months. This was just too long due to competitive pressures. The traditional approach was taken to shorten the critical path by applying more resources. The result was a plan shorter by 4 months, but much higher in cost.

Then the approach in this section was taken. It was found that people had made many assumptions related to dependencies. Also, there were a number of issues that could be resolved in project planning. After 2 weeks of effort by the project leaders, the team, and management the time was reduced by 6 months! Not bad, eh? A side benefit was that people had a much better idea of what was involved in the project—**they participated in the analysis and so supported and understood the work involved in more detail**.

Evaluate Your Plan

You are sitting back having gone through the arduous work of developing the schedule. Are you finished? Not yet. There are some additional steps that you can take to review the overall schedule.

- What happens if the project is reduced in scope?
- What will occur if the scope of the project is widened?
- What if management wants to speed up the project?
- What if one location is "too busy" to participate much?
- What if a critical person leaves the project?
- What if issues are not handled quickly and in a timely manner?
- What if a dependent project is changed?

Figure 5.6 Questions to Ask in Reviewing the Project Plan

- Look at the areas of the project that have tasks with major issues. If these issues were not to be resolved quickly, what would happen? Do you have an adequate list of contingency tasks?
- Review the detailed tasks. Are there tasks that go for, say, 1 month and that have issues associated with them. These are likely to be trouble later. What do you do? Have the team members who are assigned to these tasks break up the tasks into 1–2 week tasks.
- Consider the milestones of the project. International projects benefit from many milestones. Why? Because that is what you can review. If you are reviewing work in progress, then it is just verbal review—not very effective. There should be milestones showing up every 2 weeks in each subproject. This not only aids tracking of the work by the project leaders, it also raises the morale of the team since they will feel that they are making more progress.

In addition to these steps, you should answer and address the list of questions that are posed in Fig. 5.6.

ESTABLISH THE ROLE OF A CENTRAL INTERNATIONAL PROJECT COORDINATOR

This chapter has identified a central theme in the management of international projects—standardization at the higher levels and individual detailed schedules and issues at the lower level. This approach provides both standardization and flexibility. Flexibility is achieved where it is most needed—at the detailed level where the work is performed.

Classically, in project management, there was support for the idea of a project office. A **project office** consists of a group of project coordinators who develop plans and do other work across projects to ensure standardization. However, the project office suffers from a number of drawbacks. First, it is pure overhead. Second, many of the people in the project office do not have in-country experience—making coordination more difficult. Third, the effect of the project office was often to slow the projects down.

- Maintain and oversee the templates, issues, and lessons learned databases.
- Provide input to management on issues.
- Review project plans.
- Coordinate the development and refinement of templates.
- Conduct project reviews on a selective basis.
- Conduct measurements and the development of score cards for projects, business processes, and vendors.
- Familiarize new employees, contractors, etc., with the use of the templates, issues, and lessons learned.
- Conduct analysis of issues.
- Prepare summary analysis of all projects.
- Provide trend analysis for projects.
- Support updating template, issues, and lessons learned databases.
- Monitor usage of databases.
- Ensure that all plans adhere to templates.
- Maintain a history of projects.
- Ensure that projects are on the network for access both at headquarters and in the field.

Figure 5.7   Roles and Responsibilities for the International Project Coordinator

In the approach here, you want to have participation and not overhead. So you should consider the role of the International Project Coordinator. This is a person who is a project leader and has experience. The position rotates every 6 months or so among different project leaders so that everyone gets a turn.

The roles and responsibilities of the International Project Coordinator are listed in Fig. 5.7. There are a number of benefits to the organization. First, standardization is supported. As you can see, the databases of templates, issues, and lessons learned are overseen and maintained. The International Project Coordinator can provide a separate input to management on schedules, plans, and issues.

There are also benefits to the people who serve as coordinators. They get an opportunity to get an overall view of all of the international projects. They can use the perspective to perform better in their next projects. The coordinator role gives them a chance to unwind after doing projects that have stress.

WHAT CAN GO WRONG?

One point that will often arise is resistance to using templates. There are many arguments that have been used in the past. Here are several and your potential response:

- "We don't need templates because every international project is different." Yes, they are different in the details. However, projects of the same type are not different at the template level.

- "Using templates, issues, and lessons learned will take more time."
Actually, it will take less time since more time can be expended on the detailed tasks and work.
- "We have gotten along without templates in the past. Why use them now?" Ah, the fear of change again! Templates help to capture experience and to do a better job in the present and future.
- "There is nothing in this method for me." Now we are getting at self-interest. The project leader and the team are more effective. There is a wider common understanding of what is to be done.
- "Using templates, issues, and lessons learned will take more time." This is only true when they are set up. After this, time will be saved.

What is behind this resistance? Individuals, even those involved in carrying out change, will sometimes resist change. Another fear is loss of control. However, the bottom line is that with templates, the issues database, and lesson learned database, there is standardization at the higher levels. But the detailed tasks can be anything the team and leaders want them to be—giving them flexibility and control at the individual project level.

MARKET THE PLAN TO MANAGEMENT

If you are expecting some flashy presentation ideas here, forget it! The key to marketing the plan to management is to get them involved in some of the trade-off analysis. You should never present the finished plan. Instead, make them aware of some of the issues and the project plan at the high level. Then you can drill down to give a detailed picture of an area with risk and issues.

Another guideline in marketing is to avoid fairness. That is, don't give all parts of the project equal time. Go right to and focus on the subprojects where there are issues. Point out the resource conflicts that are likely. In short, follow what the famous actress, Bette Davis, said—"Fasten your seatbelt, baby. It's going to be a bumpy ride." You are preparing managers for dealing with issues when you do the marketing. Another way to frame this is that you should not just give attention to the positive. You are not trying to negative, just realistic based upon your experience. By drawing on experience from past projects, you are more credible with management.

EXAMPLES

SAMBAC ENERGY

Recall that Sambac is a joint venture between two major firms. Each firm tended to use their own plans and planning methods. Every time management changed, the plans changed. This consumed a great deal of time and slowed the projects down. It was first decided to have each firm produce a set of templates and list of issues. This was not productive. It took too much time and did not yield results for in-country operations. The second time around the method was different. The templates were generated locally. The existing project plans were retrofitted into the template. Issues were defined and associated with the plan and template. These were then provided to the two companies. It was very success-ful, because they could come up with a better idea. One company began soon after to employ the templates on their own. They even sent people out into the field to learn how to do it!

WHITMORE BANK

Whitmore was discussed earlier in setting up the structure of the project. In this case, people had not employed templates before. The project leaders con-structed an initial version of the templates for people to react to and change. Another technique that was useful was to establish a forum in the team to share lessons learned in setting up the template and defining issues. Often encountered is the problem of deciding when an issue is a major issue. Rather than consider-ing who or what is involved in the issue, the criterion that was used was to answer the questions, "What if this issue is not resolved? What will happen?"

LESSONS LEARNED

• When discussing the project plan with management, give them a role. Do not let people just sit passively by and look at the plan. They will not buy into the results. Get them involved in trade-offs to speed up the plan and address issues.

• How do you develop templates? Take the existing plans that you have and extract the high-level tasks. Group the projects into types or categories. These steps serve as the basis for creating your first set of templates.

• How do you develop issues? Get hold of one project. Make a list of the current major issues. Do the same for other projects. You will find a recurring pattern of the same issues surfacing again and again—sometimes in different forms and sometimes in the same form.

• What about the lessons learned? Gather these more slowly in project meetings. We'll give tips for this in several chapters later.

• Get started slowly. If you are a manager, don't impose the method on people. They will resent it. Start using the method on one or more subprojects. Then build up to the project level.

• Should you appoint a coordinator right away? No. It can wait until there is a sufficient body of templates and issues.

• Should you impose standardization? You can try, but in international projects you cannot control what people are doing on a daily basis halfway around the world. Thus, a better approach is to show success by example. **Then people will see that it is in their self-interest to adopt the methods**.

EXERCISES

1. Take a project plan that you currently are using and extract the high-level tasks. Start with as few as 20–30 tasks and 10 milestones. Then refine this. Get people's feedback after you have the initial list. This will get people involved. Do not develop templates from a blank piece of paper.

2. Take the issues in the last part of the book and use this as your initial list. Now go through one project and start to add more issues. You can discover still more by reviewing project notes.

SUMMARY

In international projects it is imperative that you do anything that you can to save time so that you can deal with issues and opportunities, and communicate with the team and management. You cannot afford to be stuck in front of some computer doing data entry or reinventing the wheel. The unified approach of templates, issues, and lessons learned will save you a great deal of effort. Moreover, you will begin to see the payoff in improved communications and reduced effort in your current and future international projects.

Chapter 6

Use Technology to Your Advantage

INTRODUCTION

In a small and local project, you can get by without any automated tools. You can probably manage the project on the "back of an envelope." Even though we employ technology in many projects, we are not great fans. From experience, the basic guideline is:

Use as little technology-based methods and tools as possible.

This seems odd. Isn't technology good? Some is and some is not. The problem is that every time you introduce some new technology into a project, you increase the risks. Let's take an example. A company that had a number of international projects gave each project leader a palmtop organizer that could set up and link to calendars of managers in the network. The goal was to increase productivity. Well, it was a failure that impacted the productivity of the managers in a negative way along with their projects. Managers were attempting to synchronize meetings with higher-level managers. However, very few of these managers put their schedules on the network. Other managers did not use a computer at all; they relied on their assistants and secretaries to print out e-mails and other items. Many project leaders started to use the devices for games and entertainment—an expensive "GameBoy." What was the solution? Confiscate all of the devices and ban them until the rules had been worked out.

Behind this simple example, there are a number of fundamental lessons learned:

- Consider always the method and why and how technology will be used first—before the tool itself.
- Technology playing around can divert people from the real work.

- Simulate and determine how the technology will be used, misused, and abused.
- Make sure that you evaluate the combination of the new technology with the current technology. There can be interface problems as well as one technology negating the benefits of another.
- Use technologies where they will be used on an almost daily basis.
- Ensure that the technology is scalable. That is, it can be employed on small as well as large projects.
- Have an expert in the technology available to provide support. Otherwise, the users of the technology will end up flailing around for a long time—more wasted effort.

Only proven useful technologies will be considered here. However, use the above list as a checklist to evaluate potential technologies.

PURPOSE AND SCOPE

TECHNICAL PURPOSE

The technical purpose of a technology-based tool is to make the underlying method more efficient and effective. As an example, e-mail automates some simple communications by substituting for fax machines. The underlying method is communications.

A second technical purpose is that the technology be simple to use around the world. It often does not help if the technology is only available in one country for an international project. Going into a related subject, the technology must be supported in the countries in which it is used. As an example, suppose that you were using a new mobile communications device that worked in Europe or Japan, but did not function in North America due to different communications protocols. Figure 6.1 presents a checklist for evaluating new technologies. A basic question to answer is always:

If you did not use the technology, what would you do and use?

Addressing this question helps you sort out whether you are looking at a technology in search of a problem or a technology that has real use.

BUSINESS PURPOSE

The business purpose is that the use of the technology product will make the project leaders, managers, and team members more useful and productive. Hope-

- Can the device or software be employed in all of the locations in which you are undertaking projects?
- Is there local support for the technology in each location?
- How will help be provided for the technology from headquarters? From the vendor?
- Are there examples of real firms using the technology? If so, what were the benefits? What problems were encountered?
- Is the technology compatible and not conflicting with what you already use?
- What is the learning curve for the technology? A person typically goes through several learning curves for anything new. First, they get some basic understanding so that they can function at a low level. Initial usage then propels them to the second stage in which they pick up more skills. There is then typically a third stage of additional learning. After this, most people are either satisfied with their skill level or they just drop the use of the thing.
- How can success, failure, and usage be measured?
- How long will it be before the technology product becomes obsolete and replaced by a new version?
- Are there any legal or competitive risks in using the technology? E-mail use has spread like wildfire in most organizations. Yet, it can create an awkward audit trail as the American White House, Enron, Arthur Anderson, and others have found—to their dismay.
- How will the technology be introduced?
- How can the technology be abused or misused?

Figure 6.1   Checklist for Evaluating and Selecting New Technology Products

fully, they will then spend less time in administrative work and more time doing technical or management work.

Another business goal is that through the use of a common set of technology-based tools and methods, you can achieve greater standardization. This has a benefit similar to that of templates cited earlier. In fact, templates, issues, and lessons learned cry out for technology-supported tools. It is difficult to imagine how these could be easily employed in a manual mode.

POLITICAL PURPOSE

One potential political purpose is to show the outside world that you are on top of the technology. This can be a useful point when you are competing for a contract. The technology shows to people that you are really organized. However, if the technology is not well organized, your firm can look like a fool.

An internal political purpose is to show the employees that you take the methods seriously enough that you are willing to invest in technology-based products to support the methods. This can help get people behind the use of the technology.

END PRODUCTS

The overall end product is to identify and implement a complete and interrelated set of technologies that will support the project management method and approach you are following. This says that the whole is greater than the sum of the individual technologies.

For each technology the end product is a working tool that supports the established and accepted method and that can be measured in terms of benefits and use. The technology must be supported and stable; you can't afford to invest in something that is too new or that can fail at critical times.

APPROACH

DEFINE YOUR NEEDS FOR TECHNOLOGY

You can first identify your needs in international projects for technologies. To do this you first make a list of what you do in managing projects and the work involved. Make this list the first column in a table. The second column contains entries for what you do now to perform the functions in the first column. In the third column go the issues and problems with the current approach. New technologies of potential interest go in the fourth column. The last, or fifth, column contains statements of how the new technology resolves the issues and problems of the third column. An example is given in Fig. 6.2. Use this as a starting point for your own table.

There are several benefits to this table. First, you show managers that you are organized. Second, the table can help identify areas where you really do need to investigate new technology. A third benefit is that it helps you narrow the focus in searching for technology. That is, you can largely ignore technologies that do not fit in any row of the table.

Where can you find out about new technologies? Check out the magazines and sources in the References appendix. What are you looking for? Articles that describe how a firm used the technology in its projects and what the benefits and lessons learned were. You can also visit vendor Web sites to see if there are new versions coming out.

Now let's now consider a range of specific technologies that are useful in project management. Specific guidelines will be provided for using the technology effectively.

GUIDELINES FOR COMMUNICATIONS AND NETWORKING

International project management is about global communications and networking. You need to be in touch with people in the various locations in which

Activity of project mgmt.	What you currently use	Issues and problems	Potential new technology	Benefits
Noncritical communications				
Critical communications				
Tracking the project				
Project costing and budgeting				
Communications to management				
Issues and lessons learned databases				
Repository of project information				
Sharing of project information				
Addressing issues				
Updating the plan and project status				

Figure 6.2   Technology Evaluation Table

project work is being performed. These statements are obvious. Now look behind the lines at the fine print of requirements. Do you need extremely rapid communications? Sometimes. An example might be videoconferencing. But you don't require it all of the time. So you don't want to pay for capabilities that you will rarely use. It is better to rent or use someone else's facilities.

Does the technology always have to be available? For some things such as defense or banking operations it does. For standard projects this is not necessary. Let's consider an example. One of us managed a project using programmers in India. The location in India had very poor communications. Internet speeds were pathetic, but the Internet was available. How could the programmers be managed and the program code and programs reviewed? The solution was to sometimes use a delivery service for large files. At other times if someone was going to a city that had rapid Internet speeds, they took files with them and transmitted them. At other times for limited e-mail and other documents, the files could be compressed or zipped and then transmitted. The approach worked fine. This is an example of learning to live with what you have available. A basic guideline is:

The project cannot afford to invest in new technology for the project itself in most cases.

Not only is this guideline useful, but you have to consider the overall cost of the technology. Figure 6.3 gives a list of cost factors to consider. Note in this table the phrase "supporting technologies." Most technologies do not come in alone. They require some technological infrastructure or related products. Vendors push this since they want to sell you a range of products.

How do you use communications and networks in project management? Consider creating a table such as that in Fig. 6.4.

Here are some guidelines for communications and networking.

• In countries where there is a modern infrastructure, use what the people in the location are already working with. It is too difficult to teach old dogs new tricks.

• In locations where there is a lack of infrastructure and technology, then each place will have to be considered on a case-by-case basis.

• Instead of investing in more technology, try to think of ways to work smarter. Plan when to communicate. Develop outlines and forms to shorten the communications.

• Define how to communicate as an issue at the start of the international project and have team members explore in their locations the cheapest and easiest way to communicate with you and each other. In one case, the simplest and cheapest was to buy someone a coffee at an Internet café.

• Accept the fact that in a wide-ranging international project, there will have to be more than one standard communications solution.

• Acquiring cost of the technology
• Gaining expertise and developing guidelines for the technology
• Training in the use of the technology
• Measuring and monitoring the use of the technology
• Supporting the use of the technology
• Upgrading the technology
• Providing a help function for the technology
• Maintenance cost of the technology
• Cost of supporting technologies

Figure 6.3   Examples of Cost Factors in Using a Technology

Type of project management communication	Frequency	Comments
Build the project plan	High at the start	Need in-depth communications
Deal with issues	Moderate–high	Need in-depth communications
Collect lessons learned	Moderate	Need in-depth communications
Determine status of work	Often and high volume	Better if you can talk to people
Do team building	Moderate	Need in-depth communications
Communicate with management	Often and cannot be predicted	Variable amount of time
Network with vendors	Often with multiple vendors	Variable amount of time
Perform milestone reviews	Large scale; moderate	Need in-depth communications
Get answers to questions	Often, on demand	Variable amount of time

Figure 6.4   Types of Communications in International Project Management

GUIDELINES FOR SOFTWARE TOOLS

Project management relies on a variety of software tools that run on top of the networks. These include e-mail, electronic forms, groupware, database management, videoconferencing, and project management software. Before plunging into each category for specific guidelines, it is useful to review some basic rules first.

• Your budget in the project for tools or new methods will be very limited. At the most, you might be able to acquire some hardware and software licenses. That is about it. Therefore, there is no use in doing a big survey of technologies available.

• If you are considering software tools for the entire organization and all of its projects, then you want to develop the portfolio approach that was discussed at the start of the chapter with Fig. 6.2.

• It will be difficult to get all of the software from one vendor. While Microsoft can fit the widest range of needs in project management, there will still likely be other tools that will come from different vendors.

• Consider the life cycle cost of the software tool in terms of training, upgrades, and support as well as acquisition.

For any software tool that you have or that you select, there will be a substantial effort needed to have the software tool usefully and consistently employed. Notice the word consistent. If you deploy any software tool in a variety of locations, you have to assume that people will tend to use it in different and inconsistent ways. The only way that you can discourage this is to provide guidance at the start of the use of the tool so that the people see consistency in their self-interest. Figure 6.5 describes the actions needed to successfully implement a software tool. As you can see from the effort behind the items in the list, you should embark upon a new software tool with trepidation.

You can employ Fig. 6.6 as a table to summarize your use of software tools. You should prepare this table and review it with all locations and any vendors or consultants that you are employing. The table is also useful as a handy reference by employees to show them that there is an organized approach. Having the table can discourage people from going out on their own to find tools that duplicate the functions that you already have. The columns are described as follows:

• Comparative analysis with other software tools that perform the same or similar functions
• Comparison with doing nothing in terms of acquiring the software tool
• Involvement of employees in the software tool evaluation
• Identification of the key employees who will initially learn and apply the software tool
• Directions on how the tool should be used and what is expected of the people
• Development of lessons learned and guidelines from using the software tool in a project
• Formulation of management expectation as to the benefits of the software tool
• Definition of the approach for measuring the use and effectiveness of the software tool
• Determination of the types of international projects that are most appropriate for the software tool
• Definition of how the software tool will interface with other software tools
• Customization of the tool to suit your international projects
• Preparation of training materials and procedures
• Identification of an expert to provide ongoing guidance
• Facilitation of gathering of lessons learned and experience as the tool is used

Figure 6.5 Actions Necessary in Implementing a Software Tool

Area or activity	Method	Software tool	Guidelines	Management expectations	Expert

Figure 6.6 Method and Tool Table

- Area or activity of project management—specific activities are listed here.
- Method—software tools have to support some method or approach.
- Guidelines—guidelines should be provided for effective use of the tool.
- Management expectation—this identifies the objectives of the tool from a management view; it helps in measuring whether it is effective.
- Expert—this indicates if there is an expert available to help with the tool and who that person is.

INFORMATION SHARING

When you think of information sharing, you might think of fax machines, telephone, e-mail, and similar tools. The most popular of these is obviously e-mail next to the telephone. It is amazing that people are taught how to use an e-mail system, but are not provided with any guidelines on effective use. Instead, they are taught a hundred specific actions in using the software. This is the difference between training in the software tool and training in the method of how best to use it.

Here are some specific guidelines for using e-mail in international projects:

- Avoid using e-mail for any sensitive topics.
- Assume that everyone in the company will read your e-mails.
- Think about what medium to use for communications before you resort to e-mail.
- Compose an e-mail and then save it in a temporary folder. Review it after a few hours to check the tone and determine if it is complete. Then you can send it.
- Make sure that the title of the e-mail is either very specific or very general. Experience has shown that titles in between result in e-mails being discarded.
- When you open an e-mail in most e-mail systems, you only can read the first 6–8 lines of the e-mail. Many people, especially busy people, read this amount and decide whether to trash the message or read it. Make sure that you get your point across.
- Avoid using e-mail for people in the same room or floor of a building. It is ridiculous to not just walk over to them and socialize rather than resorting to e-mail.
- Be sensitive to the fact that people get many e-mail messages. In one seminar we gave in the first two hours, the average attendee had received 50 (yes, fifty) e-mails. Talk about information overload!
- Maintain a copy of any important e-mail so that you can remember what you said.

• Avoid using e-mail to discuss an issue in any depth. E-mail was never intended to be used as groupware.

• Organize your e-mail into folders that are appropriate for use in project management. You might create a folder for each major subproject, for personnel matters, for budget matters, for project status, etc.

• Have each team member establish an e-mail account outside of the company. Why do this? Because you may find that you cannot access your e-mail in the company from a remote location. You also may find that firewalls inhibit remote access. Make sure that the team members are told that this e-mail account is to be used for the project only. If they want to use e-mail for personal use, they can set another free e-mail account. Pay for additional storage of messages. Encourage team members to periodically go in and clean up the e-mail account so that it is efficiently and effectively used.

Now let's prioritize communications and information sharing for international projects.

1. In person. The best communication is still face-to-face. You see the person's body language and get their tone and nuances. Very important and it often tells you more about what is going on in the project.

2. Telephone. You can still get tone of voice here. Note that you should always smile into the telephone. It gives people a feeling that you are more confident and upbeat about the project.

3. Videoconferencing is very useful in communications in a project to save travel costs. Organize the videoconference ahead of time. Try to rent a facility that has a white board and other aids.

4. Voice mail. Yes, voice mail is better than e-mail since you can give your tone of voice. Always rehearse or write down what you are going to say first. Otherwise, most people tend to leave long and rambling messages.

5. E-mail. Here it is at number 5 for the reasons given above.

6. Fax. This is probably the worse of the lot. Who knows if the fax is received? Who will read the fax? In one international project, a manager sent a fax regarding a sensitive personnel matter. It ended up being posted on a bulletin board.

Avoid leaving messages with an intermediary since the message can be garbled or not delivered. This is especially valid when you call overseas.

Another guideline is to use telephone cards for international projects. This is one of our favorite methods of saving money in a project. At the project kickoff we distribute telephone cards to everyone on the team. The telephone cards should be rechargeable using a credit card so that people don't have to keep running around for new cards. You will have to consider getting different cards for each country since the normal card allows you to call out from one country and back into that country. The telephone card approach also allows them to use the card to make personal calls back home—very important for morale!

PROJECT MANAGEMENT SOFTWARE

The most popular PC-based project management software is Microsoft Project. However, the guidelines that will be provided here apply to similar software from other vendors. Some specific guidelines are given in Fig. 6.7. You can find more detailed guidelines in the book, *Breakthrough Technology Project Management*, second ed., by the same authors.

There are some basic problems with most of the existing project management software packages. First, they were initially designed for use by single users. Hooks have been provided for collaboration, but at the heart they are still single-user-oriented systems. Project management in modern international projects is a collaborative widespread activity. Thus, the most suitable project management tools would be based on the Internet and would employ a Web browser.

A second problem is that the existing software allows either total read-only or read–write access at the file level. If you are going to do collaborative project management, team members have to update their own individual tasks within the project plan. Therefore, they require write access to only specific tasks.

A third disadvantage is that many of the software tools have excessive features. Some of the features that should be discouraged are:

- Adopt a standard set of abbreviations for terms such as review, design, etc, to be used in task names. This leads to greater consistency.
- Number all tasks and milestones. This shows to management that you are organized. It also makes it easier to refer to and save time during long distance calls and videoconferencing.
- Make sure that your customization of the project management software includes fields for issues, lessons learned, indicator of whether the task is risky, area of responsibility of the task (not the same as the resource field), date the task was created, who created the task, reason that the task was created, requirements that gave rise to the task.
- Try to keep task names down to 25–30 characters at most. This will give room for the GANTT chart.
- Customize the views, forms, tables, and filters in the software. These are terms used in Microsoft Project, but there are equivalent terms for other software. This gives consistency.
- Adopt a standard project file naming convention to make it easy to track down projects.
- Maintain files of earlier forms of the project so that you can retrace history if you have a dispute or problem.
- Train employees and team members in the method of project management. Then provide training in the use of the project management software tool. In that way, they don't become enamored of the tool, but instead focus on the method.

Figure 6.7   Some Guidelines for Using Project Management Software

- Spell checking. This is not a good feature since you will have to employ standard abbreviations for most tasks to keep the length small to show the GANTT chart.
- PERT chart. Try to avoid PERT or sequential views of the project. This is especially true in international projects. Why? A PERT chart can encourage sequential thinking. People will not start a task until the predecessor is completed.
- Automated resource leveling. This should be done manually and in a collaborative way.
- Most of the reports that can be generated. The problem here is that the reports cannot easily be customized.

As a rule of thumb, it is recommended that you will end up using about 10–15% of the software. But it is a useful percentage. If the percentage is so low, why use the tool? Politics. There is nothing like a GANTT chart in which you have highlighted the tasks with issues and risk in a different color. This will give you support and put pressure on management to resolve issues.

All that aside, a key benefit of project management software is that you can customize the data elements in the software. After all, behind the project management software is a database. Another benefit is that you can customize the views and form as well as database queries or filters for the project data.

COLLABORATIVE TOOLS

Groupware is an excellent category of software for project management. Lotus Notes is probably the best known and most widely used software in this category. Groupware allows you to organize folders in the project. Groupware also allows you to establish a folder for each specific issue or lesson learned. This is much easier in managing, dealing with, and tracking issues than e-mail.

Let's give two examples of successful use. A firm that is involved in launching satellites into space had many difficulties in sharing information between the remote satellite launch site and home offices. Groupware was implemented. The benefits were immediately felt. Lessons learned and issues were available on-line at any time. Project plans were immediately available and could be viewed anywhere in the world. The groupware provided the structure for useful collaboration. The second example had the same benefits for the deployment of new banking products in South America.

USE THE INTERNET AND WEB

Obviously, most of the team members are already well versed in using the Web and Internet. How can you employ this technology for international projects? The first way is for e-mail and was discussed earlier. Another use of the Web is to explore literature and magazines for project management lessons learned and issues (see the References listed in Appendix 3). You can also use the Internet to view the Web sites of vendors and products that apply to the project. Another application is to check up on what competitors are doing and what they see as important.

HOW TECHNOLOGY CREATES BENEFITS AND PROBLEMS

Technology can provide many benefits if you believe the specific vendor claims. Stripping off the claims, let's get down to reality. Here are some of the benefits that have been experienced in projects from using technology and in particular software tools. Note that getting these benefits assumes that you have followed the actions in Fig. 6.5.

• A technology can enforce company rules and policies by encouraging a specific way of doing things.
• Use of a technology across an organization can be self-sustaining, requiring little enforcement for the use of the tool.
• Widespread use of a technology encourages consistency.
• Use of a technology can encourage collaboration and information sharing that would be otherwise difficult or impossible.
• Use of the technology can reduce the cost and effort of performing the activity as compared to what it replaced.
• A technology or tool can reduce the time it takes to make decisions and may support better decisions by providing better quality and more timely information.

A number of problems have already been identified with tools and technology. Here let's examine the following list:

• A software tool is acquired, but not properly supported so that it languishes and is only used by a few people.
• The software tool is easy to learn at a basic level, but difficult and complex to master in detail.
• While the tool can be used by one person, it is really not suitable for use in a collaborative environment.
• The tool was selected too soon. Now there are better tools available from different vendors. The employees think that they are stuck with a lemon. Remember what happened with companies who stuck with old word processing tools for too long?
• The functions of the tool overlap with those of other tools in use so that redundant effort is needed in data entry and use—reducing the extent of usage of the tool.

Element of score card	Score (1–5; 1, low; 5, high)
How widespread is the use of the tool?	
Do people use other tools instead of this one?	
Have there been guidelines issued?	
Are lessons learned gathered about the tool?	
Does management measure and assess the value of the tool?	
Is the tool supported by an internal expert?	
Are there internal training materials?	
Are there detailed procedures for the tool?	
Are there new, competing tools available?	
Has the vendor issued new versions of the tool?	
Is the tool used and available in remote locations?	
Is the tool widely used by your vendors?	

Figure 6.8   Score Card for Technology and Tools

To put it all together, Fig. 6.8 provides a score card for your use. We suggest that you apply this to your current software tools.

EXAMPLES

Sᴀᴍʙᴀᴄ Eɴᴇʀɢʏ

Each company that participated in Sambac had their own technologies and tools. In most cases, the two firms had (by chance) chosen the same tools. However, the e-mail systems were different. This created many problems in interfaces. Custom interfaces were created by each company to share the e-mail messages. It was not effective since the software changed with new versions.

In this difficult situation, the approach was taken at Sambac to use Yahoo Mail. Yahoo is one of the most widely used free e-mail systems. This worked out quite well. Even today, the same solution is being used. The internal politics and bickering were avoided.

WHITMORE BANK

Whitmore deployed new offices into a region. Each office had its own unique issues. However, with the use of templates, issues, and lessons learned in groupware, the implementation period was reduced by 30% as later offices learned from experiences of the earlier offices.

LESSONS LEARNED

- The functions versus technology table in Fig. 6.2 is useful with vendors in that you can establish a common set of technologies that you will employ in an international project. This will minimize incompatibilities.
- Resist acquiring new technology tools that promise to do many functions. Often, they represent overkill in use except in very large projects.
- Review your methods and tools on an annual basis to see what is new and if people are using the current methods and tools effectively.
- Gather lessons learned on the use of the technology during the projects as part of the project. Make sure that this experience is shared with people in other projects.

EXERCISES

1. Try to use the Web to find what is available in project management software that is Internet based.
2. On the Web sign up at two sites that are very useful for project management—www.gantthead.com and www.techrepublic.com. These sites have many useful tips for using project management software and for project management.
3. Use the table of methods and tools to determine where the gaps are in the methods and tools that you are using now.
4. Apply the score card for the software tools to the tools that you are using now.

SUMMARY

A key idea in this chapter has been that it is not how much technology you employ in international projects; it is that you employ the minimal number of tools in an effective and efficient manner. Always, concentrate on the tangible benefits of the tools. Do they save you time? Do they produce better results?

Avoid the "wiz-bang" features of the technology. And remember the learning curve. If you have to take the time to learn some new technology, that time will have to come from somewhere—likely from areas that need more of your attention.

Part II

Manage Your International Effort for Success

Chapter 7

Manage the International Team and the Work

INTRODUCTION

Work has begun on the project. Given that this is going on in multiple locations, a key issue relates to the techniques for effectively and efficiently managing both the people and the work. If this was a simple, single-culture and -location project, then you would be provided with guidelines to cover the entire project so as to be complete. Forget it. You cannot be complete or cover all bases. There are too many people, locations, and managers to deal with. This gives you your first guideline:

**Be selective in terms of how you manage the people
and the work in an international project.**

There will be times when you feel guilty because you could not talk to all of the team members in a given week. Some things are bound to "fall through the cracks."

A related question to ask is "What is success in managing the work and people?" Is it that you do project administration well? No. Is it that you are aware of the status of the project at all times? Getting closer. Here are some measures of success in management:

• Management never comes to you with an issue. You always go to them and keep them up-to-date. This shows that you are on top of the project.

• You take time to analyze the issues and work in the project—not just oversee it.

• You are very much involved with issues and problems and the related team members and tasks.

• Morale among project members is high as is evident by how they discuss the project.

Note that these are indirect signs of success. In all of international projects we have been involved with, there were few times where people came up and said what a success the project was. In general, things are going well if there are no major complaints or issues and you hear the team talking about their work in the project.

From experience a list of key activities in managing the project when it is underway is given in Fig. 7.1. As with many things in this book, this is organized into a table for your later use. The type of activity is given in the first column. Activities are listed in the second column. Some of the potential problems that you might encounter and comments are in the third column of the table. The last column indicates whether the activity should be treated as foreground or background, based on the following discussion:

How do you manage your time among these activities in general? Consider yourself as an operating systems on a computer. Operating systems perform foreground and background tasks at the same time. A foreground task is higher priority and what you are concentrating on. A background activity is what is lower priority and can go on when you are not busy with foreground activities. At any given time as a project leader you should have two lists: one for foreground tasks and the other for background work. This method has several benefits for you.

• You force yourself to divide up what you do into two simple priority categories.

• You ensure that foreground tasks are given a higher priority than background work.

• You give a higher priority to action-oriented work and a lower priority to administrative tasks.

• You can assess how you are doing by seeing how many activities in each category have been addressed.

• Over time as you become more experienced, you can add to the number of things that you are doing simultaneously. When you later measure this, you can see how efficient you are.

PURPOSE AND SCOPE

For each purpose there are goals for you as the project leader and for the international project overall.

Type/category	Activity	Potential problems and comments	Foreground/ background
Management	Informal communications with managers	Uneven contacts; get too busy to do this	Foreground
Management	Status reporting	You can get carried away with this	Background
Management	Presentations on the project	You give too many of these and devote too much time here	Foreground when needed; otherwise, background
Management	Vendor coordination	Too much is delegated; need to stay on top of this	Foreground
Analysis	Project issues	Not enough time is spent here	Foreground
Analysis	Schedule status	Too much analysis is performed	Background
Problem solving	Dealing with issues	Too much time is spent in analysis or people jump too early to solve problems	Foreground
Project team	Team communications	You attempt to contact everyone on a regular basis	Foreground
Project team	Lessons learned	Not given sufficient priority	Foreground
Project team	Reviewing milestones	Do not apply time evenly—go for the ones with risk and issues	Foreground for risky ones; background for others
Project team	Update the schedule	Project leaders should not be doing this	Should not be done
Project	Doing work in the project	Need to do some of this to be hands-on	Background
Administrative	Doing budget analysis	A limited amount of time here is OK	Background
Administrative	Working with project management software	This can be a bottomless pit for time	Background

Figure 7.1   Critical Project Management Activities during Project Work

TECHNICAL PURPOSE

For the project, the technical goal is get high-quality work produced with a minimum of problems and issues. Doing the work on time and within budget is a business purpose. Another related technical objective is to ensure that the project state is known at all time.

Your own technical objective is to improve your project management skills so that you can be more efficient and effective later in the project and in future projects. Keep this in mind always and you will spend less time in administrative overhead work. Let's get something out on the table about administrative work. It is essential, but it is overhead and takes time away from other things. Remember that one of your biggest enemies is time. In general,

In international projects time is more important than money.

You can always find money if the project is making progress and the need is clear. No one has yet figured out how to change time.

BUSINESS PURPOSE

For the project, the business purpose is to accomplish the goals of the project within the constraints of money and time. Beyond this, the overall goal is that the results of the project yield the benefits that were expected. After all, it doesn't do much good if the project is a roaring success and the results of the project are either a stinking failure or are not used. Another business goal is the milestones and work be measurable so that the information about the project is accurate.

Your business goal as a project leader is to get issues understood, analyzed, and resolved. You do not want unpleasant surprises toward the end of the project. Another business goal is that the project team work well together in their work.

POLITICAL PURPOSE

The project goal is to build a culture of collaboration during the international project that will last after the project is completed. At the local level you want to build greater cooperation and understand with other locations and with headquarters. For headquarters you will want the headquarters managers and others involved in the project to be more sensitive to the activities and needs of the in-country operations. Aren't these goals too ambitious? Probably, but that is what goals are for.

How would you measure whether you are making progress toward these objectives? Take notice of people's attitudes at the start of the project. Do headquarters people make derisive statements about one or more in-country locations? Do the local operations managers and staff complain a great deal about headquarters not making decisions, interfering in their work, and imposing unrealistic activities on them? Then notice if there is an attitude change as the work progresses. If there is a change, then you are on the road to a success.

What is your political goal? You want to build relationships with as many people as you can for the project duration and for your future. While being a project leader is very stressful and demanding, it can also be a key to moving ahead in the organization or in advancing in another company.

END PRODUCTS

A realistic set of end products for your international project includes the following:

- Reviewed milestones;
- Issues being tracked and resolved;
- Lessons learned being collected and used;
- Up-to-date schedule and plan that are accurate;
- Management aware of issues and status of the project;
- Team members working together on tasks;
- An effective method for allocating resources and dealing with resource conflicts.

APPROACH

CARRY OUT PROACTIVE RESOURCE ALLOCATION

From the very start of this book, it has been emphasized that a major problem in international projects is that people in a location can be drawn away from the project to do other work. Often, if they do not tell you, then you will not know this has happened until you inquire about the status of the work. Moreover, this approach is reactive.

The goal here is to define a proactive approach that heads off or at least minimizes the extent to which people are pulled from the project. Here is a technique that works:

- Identify the critical resources to the project. These may be individual who are working on tasks with risk or on tasks where there is severe time pressure.

• Arrange a weekly meeting with the appropriate line manager(s) to review the use of their resources in the project and the projected use of the resources in the upcoming week. Since there are often multiple locations, you will have to resort to telephone or videoconferencing. A good day to do this is Thursday—before the end of the week, but also far enough in the work week.

• At the meeting, you will first review how the current week went. Identify any times when the person was pulled from the project. Discuss why and how this happened. This will indicate to them that you are aware of what is going on. They will be more reluctant to do this in the future. Now turn to the upcoming week. Ask what is going on that would interfere with their work in the project. This may force some of the hidden agendas out in the open. Discuss what they will be working on in the project. Agree on what is to be done. In general, you should have people work on your project on Tuesday and Wednesday. Why these particular days? Well, Monday is just after the weekend and there may have been problems over the weekend that have to be addressed. Thursday and Friday are days when people are getting ready for the weekend.

UPDATE THE PLAN

In traditional project management, the project leader updates the plan in a meeting or through contact with team members. This has several drawbacks in international projects. First, it is almost impossible to reach everyone. You would be on the telephone all of the time. You could do no other work. Second, it lowers the project leader to the position of a clerk—demeaning. Third, the team does not participate.

You require a better and faster method in which team members collaborate and participate. Here are the steps of a winning method:

• Provide network access to all team members so that they can view and update their tasks in the plan.

• Supply a minimum amount of training in the project management software (about 4 hours) so that they know how to open the plan, enter tasks, update tasks, and save the results.

• Have each team member update their tasks twice a week. Since the detailed tasks are 1–2 weeks in duration, this is not an undue effort. There are typically only a handful of active tasks at any given time. The method for updating is as follows: mark all completed tasks as complete; if there is slippage in a task, then a new task is created that links to the original task, indicating the date created and reason for the task; new tasks are also entered in this way. Recall that there is detail for 3–4 months in advance so the team members will also enter detailed tasks in the future so that you always have the future 3–4 months of the plan in detail.

• After the plan has been updated, the project leader reviews the plan to see what changed overall. Has there been a slippage? If so, then you can filter the plan and examine what changed. You can then contact the specific team members that caused the schedule to shift. More issues may be added.

This is a proactive approach that gets the team members to participate and define and update their work. The project leader is then really functioning as the project leader and not doing clerical work. Look at the third step again. Notice that team members cannot just slip a task and input a new duration. If you allow people to do this, you will lose traceability in the plan. Accountability will also suffer. Another benefit of the method is that it saves time since updating is being performed in parallel. In addition, the project leaders' time is focused on where there are problems.

TRACK PROJECT WORK

This section deals with your overall involvement with the project team as work is being done. Your goal here is to gain a better understanding of what is going on and how the work is being done. Through this you will gain insight into the real state of the project. You also may uncover more issues.

In communications the emphasis is on informal contact. Never have team members come to you. Always call them or go to them. This shows that you care enough to get out there. Try to go to team members unannounced frequently. If you always announce your visits, then people will change to show you and tell you what you want to hear. This is like Potemkin villages in the days of the czars in Russia. The czarina, Catherine the Great, wanted to see how the people lived. The officials were aghast. Potemkin came up with the solution. The czarina would take a boat down the main river and she could then see the villages and talk to people. Potemkin arranged for a model village to be created so that wheels could be attached to the houses. During the day the czarina saw a happy village which was very clean. As she slept on the boat, the village was moved down the river and changed. The same scene was repeated for several days—a small, but interesting project.

When you encounter the team member, talk in generalities at the start. Inquire about their personal life. Try to remember the names of their spouses and some personal fact. This shows that you care about them and more than just the work. After this, you can then ask how the work is going in terms of any problems that they are facing. You can also here ask about other work that they are doing beyond the project. Listen for the tone of voice. What is more exciting to them—the project or the regular work? Work to uncover any new issues. Volunteer to help them. Then you can get to status.

You will encounter some difficult personnel situations. People may not get along with each other. A team member is not doing work in the project even though you have talked about this repeatedly. How do you handle situations such as these? Begin to contact them more frequently. If they see you coming or hear from you more often, they will begin to realize that their work is really important to the project. If you fail to do this, then they may feel that there is no big problem. Remember it is what you do that is more important than what you say in project management.

Even after visiting them repeatedly, nothing happens. Then what? One of us has adopted an extreme approach. You move in with them where they are working. Now the pressure is really on. In one case, this took a long time to get across. It finally worked, but it was an ordeal. The person was quite dense.

REVIEW MILESTONES

You have no time to review all of the milestones in an international project. There are too many and there is too little time. You have to be selective in reviewing milestones. Which ones do you review? Concentrate on the milestones that have risky tasks and issues associated with them. Milestones that are routine and not critical in that mistakes can be easily corrected can be given less attention.

Here is a proven method for selecting which milestones to review? At the start of the project rate each milestone on a scale of 0 to 3 as follows:

• Level 0, no review. This category is reserved for simple situations.
• Level 1, existence. Here you just check to see if there is evidence of the work.
• Level 2, structure. The end product is in 14 parts. Are there 14 parts?
• Level 3, content. This category is reserved for areas of risk and where the work leading up to the milestone has issues.

Update the rating as time goes by.

How do you review a level 3 milestone? Obviously, it depends upon the nature of the project and that of the specific milestone. However, many milestones are reports, analysis, and similar things. You don't have time to read all of the documents. Also, how could you determine where there are problems and weaknesses? A proven method is to have the two team members who performed the work make a presentation of their work in a lessons learned meeting. During the meeting watch their body language and listen to their tone of voice. Look for topics that they gloss over. This will tell you a great deal about the parts of the document or end product that should be reviewed in detail after the meeting. Of course, if you have followed the method of successive outlining that was discussed earlier, then the problems will be lessened.

DETERMINE THE STATE OF THE PROJECT

The state of an international project is the real status and condition of the project. It is an overall view of the project as opposed to the status. The project score card that is addressed next is another method for determining the state of the project.

How do you determine the state of a project? Let's put it differently. Suppose that you are appointed to take over an international project that was in trouble. What would you do and ask? Here is a list of questions:

• What is the status of the oldest outstanding issue? Why is it still unresolved?

• If you take the latest version of the plan and go out to the team members, would you find that what they are working on is accurately reflected in the plan?

• Are team members working in isolation to each other or are they working together?

The second question is of particular interest. Several things may be observed. First, they may not be working on the project at all—not a good sign. Second, the plan may be accurate—very good. Third, the team members may be working on the project, but they are doing work that is not in the plan. However, it is important work. What does this mean? First, the plan does not accurately reflect the extent of the work that is required. This means that the schedule for the project is probably faulty and too optimistic. Second, it means that you may have encountered an example of an iceberg project. What is this? An **iceberg project** is one in which a substantial part of the work is being performed unmanaged and undetected—just like the percentage of the ice that is above the water line. What should you do if you meet up with this situation? Assume that you have just touched on the tip of the iceberg. Gather more information and develop a more complete plan.

EMPLOY A PROJECT SCORE CARD

A score card approach is useful because it allows you to measure an international project in a consistent manner over time. It can also be employed to measure multiple projects. Score cards are also valuable because they give you the opportunity to measure more than just budget and schedule. Fig. 7.2 presents a score card that includes a number of subjective factors. Like the other score cards in this book, you will want to adopt and change it to fit your requirements.

Here are comments on some of the elements of the score card in Fig. 7.2. Some of the items on issues will be discussed in Chapter 10:

• Number of people involved in the project. In general, in an international project you seek to involve more, rather than fewer people. Involving more people increases the support for the project. Also, you are less dependent on one person if people are being rotated in and out of the project. The impact on a department is reduced since no one person is being kept from the work for too long.

Score Card Factor	Score (1–5; 1, low; 5, high)
Number of people involved in the project	
Turnover in the project team	
% of tasks ahead with risk and issues	
Age of the oldest outstanding issue	
Budget versus actual	
Schedule versus planned dates	
Number of outstanding issues	
Ratio of controllable open issues/total open issues	
% of milestones achieved on time	
Number of lessons learned captured in the project	
% of tasks that are jointly assigned	
Tasks defined-team members?	
Tasks updated by team members?	
Are issues associated with tasks?	
Number of contacts with management	
Number of contacts with remote locations	
Weekly resource allocation being used?	

Figure 7.2   Score Card for an Ongoing International Project

- Turnover of staff in the team. Some turnover is good; a great deal of turnover is negative.
- % of tasks ahead with risk. This is to measure the percentage of hours in future work in the project that has risk and issues.
- Ratio of controllable issues to total issues. Controllable issues are those that can be decided by the project with minimal management involvement. Obviously, the lower the ratio, the higher the risk.
- Number of lessons learned in the project. If there are only a few lessons learned, then either the project is very routine or else lessons learned are not being captured.

As you review the score card, you can see that it goes beyond simple budget and scheduling measurement. You can also see that many of the items relate to themes in this book. This is done by intent.

To reinforce the project management methods, score cards must use these factors.

Otherwise, people will tend to ignore the methods since they do not see them being reinforced.

How often should you build the score card? Every 3 months might be useful. If it is done more frequently, there is too much effort. If it is done less frequently, then the value is reduced. Who should build the score cards? The project leaders with the international project coordinator.

CARRY OUT CHANGE MANAGEMENT

International projects often involve change. People tend to resist change. However, if there is no change, then the results of the project may either be failure or a lack of benefits. Change management often goes hat in hand with project management.

You must first get the people who will be using the results of the project to admit that the way they do their work now is not good and has problems. This is consistent with drug and alcohol addiction in which the person must first admit that they have a problem. Once they admit that they have problems, then they are on the road to a cure. It is the same in international projects. If people don't feel that they need to change, then they will resist using the results of the project. After the project is turned over, they may just return to their old ways!! It has happened many times.

How do you accomplish this? Early in the project, you must analyze the situation that the project is to address. Get people involved to talk about their work and problems. As they discuss their problems, they will begin to wonder if the problems cannot be fixed. This will start to give you support for change.

Later you will likely run into another barrier to change. People will say that many efforts have been tried before, but that there have been no real lasting improvements. They lack confidence that you can deliver results. What should you do in this situation? A possible answer is to implement improvements that lead up to the final project results. This approach is called **Quick Hits** or **Quick Wins**. The basic idea is that implementing the project results is too traumatic in one step and it may be too long so that people lose both confidence and interest. The alternative is to implement several waves of changes or Quick Hits that yield benefits, raise confidence, and prepare the way for the results of the project.

Figure 7.3 compares the Quick Win and traditional approaches. In this figure there are two solid lines for the Big Bang and two dotted lines for Quick Hits. One line shows the implementation method. The other shows confidence in the project. In the Quick Hit approach confidence builds. In the Big Bang graph confidence increases, but then declines because nothing is happening.

Of course, not all projects are amenable to Quick Wins. However, changing processes, implementing new systems, and putting in new policies do fit within this. Care must be taken when using this approach.

• The changes that you make must be consistent with the results of the project. Otherwise, they will have to be reversed or undone—causing more problems.

• Care must be taken to ensure that the project does not get sidetracked into just doing Quick Hits.

• Management may want to stop with the Quick Hits. Be on guard for this.

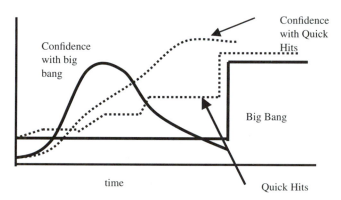

Figure 7.3   Big Bang and Quick Win Approaches to Project Implementation

Nevertheless, this is a useful way to introduce change that is an alternative to the "big bang" approach followed in many cases.

DEAL WITH SCOPE CREEP

Scope creep is an infamous phrase that is as old as projects are. **Scope creep** can be defined as the unplanned expansion or change of a project after it has been started. How does scope creep arise? Here are some reasons.

- The project was not carefully defined at the start. People just started into planning.
- There was no consensus or agreement on what was to be done in the project. People just assumed. Like the old saying, "Making assumptions makes asses out of you and me."
- There is lack of communications to detect potential scope creep and change. When change comes, it is often too late to be handled well. Much of the project may have to redone.
- There is no method or approach for dealing with changes. It is all ad hoc, reactive mode—deadly. The project leaders lose control.

Many people accept scope creep as a fact of life in every project. However, it does not have to be this way. If you carefully plan and keep people informed as well as make provisions for dealing with change when it comes, it can be managed better.

Some useful guidelines for dealing with scope creep are the following:

- *Planning for the project.* In the second chapter, the project concept was presented as something that is essential to get consensus and understanding of purpose, scope, issues, and other factors.
- *Extensive informal communications.* This is stressed in Chapter 9. By communicating with both headquarters and field locations, you can pick up on potential factors that could affect the international project.
- *Contingency planning for potential changes.* At the start of the project, you should express the idea that people will want to make changes. Indicate that this is natural. However, also tell them that the following questions will have to be addressed. Then when someone proposes a change ask the questions. It is also a good idea to run through several examples of change so that they fully understand the process to be followed.
  — What is the change?
  — What other changes are there?
  — What are the business and political factors behind the change?
  — What will happen if the change is not carried out in the project?

— What will happen if the change is made later after the project is completed?

— If the change is made, what will happen to the budget, schedule, and resources?

— What are the real benefits of the change?

— How will the benefits of the change be measured?

— Will the original benefits of the project be affected if the change is not made?

— What will be the role of the person or group that is suggesting the change? Will they have "skin in the game"?

• *Periodic review of scope.* Sit down with the team and review the project with the view of detecting potential changes.

ALTER PROJECT DIRECTION

During a longer international project, it is possible that the project will have its direction changed due to internal business needs or outside factors. In traditional project management, there is no organized way to deal with this. With the lack of a method, many project leaders just change the project plan and keep going. They do this after every change. After a few changes, it becomes very difficult, if not impossible, to track changes and find out what happened. The baseline schedule becomes meaningless. People lose confidence in the project. The team morale plummets.

The use of templates can help shield the project plan from changes.

Unless the project changes dramatically, project changes can be accommodated within the template.

This provides for greater stability. It also reveals the flexibility inherent in using templates.

Here is another guideline. Do not respond to each change separately. Instead, bundle several changes into a new release of the project plan. This is the same technique employed with software and engineering releases of upgraded products.

MEASURE PROJECT RESULTS

There are several things to measure after a project is completed. One is the project itself and the other is the result derived from the project. Let's consider each of these. To measure the project you can use the following:

- The project score card;
- Budget versus actual analysis;
- Issue analysis as described in Chapter 10;
- Assessment of lessons learned from the project.

In order to measure the results of the project, you have to have measurements from the situation before the project was started. Incredibly, many organizations do not carry out these measurements. They never really know if they are any better off, other than a vague feeling. Here are some techniques to employ:

- Undertake comparison of score cards between the old and new situations.
- Have individuals involved in the work make comparisons between the old and new. This approach can be very useful to management—especially if it is conducted at the in-country level.
- Conduct surveys of customers, suppliers, or employees.

When should you carry out this analysis? Do the project analysis at the end of the project. Otherwise, people will have moved on to other work.

At the end of a project there is likely to be some unfinished business. There are some things for follow up. Should you not stop the project and keep it going to finish these things up? No. Gather the data and start a new small project. Remember that some people may want to use this as an opportunity to not use the results of the project.

If you have defined the scope of the project properly, then the project results will be used. However, if the scope of the project was not created right, then the project may end, but there may be no benefits since there are additional steps that must be taken. As an example, consider the implementation of new software in five locations. Assume that the scope was restricted to the IT work. The project ends when the system is installed and working. But who is to say that it is being used? After a system is installed, there must be training and conversion to new business processes that are consistent with the new system. If these are formally in the project plan, then there is likely to be system success and overall project failure.

EXAMPLES

SAMBAC ENERGY

At Sambac every project was managed according to the experience and approach of the individual project manager. Thus, if there were five different projects, each with different project managers, the result would be five variations of project management. This made it impossible for management to track the projects overall. Each project manager handled issues differently. A few managers gathered some lessons learned; most did not. In essence each project was treated as unique.

The implementation method was to begin in one project. This was a moderately sized project with many issues. It was felt to be a good test of the methods in this and other chapters. It did work, but in retrospect the choice of projects was poor. A project with fewer issues would have been a better place to start since more attention could have been given to lessons learned and other areas. Instead, issues dominated the project—highlighting the value of the method for dealing with issues.

WHITMORE BANK

The problems in the first project attempt for credit card became apparent during a project review. The methods of this chapter were applied and the project was found to be a true iceberg project. When the additional tasks were added, it became clear that the project would be a year late! This was the trigger to start over again. Using the new methods the project finished ahead of where the original project would have been.

LESSONS LEARNED

An important consideration is how to introduce a change in project management methods. This subject arises here because much of the attention in projects is on the ones that are active. One approach to implementing change is for management to announce a new method and then follow it up with training. This is not a good method. People feel defensive and resentful. They feel that management is throwing away what worked for them. They also may feel that they are being grouped in with other project leaders whom they view as marginally competent.

A better technique is to introduce the methods informally in one or two projects where the project leaders are amenable to changes. This is a useful low-profile approach that works. As the methods are applied in these projects, you can gather lessons learned and additional guidelines to make the methods work even better in the future. This also reinforces the value of lessons learned.

As the projects are successful, you can expand to other projects. You can announce a policy after most of the projects are working under the new methods. Then it is a fait accompli. Use the project leaders who applied the methods first to give training and testimonials on the value of the methods. If people hear from their peers about the benefits and ease of use, they will be more accepting of change. You also form focus groups to have project leaders express their frustration and define problems associated with the old techniques.

EXERCISES

1. Review how your international projects are managed. Is there a consistent approach or does the method depend on the specific project leader and situation.

2. Have there been any attempts to improve the management of ongoing projects? Or have the pressures of time and money made this impossible?

3. Have new methods been tried? What happened? Were they given a fair trial? Were the results measured?

SUMMARY

A substantial number of guidelines have been presented to make you more effective as a project leader and to better ensure the success of your international project. Keep in mind that these ideas are proven and that they support the major themes given in earlier chapters. These themes included the use of templates and standardization at the higher levels. Another theme was the use of issues and lessons learned. A third theme was collaboration and communication. As you can see, the themes are carried out in updating, measuring, reviewing, managing, and doing the work in the international project.

Chapter 8

Manage Outsourcing and Vendors

INTRODUCTION

In a project, when you hire someone or a company to do part or all of the work in the project, it is called **outsourcing**. The use of outsourcing goes back thousands of years. Machiavelli referred to outsourcing when he discussed using mercenary troops, for example.

In international projects, there are many varieties of outsourcing. Three types are:

• Outsource one or more activities across all locations. Examples here might be construction oversight, project management, or communications.
• Outsource specific or general activities within one location. Here you are drawing on the experience and ties of the outsourcing firm to get started in this country, as an example.
• Outsource a short-term piece of work across multiple locations. This can be viewed as a one-time situation.
• Outsource part of the ownership of the firm in the country—franchising or affiliation.

The outsourcing firm can be local, international, or the local franchise of an international firm. All of this matters since it may indicate how much communications and coordination there is in the firm.

There are a number of benefits to outsourcing for international projects:

• You literally may not be able to do business without a tie to a local firm.
• Your learning curve in the country is reduced if you can pick up the knowledge from the outsourcing firm.

- Members of the staff can be freed up to do other work due to the outsourcer's presence.
  - You may have greater business success by having a local partner.
  - Costs will be lower by using local firms with their competitive labor rates.

Outsourcing is often a major part of modern international projects. There are a number of reasons for this. Some of these are:

- Your company lacks the experience and expertise in a particular country or region.
  - You lack political ties to the government which may be essential to gain licenses and permits.
  - It is just too expensive to bring in overseas people to do the work.
  - Local regulations may require that native firms be employed.

However, there are also disadvantages.

- You become dependent upon this firm. In some cases in Asia, the firm gained the experience and expertise to do manufacturing better than the western partner firm. They then established a duplicate plant and made similar or better products for less. A basic lesson learned here—"Watch out who you trust."
  - The outsourcing firm takes on more of the work and visibility—affecting products and market share.
  - Management of the outsourcing firm may increase costs because they know that you are dependent upon them.
  - Knowledge is not transferred as planned.
  - The outsourcing firm has a falling out with the government, or a new government comes into power that is not as friendly as the previous one.
  - Your flexibility to change and maneuvering room are much less. It may take much longer to make decisions.
  - You become reliant on the methods, software, or tools that the vendor uses and your employees lack expertise in these areas. This can create a long-term relationship that you may not have wanted.

It is not that you can trade-off between the advantages and disadvantages. For many international projects, there is no choice. It may be a requirement to do business in a particular location.

Because of the extent of its use and importance in a project, it is imperative that you plan in detail and then manage the outsourced work. In international projects, things can slip by. You must manage it like you would the rest of the project.

Another note here is needed for the situation with multiple consultants and vendors. This is not unusual in a larger international project with several locations. Normally, in work within one city, we would discuss how the vendors would get along and share knowledge. This is not true here. Your best and safest route is to compartmentalize the consultants so that they have little contact with each other. The only exception for this is when you are dealing with technical work wherein they must work and interface with each other.

PURPOSE AND SCOPE

TECHNICAL PURPOSE

One technical purpose is that the work performed by outsourcing firms is of high quality. Quality is a subjective term so that means that standards have to be set and enforced. If this was a more localized book, then you would see here an extensive discussion of quality. The problem in international projects is that there are other factors involved. Politically, you may have to accept a specific partner who, in effect, is an outsourcer. Then the technical purpose is to get the most work done for the limited amount of money and effort.

Even if the relationship is entirely political, the focus is on performance. What was done over a specific period with respect to work by the vendor or partner? In order to answer this question, you also have to address what is really important in the vendor relationship.

Another technical purpose is that knowledge gained and used by the vendors is transferred to your people. How do you test for this? Try a variety of situations out on the staff who have interacted with the vendor and see what happens.

BUSINESS PURPOSE

Here you must separate the vendors into two groups—those that you require from a technical view and those that you need politically. For the first, the business goal is the work performed by the vendors gets done on time and within budget. This is more traditional outsourcing. For the second group, you are on more fuzzy turf. You have to determine what the relationship has brought you in terms of the business. You may be met with promises that things will happen in your favor. This sounds fine the first time, but it is tiring the fifth time. You have to set a cutoff for performance—otherwise, you risk being bled dry.

POLITICAL PURPOSE

For international projects, there can be a variety of political objectives. Some that have surfaced in the past include:

• Generate sufficient revenue to justify the expense of having the vendor firm.

• Get a positive return when you calculate what would have happened without the consultant. This is a good test since it starts to examine what would have happened if you had not hired the consultant or vendor.

• Gain independence through acquiring knowledge, contacts, and expertise through the vendor.

END PRODUCTS

Specific end products related to outsourcing include the following:

• Agreement on what services will be provided under what terms.
• Measurement of what the vendor does.
• Transfer of knowledge from the vendor to internal staff.
• Performance of the vendor on specific tasks.

As you can imagine, doing this for political-type vendors is more difficult than for technical vendors. Yet, it must be done. Otherwise, you will be paying out money to a vendor for months and then later find out that nothing happened. That is what occurred to many European powers when they first worked in the Orient! It is, in short, an old story.

APPROACH

THE GENERAL STEPS IN OUTSOURCING

You need an organized approach for both types of outsourcing—technical and political. These types are surfaced here because the introduction has been paved with the preceding discussion. A technical vendor is one that will perform specific business or technical work, independent of politics. A political vendor is someone that you require to do business in the specific location. So there are many combinations of these two. You can, for example, have many political vendors and only one or two technical vendors. A political vendor is usually limited to a specific country.

The steps in outsourcing are shown in Fig. 8.1. In the first step, you want to identify what can be outsourced. You will have to be creative in an international project since you have to include political factors. You should consider hiring one consultant to determine what you need in political outsourcing. Then you would hire another, different vendor for the political work. This sounds weird to people academically, but in the real world you are dealing with a culture about which

Identify what can be outsourced

Analyze the risks and benefits

Determine what is to be outsourced

Prepare for outsourcing

Evaluate and select vendors

Build the vendor relationship and manage the outsourcing

Figure 8.1   General Steps in Outsourcing

you have limited knowledge. The National Geographic or the Discovery Channel don't help much here—this is the seamy world of politics in a locale strange to you. Get used to it!

Assessing the risks and benefits forces you to determine in more detail what the vendors will do. You have to weigh what would happen if you didn't have a vendor, remembering that in many cases you have no choice.

The third step is to determine what is to be outsourced. In the first step you have defined the potential scope and then you analyzed it in the second step.

Preparing for outsourcing can mean getting the organization ready to accept the outsourcing firm. If the employees and managers are not used to international projects, then they will likely question having some of the vendors. You should mount an education campaign to inform them of the alternative of doing it themselves. Here it is useful to highlight a few language and cultural issues. This will bring them down to earth rather quickly from experience.

OUTSOURCING FROM THE VENDOR'S PERSPECTIVE

How does an outsourcing firm survive and grow? Obviously, they have to build good relationships with customers. Here are some other factors behind outsourcing:

• The vendor may have unique ties with the government in a country.
• There may be useful family and other ties involving managers in the outsourcing firm.
• The vendor has unique expertise and knowledge about a particular country.

Most vendors want to build long-term relationships because of the cost of starting up the relationship and building ties. This is especially true in some countries where cultural factors dictate that it takes substantial elapsed time to become familiar with another firm.

Technical vendors see your project as a means to build their capabilities to market to other firms, including your competitors. You should always assume in an international project that the firms will immediately begin to market to your competitors after they sign a deal with you. For political vendors, the situation is different. You will likely select the vendor based on political and cultural factors. This evaluation will be very subjective.

DETERMINE OBJECTIVES AND WHAT IS TO BE OUTSOURCED

Let's first address objectives. From experience it is useful to define political, business, and technical objectives for each type of outsourcing that you will consider. If you just consider the technical objectives, then your evaluation could select a technically qualified vendor, but one that is poison for a specific country or region. You must balance the objectives.

The potential areas to be outsourced are many and depend on the specific project. Figure 8.2 gives a sample list. It is not intended to be comprehensive, but merely to show what you have to consider. Notice that many of these are political—ah, this is the real world.

How do you determine what is to be outsourced? Well, you would make a list of the various activities and task areas that will have to be addressed in the project. That is a start. Then you have to add to it the political areas. You should consider what other companies who have been successful have done. This is very important. A fundamental guideline is that:

You don't want to be first in a country to do some kind of work.

- Political ties to gain work
- Political ties to carry out the work
- Technical work in specific areas
- Political ties to handle potential issues and problems
- Project management for multiple countries
- Technical infrastructure work in different countries
- IT work in communications, hardware, or software
- Logistics support
- Testing and installation support
- Software vendors for specific software packages
- Auditing and accounting support

Figure 8.2   Examples of Potential Outsourcing Areas

If you are first, you are a pioneer and you will likely get many arrows in your back! If you are first, then you have to establish a new way for firms like yours to work with the government. Here is another guideline:

Hire a consultant who worked with an earlier, on-the-spot firm.

This person can provide valuable insight into what is needed and what works and what doesn't work. You cannot underrate experience. If you do it yourself, you are likely to repeat the mistakes of your predecessors. For a fast food and convenience chain, we suggested that they hire someone who worked with a fast food company to get them started. This can work to your advantage. Many of the people who are good at setting up a company operation are not good at maintenance and operations. They do not fit in. These people have a tremendous amount of knowledge and expertise that will be useful to you.

You also want to be concerned about measurements at this stage. How will you evaluate the vendor's performance? Can you identify specific milestones and quality standards? For construction or engineering this is rather straightforward. However, for marketing, software, political outsourcing, and other activities, the situation is not crisply defined. Before you go any further, this is the time and opportunity to discuss what constitutes acceptable and unacceptable work. How will the work products be evaluated?

In general, you will be outsourcing more than one activity in international projects. There may be outsourcing in specific countries as well as general outsourcing of a function. Many firms make a basic mistake here. They do not look at what is to be outsourced overall; instead, they address in a piecemeal, ad hoc way one area at a time. This can be a problem for the following reasons:

• The activities to be outsourced may interrelate to each other. If there are problems in this interface, then you are in trouble.

• There may be some economies of scale in outsourcing in which you can combine several activities for one vendor.

IDENTIFY VENDOR REQUIREMENTS

Having identified potentials for outsourcing, you can begin to list requirements for vendors. These should be divided into technical and political categories. Don't even think that one vendor can do all of it. It is very useful to have a technical vendor and a political vendor for the same type of work. The technical vendor can tell you what is needed to achieve the desired results from a work point of view. The political vendor can act as a counterpoise to indicate how and what is possible. You want to listen to both.

In general, vendor requirements constitute a list of the vendor will do and how this work relates to the overall project plan. The more complete the list the better. Here is another guideline:

Associate each task area with potential outsourcing vendors.

At this point it pays to be very open as to what is needed.

PREPARE FOR OUTSOURCING

For technical vendors you want to define the following:

- Define how the vendor and your staff will collaborate.
- Identify specific milestones that the vendor will be responsible for.
- Determine how vendor work will be reviewed.
- Develop a method for identifying, analyzing, and resolving issues.

In some cases, you are going to want to outsource a specific business activity or process. For political vendors the situation is fuzzier. You should define a specific set of milestones related to permits, licenses, permissions, and other work. Then you can begin to assess how you will measure the performance of the political vendor.

SELECT THE RIGHT VENDORS FOR INTERNATIONAL PROJECTS

How do you identify specific vendors? One approach is to employ the in-country employees to ascertain what vendors are being used and what results have been obtained. This is good for several reasons. First, it gets the local office involved in the process so that they are part of the solution as opposed to a problem. Second, you probably will get better information than from their head office.

In parallel, work from headquarters to identify potential firms through the accounting and consulting relationships that you already have. You will want to coordinate this with the local office work and indicate to the consultants that you are also doing a local search.

Another approach is to use the Web if you are looking for specific types of expertise. This is a general search and may not yield much. However, every now and then the limited effort has proven worthwhile.

What is right in a standard project often depends on various attributes of their technical capabilities. Do they have a track record and presence in a specific country? What is the staffing and relationship of the in-country office with the headquarters of the vendor firm?

Figure 8.3 gives several areas for vendor evaluation beyond the normal ones of firm history, financial condition, and track record. You should probably start raising these questions and areas early. That will help narrow the field of potential firms.

Your company already probably has an established method for procurement. Typically, you construct a document in which the requirements for the vendor are spelled out. Then purchasing adds the necessary boilerplate and a Request for Quotation (RFQ) or a Request for Proposal (RFP) is issued. Make sure that your RFP or RFQ contains the following items:

- Exact tasks that the vendor will be required to perform;
- Milestones associated with these tasks;
- How milestones and work will be assessed in terms of quality;
- How the vendor is expected to interact with headquarters and project management;
- How the vendor is expected to interact with local office managers and staff;
- How issues are to be resolved;
- How decisions are to be made;
- The project template and plan;
- Initial list of issues and potential problems.

You want to make it clear that there is to be a common project plan. You cannot afford to spend hours in meetings reconciling their plans with yours. There should

---

- *Understanding of the local culture and regulations.* Have the local office prepare a list of questions and issues to pose to potential vendors. Even better, involve a member from the local office in the evaluation.
- *How they deal with issues and problems.* General qualifications are good, but what will count when it comes down to it is how they address problems. Do they handle these locally? What degree of discretion does the local office have? How much do they have to consult head office? How do you test this out? You should make a list of potential problems and see how they would handle these.
- *Availability of specific skills and knowledge.* Companies can claim that they have a wide range of skills, but it will come down to their people in the end. If you ask general questions, you will get general answers. It is better to take the project template that you are using and identify some specific tasks that require the skills that you are interested in. Point to these areas in the template.
- *Decision-making process.* How does the firm make decisions? This is important because if they are bureaucratic, then getting a decision may take longer for them than for you. Remember too that you have less leverage on the vendor once they are involved in the work.

Figure 8.3 Evaluation of Potential Vendors

be an agreed upon approach for tracking issues. We suggest a common issues database. Another thing to insist on in the RFP is that you expect that the vendor staff will participate in lessons learned meetings in which knowledge is to be transferred from them to internal employees on a regular basis—not just at the end of the work. In general, the more detail you put in here, the easier it will be later and the fewer surprises there will be.

Selecting the right vendors for political work is more complex. You have to ensure that the firm is well placed with the government. You can, of course, listen to their sales pitch. However, a better approach is to find out what other firms they have assisted and then see what happened. Again, using a separate consultant to help in this selection can be very useful.

ESTABLISH WORKING RELATIONSHIPS

The building of a working relationship does not wait until there is some magic kickoff meeting. You want to begin to use the template and start building detailed tasks with the person(s) who are designated as project leaders for the vendor. Start identifying some issues as well. Then you can discuss how the issues are to be resolved. A basic guideline is:

You want to define and agree on the issue resolution method before significant issues arise.

If you wait until an issue appears, then everyone will have to cope with solving the issue at the same time that they are working on how to resolve issues in general—too much to ask at one time.

You should do joint planning with them to define detailed tasks in the template for their work. By doing this with your employees and those of the vendor, you start to build working relationships that will be very important later. Another guideline is:

You need to create patterns of working relationships and behavior at the start of the vendor's work.

This has several benefits. First, you see how the vendor thinks and what techniques that they use. Second, your employees will start having detailed technical contacts with the vendor's employees.

Another idea is to identify joint tasks that require work by both your firm and the vendor. Joint tasks are a good method for forcing people to work together in detail. This is much more satisfactory than some general meetings.

Get some detailed tasks going right away. This shows the vendor that you are serious. If there is a big time gap between when the contract is negotiated and when work begins, the vendor may not think that you are serious and may reassign their staff to other clients. By starting work early you avoid this situation.

MONITOR AND DIRECT VENDOR WORK

The type of vendor and work will dictate the details of how the vendor will be managed. However, here are some useful guidelines:

• Meet on a regular basis to review issues and status. Do this at both headquarters and local levels. Meet more often if there are problems and less often if there is not much going on.

• Make the vendor accountable for specific issues early in the project. This starts to build a pattern for how they will resolve issues. Then you will be better prepared when a major issue appears.

• Monitor the communications and miscommunications between their local and headquarters employees. This is a major problem in some international projects in that when there are communication gaps, people on the receiving end begin to make assumptions. There may later prove to be incorrect. Work has to be redone and undone. The consulting bill to you rises. You want as few middle men as possible in communications.

• Establish a standard method of communications in terms of reporting, use of voice and e-mail, etc.

• Define how tools and methods are to be employed in the project. This should be reviewed early in the project and then reviewed on a periodic basis to ensure that there has been no change.

• Try to have 20% or more of their tasks joint between vendor staff and employees. This helps to ensure transfer of knowledge.

Implement a vendor score card. A general example is given in Fig. 8.4. Some comments on these scoring elements are as follows:

• *Ratio of local staff to total staff*. This is a good measure of whether they are taking advantage of the local talent that they have or if they are sending in headquarters people at higher cost.

• *Turnover of vendor staff*. Some turnover is acceptable. Too much means that you may be getting "churned." That is, the vendor may be moving people in and out of your project to gain experience.

• *Number of active issues over the total number of issues*. If this number is high, then they have many issues and they are not getting closed fast enough.

Area of evaluation	Score (1–5)
Number of staff assigned locally/total staff assigned	
Turnover of vendor staff	
Number of active issues assigned to them/total issues assigned to them	
Status of the oldest outstanding issue assigned to them	
Percentage of work complete versus percentage of their budget consumed	
Percentage of tasks that they have that are joint with your employees	
Percentage of lessons learned meetings in which they present	
Number of instances of miscommunications between their head and local offices that you detect	
Percentage of future tasks that involve the vendor and have risk and issues	

Figure 8.4   Vendor Evaluation Score Card

• *Age of the oldest outstanding major issue*. This is also an indicator of their decision-making abilities.

• *Percentage of work complete versus percentage of budget consumed*. This one is obvious, but it is a good indicator of what it may end up costing you at the end.

• *Percentage of tasks that they have that are joint with your employees*. This is a good indicator of collaboration and transfer of knowledge.

• *Percentage of lessons learned meetings in which they present*. This should be high indicating that knowledge is being transferred.

• *Number of instances of detected miscommunications between their local and head offices*. This is subjective, but is useful in starting to tell you if there is a problem.

• *Percentage of future tasks that involve the vendor and have issues and risk*. The higher the percentage, the more in trouble the project is likely to be.

Of course, you will want to build your own score card from this. You will then want to adapt it to each vendor. Go over the score card with the vendor so that they are clear on what is to be measured. Implement the measurement approach every 2–3 months. If you do it more frequently, it will take too much work. If you do it less often, then it has little effect.

MANAGE MULTIPLE VENDORS

International projects struggle because of multiple vendors. One way to approach this subject is to manage each vendor separately. This can be risky because you are paying enough attention to the interaction among the vendors. Knowing in advance that there can be many problems in having vendors deal peer-to-peer with each other, consider separating this out as a subproject that gets individual attention. What can go wrong?

- Each vendor will tell you a different story. If you are involved in the interface, you don't know what happened.
- No one vendor is in charge so none step up to the plate and take responsibility.
- If there is a meeting and a vendor is missing, the other vendors may jump on this and blame the problems on the missing vendor.

As its own project, it requires each vendor to provide a contact lead person who will take responsibility. You will want to generate and track issues as well as progress here as well. In some projects we have had in the past, over 40% of our time was spent in this area.

COPE WITH SOME COMMON OUTSOURCING ISSUES

A Local In-Country Vendor Is Not Meeting Expectations

If this is a political vendor, then you could have a major problem on your hands. If they are well connected, then putting pressure on them may just make your position worse. It is better to sit down with the vendor and start getting into the detail.

A similar approach works with technical vendors. As you become aware that a vendor is not working up to speed or quality, then you should increase your presence in the country and with them. Sit down and review both the plan and open issues. Initiate more joint tasks so that you can see what is going on behind the scenes. As you get more involved in their detailed work, you will acquire more knowledge of the situation.

The Vendor Changes Staff Often

Some vendors give you "stars" at the start of the project. You are really impressed. After a few weeks, you turn around and they are gone. Now you are surrounded by "turkeys." This sound humorous, but it is serious. To head off this problem, track how the vendor is applying the people to the project. Start to watch who is assigned to which tasks. If a person is being assigned to lesser tasks, then the vendor manager may be getting ready to pull them out.

If the problem occurs, then make staff turnover an issue in the project. Indicate the impact and effect on the project due to the loss of knowledge and learning curve as well as by the substitution of junior people. When you use your own employees, you don't want to cripple the department by getting the best people. For the vendor you want almost the best people. Why "almost the best?" Because the best are likely to be difficult to manage. They may view themselves as prima donnas.

The Vendor Wants to Impose Their Own Management Approach on the Project

This occurs sometimes with larger management consulting firms working with mid-sized client firms. Why do they do this? It makes it easier for them. They can make your project look like a similar one they did a year ago. Maybe they can reuse some of the work and results—it has happened before. They also want control for control's sake.

What are some signs of this occurring? One sign is that they volunteer to do project management tasks such as reports, notes of meetings, plans, etc. Another sign is that they begin to call meetings and start to direct the internal employees.

This has to be prevented unless you are planning to turn over the project management to them. The project leaders must lay down the rules at the start. Each time the vendor leader starts to intrude into project management, the project leaders need to push him/her back. This should be done directly. After a few times, the vendor should give up.

The Vendor Work and Staff Quality Vary Greatly by Country

This is the case with everything. Let's suppose you have a commercial airliner. You can get complex and any other repair done in country A. However, it is very expensive. You can get simple repairs done for far less in country B. Your plane has a problem. What do you do? The problem could turn out to be serious. You might want to try country B to see if that will work.

It is important to go over what is expected of quality for both employees and vendors in each country. Part of this is due to culture. Part is due to the level of training and education. There are many factors. It does absolutely no good to complain and lament about the work habits or work quality of people in one area or country. You have to work there—period. You must accept this as a constraint of doing business and deal with it accordingly. Therefore, the project leaders should factor this into their task planning.

The Vendor Employs Their Own Methods and Tools—Incompatible with Yours

Every vendor who comes to work for you has their own preferences for methods and tools. In many cases, this is not a problem since the method or tool is only required one time. However, there are situations in which the method or tool selected during the project will be required after the project is completed for maintenance and operations support. Then the methods and tools become critical.

You should review the methods and tools of the vendors. Use the table templates in Fig. 8.5. The first, labeled "a", deals with methods and the second, labeled "b" addresses the tools for the methods. You should fill out this table with the vendor. There are several cases to be considered:

• The methods and tools are the same. You are not out of the woods yet since you have to compare the guidelines for how to use the methods and tools.

• There is no tool available. The firm and vendor have to decide what to do.

• For a method there are different tools. This is the difficult case. You have to decide which tool is the winner. If the vendor's tool is the winner, then you have to define a plan for learning and becoming adept in the use of the tool. This can take valuable time away from the project.

a. Method Comparison

Activity	Method, firm	Method, vendor	Comparison	Comments

b. Tool Comparison

Method	Tool, firm	Tool, vendor	Comparison	Comments

Figure 8.5   Table of Methods and Tools

EXAMPLES

SAMBAC ENERGY

Each of the parent firms of Sambac favored different vendors. It was a night-mare. When there was turnover in management at the top of Sambac as was stated earlier, then there was vendor turnover. Progress was slowed. Transitions among vendors was very difficult. The situation became acute when a major project failed to meet its delivery date.

The two firms tried to select one list of approved vendors. It failed. Finally, it was handed over to local management who had dealt with all of the vendors. They came up with one list that was approved by the two firms. This example shows how political issues in management of the firm are often reflected in the vendors and outsourcing.

WHITMORE BANK

Whitmore had not very much experience in the countries of the region where the credit card services were to be offered. They did have local employees, but headquarters management was not familiar with the culture and politics of the country. As a result, the applications of the bank to the governments of the region got nowhere. They languished in some bureaucratic office. When Whitmore management pressed the government, they were told that it was "under review."

After some time, it was recommended that the applications be withdrawn. In each country a new company was established. This company had on its board of directors local dignitaries and politicians. Amazingly, the application process was swift. Not only did Whitmore involve local people at higher levels, they also showed respect for the culture and political workings of the country.

LESSONS LEARNED

• Unless the work to be performed is very narrow and technically focused, you should assume that there will be a political and cultural dimension. This cannot be ignored. It is best to openly find out how things work. You want to indicate that you are sensitive to the culture of the area.

• The project leaders should spend proportionately more time with the vendors than with employees. This is because the vendors are often doing critical work. Also, it is where the costs are greater. A third reason is that the risks and issues are more here.

• The project leaders should rate themselves on their vendor contacts. You can create a mini score card that includes items like amount of contact with the vendor staff; amount of contact with the vendor manager; number of visits to the vendor offices; etc.

EXERCISES

1. Look around for international projects that are cancelled. Behind many of these are vendor issues. If there is a local project with local people only, then the project can be salvaged or changed easily. It is more visible with vendor involvement. Try to gather lessons learned.

2. Consider the field of system integration. Oracle, IBM, and other firms do this work. Go to their Web sites and see if you can gather additional lessons learned.

SUMMARY

Because vendor relationship and outsourcing are so prominent in international projects, an entire chapter has been devoted to this subject. You will notice that outsourcing has been treated in a political as well as technical manner. That is because of the importance of politics and culture.

Chapter 9

Sustain Effective Communications

INTRODUCTION

Communications must be effective in even small projects. It becomes critical in international projects. The uniqueness of international projects creates special problems.

- If communications is not achieved, then there may be a delay of a day or more before you can try again.
- Different countries have widely different holidays and varying work schedules. This adds to the communications burden.
- Many people think that they can just communicate through e-mail or telephone or fax at any time. This places an undue burden on the people at the other end who must remain at work for hours or get up in the middle of the night to communicate with you. No wonder this approach builds resentment.

In many international projects, people start out without a plan or an approach. The haphazard, ad hoc approach seems to work until an important issue or problem arises. Then there is a crisis and people are kept up for hours—not good for either resolving problems or being useful.

The golden word in international communications is planning. You have to plan ahead. The second rule is that there must be minimum overhead in preparing reports and presentations. This supports the use of templates for reporting and presentations. What is a template here? It is a high-level outline of a report or presentation. These outlines can then be improved and reused over time. By using the same general outline for a category of presentation or report, the audience is not concerned about the structure; they have seen it before many times. They can then focus on the content of the material.

Let's summarize what has been discussed so far:

- The major project management documents and reporting, including the plan, project status, and issues employ templates.
- All presentations and plans should be stored on the network so that people can read them over and learn. They can also steal ideas from them for their own work. Nothing wrong with this—it is to save time and to improve the end product.
- The outlines are improved and refined over time as are the templates for the project plans.

PURPOSE AND SCOPE

TECHNICAL PURPOSE

The technical purpose is to get your ideas and information across to the audience, whomever they may be, in a clear, concise, and understandable manner. You can also add the phrase "with limited effort." In international projects your communications efforts could consume much of your time as you try to reach people, retrieve information sent to you, etc. In standard projects you can afford to be slack and not well organized. Lack of organization in international projects can cause you more pain, distress, and extra work.

What types of things can go wrong in communications for an international project?

- *People misunderstand the words and take offense.* It then takes weeks to recover. Some words that are acceptable in one language can end up being offensive in another language. For example, a major drug store chain renamed itself in the signage in over 1,000 stores. No one considered what the word meant in Spanish. It was not nice. Sales to Hispanics in the US dropped off dramatically as a result. It took over a year to recover and go back to the old name—with many lost sales.
- *People are not sensitive to dates.* This is not just holidays. It includes the vacations of the team members, when major activities (like year-end closing or inventory counting) go on, and so on.
- *People use the software tools in different ways in different cultures.* This seems strange, but it is true. Each country tends to adapt software tools such as e-mail, etc., to fit their established culture.
- *People lack cultural sensitivity.* A project leader may make direct contact with employees in a department to gather information. In some cultures, this is an affront to the manager of the group.

Experience shows that these things occur most often among headquarters or at the dominant location. Managers think that their needs override the culture factors. This is a big mistake.

BUSINESS PURPOSE

Even with good technical communications, you may fail. The business purpose is that you communicate and get results. This is much more than just communications. It is success after you communicate. The business purpose is to be effective in communications.

POLITICAL PURPOSE

The political purpose of communications in an international project is to be successful in the project and with management and organizations in a political sense. Through communications you can build either enemies or friends and allies. You prefer the latter over the former. In most international projects if you make an enemy of someone, it is likely to come back and haunt you later. This is due to the length of the project. Typically, international projects tend to have a broader scope and last longer. The only thing comparable to an international project is an organization that has very stable staffing over a long period. An example is the faculty at most universities where a high percentage are tenured. These people have to deal with each other not for years, but for decades—a daunting prospect. Younger professors who fail to grasp this basic end up being thrown out and being denied tenure. It is also due to the fact that you will probably need their support later for some issue or other. Now this is not to say that you will make friends forever. This will never happen. Rather, it is that you not make enemies. Neutrality and indifference are OK as well.

Making enemies in an international project will exact a high price for the project and the team.

This is another reason why you want to have two project leaders. If one rubs some manager the wrong way, then the other manager can recover. In communications, one can play the role of the good guy and the other the bad guy. Then they can rotate the role. This brings up another basic point.

Communications, even informal communications, must be planned. There are too many dangers and risks to leave it to chance.

END PRODUCTS

There are a number of specific end products in communications. These include:

- Marketing and promoting the project concept;
- Marketing the project plan to management and the various location managers;
  - Marketing the project to potential and actual team members;
  - Getting issues resolved;
  - Obtaining changes to the budget, schedule, or resources for the project;
  - Communicating clearly the status of the project;
  - Managing the work in the project.

What is a common thread here?

Communications in an international project involve a great deal of marketing and sales.

Does this mean that marketing people should be project managers? It is not necessary. The project leaders and the team have to realize the importance of communications both within and external to the project team.

APPROACH

INFORMAL AND FORMAL COMMUNICATIONS

In international projects formal communications represent a risk. Every time you get up and make a formal presentation, you are risking quite a bit of the project. People may want to look good at your expense. You risk exposing your lack of knowledge and sensitivity to the culture in a location. Being in a formal presentation may feel threatening to the audience. They may feel that they have to do something. You have to make formal presentations and cannot avoid it. The guideline is:

Make as few formal presentations as possible.

What should you do? Concentrate on informal communications. Try to get to people to communicate one-on-one.

Informal communications are a critical success factor for international projects. You can bring people up-to-date on the status of the project. You can solicit their ideas about issues. You can get support in terms of resources. How do you arrange for informal, casual communications? Planning. Try to get to people in person or by telephone early in the morning in their time zone before they start work. If you can do this in person, run into them casually as they walk into work. Another good idea is to talk to them in the restroom or where they smoke (if they smoke). When people smoke, many tend to open up and talk more frankly and honestly about situations. If you are not a smoker, try to put up with second-hand smoke. These techniques sound crude and sneaky. But they work! For employees, go out where they have their breaks or lunch. Just sit there and listen. Then you can ask questions.

When you communicate with people informally, you should always have these three things ready at all times:

1. Status of the project from their point of view.
2. Issues that are active and unresolved that are of interest to them.
3. A story or anecdote from the project that might be amusing or interesting to them.

Give them the status. Then if there is interest shown, move to issues. Put the story into your discussion when discussing the issues. On issues follow these guidelines:

- Have three issues ready.
- The first issue is a very small one that be disposed of quickly. This establishes a pattern of success in the meeting for dealing with issues. People are happy.
- The second issue is a major political or business issue for which there is no immediate solution. They cannot give you one. They feel bad, because they could not help you.
- With the pattern of success in dealing with the first issue and the guilt of the second issue, you can now discuss the third issue. This is the one that you really need a decision. They will tend to make decisions more readily.

Never, ever, go to someone with one issue. They will feel that you are putting their back up against the wall. You will not likely get the result you desire. Also, by going in with a group of issues, you show that you are top of the project from technical, business, and political perspectives.

You should keep a record of what people you have communicated with informally. Try to evaluate both your informal and formal communications. Figure 9.1 consists of a score card for your formal presentations. Figure 9.2 presents one for informal communications over a period of time in the project. Here are some added comments about some of the items in these figures:

Score card element	Score (1–5; 1, low; 5, high)
% of the audience that you met prior to presentation	
Time of presentation/time of meeting	
Extent of change in presentation after meeting with managers prior to presentation	
Approval of action items	
Approval of direction	
Understanding of project by audience	
Response by audience after presentation	
Enthusiasm by audience one week after presentation	

Figure 9.1   Score Card for Formal Communications

Score card element	Score (1–5; 1, low; 5, high)
Number of contacts made	
Number of contacts made/number of contacts attempted	
Number of times issues were discussed/number of contacts	
Number of times managers brought up issues before you	
Average time of contact	

Figure 9.2   Score Card for Informal Communications over a Period of Time

- Percentage of audience reached before the presentation. This indicates your success at the reach toward the audience.
- Time of presentation/time of meeting. The numerator in this fraction is the time required without questions and interaction. The fraction indicates how much time was spent in questions and discussion.
- Extent of change in presentation before final presentation. This percentage indicates how much feedback you received after getting to managers prior to the presentation itself.
- Understanding of the project by the audience. This is often revealed by the quality of questions and comments at the end of the presentation versus at the start.
- There are two measures of response—one immediately after and a second one week after.

• Number of contacts made/number of contacts attempted. This reveals your success rate in making informal contacts.

There is also the item in informal communications of the number of times that a manager brought up an issue to you first. What is this? If a manager calls you up or comes to you with an issue before you brought it up with them, you failed in communicating. Why? Because they were taken by surprise; surprises tend to be unpleasant. The person may think that you are not on top of your project. They may now feel that they cannot trust you as the only source of information about the project.

SELLING THE PROJECT CONCEPT

One of the major things that has to be sold is the project concept. Recall from Chapter 2 that this is a predecessor to the project plan. It is where you obtain management support to create the plan and move ahead. Many good project ideas flounder here. People can misunderstand the purpose or scope of the project, for example.

It is necessary and valuable to employ an outline template and structured approach for the project concept. Before making any formal presentation including this one, you should meet with key members of the audience that will hear the project concept and make decisions. This seems unnecessary if they are going to be in the meeting. However, it is essential for a number of reasons:

• When you talk to someone about the project concept individually, you can explain the project to them in their own terms. As an example, how you would discuss a project at headquarters is different than at a specific field location.

• You want to give the person an opportunity to voice concerns and to give input to the final presentation. They become active participants and supporters, not just passive spectators.

• You will collect some ideas to improve the presentation.

• You can discuss political factors. They can alert you to the people in the audience who do not like the project idea. They may see it as a threat. They may see it as taking away their scarce resources.

You will not be able in most cases to reach all of the audience so you should concentrate on people who will make decisions and who are tuned into the politics in the specific location. Don't spend too much time with managers who already support the project. Use the reliability structure of K out of N. If any K components of N work, then the system works. It is the same with communications.

Now let's turn to the structure of the presentation. In a traditional approach you would present the background of the project and lead into the purpose, scope, schedule, cost, etc. This is too boring and the wrong type of presentation. You must be more dynamic in your presentation. Here is an outline:

• State the purpose of the project from a technical, business, and political perspective. This will indicate to the audience that you are sensitive to politics.

• Go into both the benefits of the project as well as what will happen if the project is not undertaken or if it is deferred. Many projects are approved because of the negative consequences of doing nothing. Capitalize on the fear factor. This is what happens in television commercials. Your car will fall apart if you don't have the brakes replaced or repaired.

• Discuss the scope of the project and potential issues. Issues seem to be negative. They are not here. You are warning management long in advance of some of the potential problems that lie ahead. Everyone likes to be warned in advance. You also show your qualifications and experience as well as demonstrating that you are aware of the issues and have thought about these. Get management and the audience in general to participate in the meeting to discuss how issues will be addressed in general by using one issue as an example.

• Talk about how the business will change after the project is completed. Here you can give sample transactions or examples of how work will be performed. This will get the audience excited since you are moving beyond the project work. You are showing how the benefits will be realized. This is also a positive point in the presentation to offset the negative tone of issues.

• Discuss the cost, resources, and schedule for the project. Notice that there is a break between the benefits and costs. This is by intent. The benefits get them excited. The issues and scope discussion got their involvement. Now you have some discussion of the schedule. By combining the schedule and resources with the costs, you are combining negative things (costs) with positive ideas of how long it will take and what resources are needed. People will tend to discuss the positive part more.

• Close the presentation with a list of specific actions that need to be taken to develop the plan, line up resources, etc. Notice that you are closing with specific small actions for them to approve. You are not asking for the moon. You will come back later with the project plan for their final approval. By breaking this up, you will be more politically successful in getting the concept of the project approved. Momentum will be gained so that it will be hard for people later to turn down the plan if it follows the concept.

Look at these bullets again. What do they look like? A 30-second commercial— one of the most successful advertising inventions in the past century.

How do you determine if you are successful? Well, did your action items get approved? However, you also want to follow up by going back to some of the audience and getting their reactions and thoughts. They will pick up tones, nuances, feelings, etc., that you missed because you were concentrating on the presentation.

INTERVIEWS AND DATA COLLECTION

Data collection in any project is a key activity. In international projects, you often have to collect similar information in multiple locations. What is an effective and efficient approach to get this information? Tradition says interviewing. Put together some key questions and go out and get the answers—a solid academic approach. Unfortunately, this fails in the real world. In interviews there can be many problems, including:

• The person gives you false leads or "red herrings." This misleads you and you take a wrong direction—costing time and money.
• People respond to the questions even if they do not know the answers since they do not want to appear to be dumb.
• Many managers being interviewed don't remember the details of the work since they have not performed the work in many years.
• They may get a number of people in the room for the interview. The quiet ones who know the answers do not speak up.
• In many interviews people often will tell you what they think you want to hear.

With all of these problems, should you drop the idea of doing interviews? No. Interviews are important in many cultures because you have to get through the levels and layers of middle management to get down to where the project will really be done. Interviews are then essential, but you cannot rely on them.

What should you go in with for an interview? You have the project concept or status. Discuss what is going on now from their point-of-view. You are updating them on the project. This provides them with information. Do the interview alone. If several people interview someone, they will feel outnumbered and may not talk openly. Go into the interview with 3–4 questions. Some of these might include:

• What activities are going on that might conflict with the project?
• What people might be most appropriate to gather information?
• Who might be appropriate team members?
• How do they see their role in the project?

Many international projects deal with business processes. After these interviews, you seek to get down to where the work is being performed as quickly as possible. Remember the X-Files television show—"The truth is out there." Here it is down in the detail.

Team Communications

Team communications here means communications between the project leaders and individual team members and communications among team members. There are three general areas where project leaders approach individual team members. One is status—covered later. A second is to discuss a problem or opportunity. The third is just to see how people are doing. Here are some guidelines for project leader–team member communications:

• Encourage individual and pairs of team members to come to you with issues and problems. Always be open to problems. This avoids very unpleasant surprises later.

• To find out about issues, use the third area of contact where you ask them how things are going to get issues out on the table.

• After you ask how things are going, find out what else they are working on. This will indicate to you if they are experiencing being pulled in different directions and being subjected to pressures from their other work. Then ask them what you can do to help.

• Don't accept at face value what one team member says. Always look for validation and another point of view from the other team member that is working with them. Do not attempt to do this right away; it will appear that you do not trust them. Wait a few days and then casually contact the other team member.

• Do not attempt to be fair in reaching all team members the same number of times in a given period. There is no time for this in most international projects. There is too much to do. Instead, the project leaders should concentrate on areas of the project where there are issues and risk and the areas of the international project that are critical.

• Keep a log of the contacts with the team members. Update the issues database as you uncover more issues.

In the approach of this book for international projects, team members will work together on a substantial percentage of the tasks (30–40%). Therefore, there should be a great deal of team member interaction. Do you just let this happen? Experience shows that many people are not comfortable working with someone else. It could be a culture barrier. It can also be that in past projects the people worked mainly in projects as individuals. The project leaders must provide guidelines at the start of the project work for the interaction. They should sit on some of the initial chats among the team members to kick off work in the tasks and to establish a pattern. A basic rule is:

In international projects it is always important to establish patterns of good behavior at the start of the project.

It will then be easier to monitor the work and have some confidence that things will go right.

Another guideline is to have the team members share their experiences in working together in the lessons learned meetings. In that way, other team members might pick up some useful tips in working together.

MANAGE PROJECT MEETINGS

In many companies project meetings can be characterized by the following:

- The meeting is held at the same time each week.
- The meeting is held in the same location.
- Most of the meeting is devoted to the team updating people on status.

This approach fails for a number of reasons. First, in international projects you cannot get together easily. So people tend to use voice conference calls. People find the meetings boring since they are often interested in their own status, but not that of others in the team working on things that do not affect them. Third, the project leaders' only power is that of timing. Project leaders do not, after all, control people or money. They have the use of these things, but they do not control them. When the meetings are always held at the same time and place, the project leaders give up their power. Thus, even if the project is in trouble, people are meeting in the same way. What is the impression given to the team? Even though the project leaders say the project is in trouble, it is really not. "Otherwise, why are we meeting in the same way?"

There is a better approach for meeting on international projects. Follow these guidelines and you will have more success.

- *Timing*. Stagger the meetings in time based on urgency. That is, if the project is doing fine, then have a meeting every two weeks. If the project is in trouble, have meetings twice a week. This supports one of the basic tenets of project management—what you do is more important than what you say.
- *Location*. Vary the location. Never have the meeting where the project leaders are. Go out to a department participating in the project. Go to different

locations. This will give the team a chance to be more exposed to the project culture. Visit the places where the effects and benefits of the project will be felt. This will be a strong motivating factor for the team.

• *Subjects of the meetings.* Avoid gathering status at the meeting. Status collection and reporting are discussed in a later section in this chapter. What do you talk about? Two things—issues and lessons learned. You may not resolve issues, but you can discuss most of these in the team. Issues tend to be negative since many are problems. In contrast lessons learned are positive. People in the team get something out of attending these meeting.

• *Format.* Obviously, you cannot afford to have everyone fly to a different location each time. However, since you are going to have issues and lessons learned as the focus of the meetings, not everyone has to attend every meeting. The project leaders can identify only those individuals who are concerned about an issue or what can use the specific results from experience that are covered in the lessons learned. This reduces the number of people involved. Issue meetings can be discussed using voice or videoconferencing. Lessons learned are best done in videoconferencing and in person.

In general, try to have two meetings on issues to one on lessons learned. Gather status on the project ahead of the meetings. At the start of the meeting, summarize the status of the project. In an issues meeting, try to address three issues. The people for the first two issues should be present. After the first issue is covered, then these people leave and get the individuals for the third issue. This keeps the meeting going and it minimizes the waste of time for the meeting. Why three issues? This is a number that you can get through in a time of say one hour. Never try to resolve issues in the meeting. This would put too much pressure on the people and will likely lead to bad decisions. In many different cultures, issues are never solved in meetings. They are resolved in one-on-one get-togethers after the meeting. That is the model to follow. You also avoid confrontation in the meetings.

How do you discuss an issue? Present the issue to the group and give some background. To test people's understanding of the issue, discuss what will happen if the issue is not solved. This gets people involved in the conversation and is not forcing them to think of solutions.

Now international projects tend to be complex as do their issues. If you next discuss decisions that are possible, you are likely to get some fuzzy general discussion. This is a waste of time. Instead, talk about potential actions that could be taken after the meeting. This is more productive. Actions are specific things that people can do. Once the group has discussed the actions, then you can briefly talk about decisions. However, remember again that you are not attempting to reach a decision in the meeting. If you can in a natural way, fine. In general, you are collecting information on the issue and people are getting a common understanding and vision of the issue and its various facets. Lessons learned will be discussed in the next chapter.

Who takes the minutes of the meeting? YOU DO! Whoever takes the notes of a meeting controls the truth. Do not forget this basic point. This is true even if you are highest ranking person in the room. Write up the notes of the meeting within one hour after the meeting. How should you organize the notes? Here is a suggested approach that has worked:

- Identify the issue and the impact if it is not addressed;
- Summarize the potential actions that were covered;
- Summarize the decision and what comes next—agreed upon action items;
- Make sure that, with few exceptions, that all action items are to be
followed up on within 48 hours of the meeting.

This last point addresses the problem in many international projects that people discuss and agree on items and then they just return to their work. There is no follow-up. Project leaders must follow up and soon after the meeting. Additional guidelines on handling issues will be explored in the next chapter.

MANAGEMENT COMMUNICATIONS

Informal communications are a key to management communications. You have to not only stay in touch with the managers who oversee the project, but also with the line managers who control the individual team members in each location. This group of people is very important. Here are some guidelines:

- Bring the line manager up-to-date on the status of the project overall.
- Zoom in on the contribution that their people are making to the project. This will give them a good feeling.
- Ask them about what issues they are facing. This will show that you are sensitive to what they are doing.
- If they present an issue, then try to help them. If it is appropriate, make the issue one of the issues for the project. Remember though that you are politically showing that you care. You are not trying to do their job.
- If they indicate that they need the person back from the team, try to see what you can do. Maybe, you can find someone else from the department or division. Always anticipate that they want the person back. If they never bring this subject up, then they may feel that they can get along without this person. This may give you some clues about how important they are in their own organization.

PROJECT STATUS COMMUNICATIONS

Never gather status in the project meetings. People often will not address their problems openly. A better approach is to ask how their work is going. Then this will lead to any problems that they have. After doing all of this, you can infer the true status of their work. However, you should always ask about status.

For tasks that are jointly assigned, try to get the status and information from the two people assigned to the tasks together. This may mean a meeting or conference call.

In collecting status, you should always gather status from the people working on critical tasks first. This will give you more time to deal with issues and understand them. After this, you can use this information when you gather information from other team members. Remember that gathering status on a project is a cumulative, yet sequential activity. Take advantage of this by using the information gathered earlier in later conversations.

How should you report on status to management? The major way is the informal communication method that was discussed. But there are also written reports on status. There are two types of status reports. The first is for the project overall. The second is for a part of the project. Use the form in Fig. 9.3 to report on status. It offers a number of advantages. First, you are stating and restating the **business** purpose and scope of the work. The GANTT chart gives management an overview of the work in the project. Also include in this chart the tasks that have significant issues. Thus, the GANTT chart includes summary tasks as well as those with issues. The cumulative budget versus actual chart may only be useful in the overall project status. It is an S-shaped curve.

Date:
Title of the project:
Purpose:
Scope:

GANTT chart   Cumulative budget vs actual
                                                               chart

Milestones achieved:

Upcoming milestones:

Outstanding major issues:

Figure 9.3   Sample Format of an International Project Status Report

At the bottom of the chart there are a number of items. First, you are stating what milestones were achieved. These are stated in business terminology so that the managers can understand. The same is true for upcoming milestones. Another item is a list of critical outstanding issues. Do you provide more detail than this as to status, etc.? No. You want to use the status report politically so that managers will then contact you about the issues. You are using the status report to move ahead on the issues. This is why this template for status reporting is quite useful.

ISSUE COMMUNICATIONS

Issues are a major part of international projects. When an issue first surfaces to you, the form and nature of the issue tend to be fuzzy. You don't know if you have all of the information. You don't know if you are dealing with a problem or a symptom of a problem. Yet, you want to inform management informally of the potential issue so that they are not taken by surprise.

Communicating about issues over time and distance is difficult. Therefore, you seek to have an organized approach that is followed not only by the project leaders, but also by the team members. What are your goals in issue communications?

- Management hears about the issue first from you.
- There is a gradual buildup toward action on an issue; you do not want snap decisions in most international settings.
- You want to deal with several related issues at one time.
- Most of the time when you communicate issues, you are not seeking actions and decisions. Rather you are attempting to get understanding by them.

After first communicating about an issue, you then keep the manager informed. From initial symptoms and fuzziness, you present an increased picture of clarity and focus. After there is agreement on a decision and actions, you should communicate back to the manager exactly what was agreed to—to avoid misunderstandings.

The communications doesn't end here. The managers who were involved in the decisions deserve to be told from you what happened. They want to know if they made the right decision. If the feedback comes from other people, it will tend to be a murky picture related to some side effect of an action—not very reassuring. Go back to the managers and communicate the results as well as the events of what happened in the project after the effects of the actions.

WRITTEN REPORTS

Each international project type is different. Construction projects are different from software projects, for example. Therefore, it is most useful here to provide you with some general guidelines for written reports and documents.

- At the start of the international project, identify the types of documents that will be produced.
- For each type, make sure that you have an outline for the document.
- Try to put examples of these documents from previous projects on the network. Include good and bad examples. Expunge the names of people and organizations. This will give the team members models of what is expected. We do this in our teaching. Each quarter we often put past projects on the Web or network for students to review. Since each project is different, they cannot just reuse what has been done before.
- Discuss guidelines and expectations for each document.
- Discuss how documents will be reviewed.

From experience there are some additional guidelines for preparing the documents. Do not send team members away to work on a document. They might come back weeks later with something unacceptable. That is too risky and there may be insufficient time to redo the document. Have the team members produce an outline for you in a short time. Then they can submit more detailed outlines later. The document grows and there will be no unpleasant surprises. This method is called the **method of successive refinement**. It has been employed in both teaching and projects for over two decades—always with good results.

SIGNS OF COMMUNICATIONS PROBLEMS

There are many signs of problems that you should be on the lookout for. Here are some of the common ones:

- Team members are very quiet and do not participate. Do not assume that everything is fine with them.
- When you sit and listen to what team members talk about during breaks, you find that they are never talking about the project. This is a sign of trouble. If the project was interesting or exciting, then they should be discussing their work.
- When you talk to two team members who are working together on tasks, you find that you are getting very different views of the work. What is going on? They have probably divided up the work to do it individually. You should

get them back working together. Maybe, you should have meetings with both of them at the same time.

EXAMPLES

SAMBAC ENERGY

At Sambac the communications were mainly top down. That is, the managers from the two companies would come in and make directives and issue instructions top down. This communication approach was not effective. It took too long for instructions to reach through middle management down to where the work was being performed.

To rectify this situation, the projects were divided up into subprojects that were managed and directed at lower levels. This provided for more communications and input on projects from the working levels. The managers from the two companies then functioned as steering committees with the higher-level local managers. Instructions made more sense because they were in the context of the actual work.

WHITMORE BANK

In the first attempt at the credit card project, you will recall that they attempted to entirely base the project in one location. The result was failure. This was in part due to communications. Communications were stifled at the single head location. People in other locations after voicing issues several times then just went about their other work.

Another problem was that the project leader did not want to hear about issues. He expected that the project team members would deal with issues on their own. How can they when the scope of the power and influence may be extremely limited? Managers in the other countries did not see their role as solving issues— in part due to the culture of the country.

In the new organization of the project, things got better. There was much more communications between locations since the project was organized across locations.

LESSONS LEARNED

A number of lessons learned have already been presented as guidelines in each section. Here some additional general guidelines are given:

- If things are quiet in the project, assume that things are not going well. Assume that there are issues. This is similar to that of children. If your child is very quiet playing in their room, then you can assume that they are getting into mischief.
- If you begin the project and have identified documents as milestones without outlines or templates, then there will likely be problems. The team members do not know what you are expecting. This makes it more difficult to estimate the duration of the work. As a result, they will tend to underestimate the work.
- As a project leader, after resolving issues, communications is your number two activity. You must often force yourself to get up and go out to find out what is going on. This can be a struggle, because some days the last thing you want to know about is another issue. But get out of that chair!

EXERCISES

1. Look in the literature on the Web to examine if the cause of failure in projects was a breakdown in communications.
2. Apply the communications score cards to existing projects.

SUMMARY

Communications is a major factor in any moderate-sized project. It is more so in international projects because of the range and extent of parallel work being performed. This calls for constantly reviewing the effectiveness of your communications through the score cards and through reviewing where you lack knowledge about the project.

Chapter 10

Deal with Issues and Use Experience

INTRODUCTION

All through the book two recurring themes have been issues and lessons learned. In this chapter guidelines are provided for dealing with the issues that have been identified and using the lessons learned you have collected. You want an organized, consistent approach to save time, increase productivity, and produce cumulative results and benefits over time. If you attempt to resolve issues one at a time, then you can run into the following problems:

- Every time you will have to educate management on the method you are using for dealing with issues.
- Many issues are being treated one at a time and not being grouped. Issues should be bundled.
- You and others will have to devote too much time to deal with issues because of the lack of an organized approach.

Moreover, if you use the issues database and track the issues, then you can begin to see that in similar international projects, the same issues will recur again and again. In our work we have found that the issues database seldom grows beyond 200–300 different issues. Of course, you have to analyze an issue to determine if it is a variation of an existing issue.

You have to plan ahead as a project leader for how you will surface issues and major problems to management. You really want an overall strategy for visibility to management. The graph that has been useful is shown in Fig. 10.1. This graph shows that there is great visibility at the start during the project concept. Then there is a great deal of discussion on the scope and issues. Later, there will be some visibility for the project plan. However, this is less than

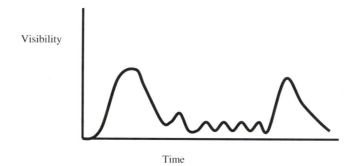

Figure 10.1   Example of Visibility of Issues to Management over the Life of the Project

the project concept because it reinforces the project concept. During the project there are times when you will be taking bundles of issues to management. Near the latter part of most international projects, there will be crises and many issues. This accounts for the final large "bump" in the graph. You will want to construct your own graph and then use it to plan for going to management with issues.

For lessons learned, a traditional approach is to gather experience at the end of the project. However, most of the people are gone and the memories of those remaining are dim. In addition, people don't see the need to do this since they sense that the lessons learned are not employed—they are filed or tossed away. The basic guideline is to collect the lessons learned as you do the project work. Then the memories are fresh and the people are there.

PURPOSE AND SCOPE

TECHNICAL PURPOSE

For issues the technical purpose is to correctly address an issue with the proper actions and decisions at the right time. Notice the phrase "right time." The right time is what a project leader must develop—the sense of timing. If you present an issue too soon, people may not think it is important. Presenting it too late may result in drastic and expensive measures.

It is a true test of any international project leader that they develop a sense of timing for issues—when to do something and work with management.

The technical goal for lessons learned is that the lessons learned be useful and applicable to the work so that the gathering and organizing of the lessons learned is worthwhile.

BUSINESS PURPOSE

The business purpose for issues is that the solutions required are done with limited cost and resources. Another goal is that the issues are processed in an orderly manner. A third business goal is to have accountability for issues.

For lessons learned, the purpose is to improve the present project performance as well as that of future similar projects. The future work should improve in terms of reduced cost and time and reduced risk.

POLITICAL PURPOSE

The political goal for issues to get these resolved so as to have a minimum of political problems and additional issues. Another goal is that the actions and decisions related to issues are agreed to and followed up on.

For lessons learned, the political goal is that the people on project teams are willing to learn from the experience of others. The goal is then to have less of the "not invented here syndrome."

END PRODUCTS

For issues the end products are:

- Complete database of issues for analysis and tracking;
- Sufficient information to support the timely resolution of issues;
- Documentation of issues, decisions, actions, and follow-up for tracking purposes and accountability;
- Analysis method and results for assessing issues.

End products for lessons learned include the following:

- Usable and appropriate lessons learned with specific guidelines;
- Method for improving and updating the lessons learned through additional experience;
- Defined approach and process for formally ensuring that lessons learned are considered, reviewed, and employed.

APPROACH

CHARACTERISTICS OF ISSUES

An issue surfaces. But it may not be an issue. It may be a symptom of a more complex problem. It may be a previous issue reappearing. Or it may just be more about an existing issue. This gives us the following guideline:

In an international project, you always want to analyze and assess an issue before making decisions and taking action.

You should not rush out and assign it to someone until you understand better what you are dealing with. The next guideline is that it is the project leaders who should undertake to do the initial analysis of an issue. Then it may end up being assigned to someone.

Issues can be considered by types. What is a type? It is a category of issue. One method of defining categories is to consider the source of the issue.

• *Management.* The issue deals with management areas such as resources, budget, and schedule.

• *Work.* The issue involves specific work in the project. Quality and completeness are issues.

• *Project team.* There can be personality conflicts in the team. People may be getting pulled off of the team to work on other things.

• *Business situation.* The underlying business situation in a country may have deteriorated, affecting the project.

• *Other projects.* Your project may be highly interdependent on other projects that have issues.

• *Government regulations.* Your project may be hung up on getting government approvals or reviews.

• *Culture.* There could be substantial cultural problems and conflicts.

• *General external factors.* These could include labor unions and the weather.

• *Competition.* The competitors may be ahead of you on a similar project, creating more pressure to get the work completed.

• *Headquarters.* There can be issues arising from headquarters such as changes in priorities.

• *In-country operations.* There could be new work or problems that interfere with the project.

• *Customers or suppliers.* There can be dynamic factors here that affect the project.

- *Business processes.* There may be issues with shadow systems, procedures, and policies.
- *Vendors and consultants.* Availability of staff and quality of work are two issues here.
- *Technology.* There may a number of systems and technology problems and opportunities.

Use the above list as a starting point for type. Another method of rating or typing an issue is by impact. This also might be considered important. A third method is by time urgency. How pressing is the issue?

Still another categorization of issue is by control. Do you have the resources and management authority to act on the issue? The killer issues for many international projects lie in those that are beyond the control of the team. It is these that you have to build contingencies for. You might want to assume the worse that can happen and then minimize the impact. This is the **minimax approach** to issues management. It sounds good, but it has several drawbacks. First, it tends to make the situation and you more negative. Second, it can lead to an overly conservative approach to a project when a more aggressive stance is required. Temerity is not often a winning trait in international projects.

Another characteristic of an issue is the status. When an issue appears, it should be given a pending status depending on investigation. Then if it becomes an issue, its status is open. When you resolve an issue, it becomes closed. An issue can also be combined with another issue.

Why do some issues fail to surface until the end of the project? There are many, often political reasons. Some people may not want to use the results of the project. When they see that it will be completed, they may raise last minute issues. Another reason is that team may be too isolated from the real world. As the project gets closer to completion, the real world starts to move in on the project—just like fog. The issues could have been there all of the time, but they went unnoticed.

POTENTIAL ACTIONS AND DECISIONS

What can you do about an issue?

Most of the time you should do nothing about an issue.

Why nothing? Because you lack information. The issue may not yet be "ripe" in terms of urgency. If you act too soon, management may not support your decision. That can look real bad. Also, you may end up treating a symptom and not the underlying problem. The issue will then surface again in another guise. It is the same with children growing up. If the parents run to the doctor with the child for treatment for every cold, the child could become overtreated with antibiotics. Then when the child really becomes sick, the antibiotics are not effective and the child gets sicker.

There is another guideline here. Many issues that surface in one country are specific to a situation. The situation may change on its own and cause the issue to change or go away. Or it could become more pressing. This is especially true with issues that you do not control.

There are political currents related to issues. You may not want to solve an issue right away. You and team might look better to management if the issue becomes more acute. This sounds perverse, but remember you are dealing in a political world. If the project and the world around it won't collapse, what is the harm in doing nothing? If you keep acting on issues quickly, you can be seen by some managers as "shooting from the hip" without thinking—not a good way to be typecasted.

You can also examine the following as decisions and actions to take. Use this as a checklist when you are evaluating an issue.

- Add resources to the work;
- Take resources away from the work;
- Stop using the method or tool;
- Enforce a different use of a method or tool;
- Change a policy to alter the scope of the project to make the issue disappear;
- Change the issue into another form that may be less political and easier to address;
- Break up an issue into parts and deal with each part;
- Combine issues so that one issue is swept up in the actions for other issues;
- Assign the issue to a different person;
- Throw money at an issue;
- Throw more technology at an issue;
- Involve a vendor in the issue;
- Take a vendor out of the issue;
- Reorganize the work;
- Move the issue away from the project to the line organization or another project;
- Restructure the project plan;
- Apply different types of resources in the project.

Follow these guidelines when getting ready to solve a group of issues:

• Make sure that the group of issues is related in some way that is acceptable to management.

• Take care to have the issues stated clearly and succinctly.

• Ensure that management is aware of the issues. Surprises are bad here.

• Examine as many alternatives as possible before making any decision.

• Weigh the effect of delaying a decision with that of making a decision.

• Make certain that the decisions that you are about to make are backed up completely by the actions.

• Work to understand the business, technical, and political implications, impacts, and effects of the actions and decision at both the local and headquarters levels.

• Define how you are going to measure the actions after they have been carried out.

Many mistakes made by many governments on the international level could have been prevented had these actions been taken.

A GENERAL PROCESS FOR MANAGING ISSUES

You should always consider groups of related issues. In an international project of any size and complexity, if you consider one issue at a time, you are going to drive yourself crazy.

The general process for handling issues is presented in steps in Fig. 10.2. Here are some additional comments on these steps:

• *The initial investigation of the issue.* The project leader should try to determine where the issue originated from. What caused it to surface now? Has it always been there? Why didn't people become aware of this issue earlier? Can you quickly group it with other issues? Can it be dealt with now?

• *Assignment of the issue.* It is good to spread the issues around the team politically. The team members become more sensitive to what is going on beyond their immediate work. Of course, this requires care so that they are not diverted off of their work in the project.

• *Tracking the issue.* Have the team members log what they are doing in the issues database rather than e-mail. E-mail lacks structure.

• *Surfacing the issues to management.* You want to alert management of the symptoms and problems. But you initially do not want to press for action. They will often just push it back to you. A gradual buildup is better.

• *Presenting the issue, and recommended actions and decision to management.* Here you want to show the impact of continuing to do nothing about the issue. It is the fear of the impact of the issue getting worse that drives people often to make decisions.

Detect an issue, symptom, or opportunity.

Log it into the issues database so that it can be tracked.

Carry out an initial in vestigation to determine characteristics of the issue.

If necessary, assign the issue to someone with specific directions.

Follow up on the progress regarding the issue.

Analyze the issue to see how it should be grouped with other issues.

Examine alternatives for dealing with the issue.

Surface the issue in the form of symptoms to management.

Present the issue and recommended decision and actions to management.

Announce the decision and the actions.

Follow up on the actions and measure the results.

Figure 10.2   Steps in Addressing Issues

ISSUES AND MULTIPLE PROJECTS

Many issues may impact several subprojects and other projects. Solving an issue for one project may make the issue worse in another setting. Thus, as part of the analysis of issues, you should employ the table in Fig. 10.3. In the table the rows are issues and the columns are the projects or subprojects. There are several ways to fill the table. One approach is to use "X's". You put in an X if the issue pertains to the specific subproject or project. A second method is to put text in each box that explains in a summary form the impact of the issue on the subproject or project.

There is another approach. Return to the GANTT chart. Since you are employing standardized templates, you can create an overall GANTT chart that contains summary tasks from all of the projects along with the tasks that are affected by the specific issue. This is often a good graphic method for getting management to sit up and take the issue seriously. You can do the same with groups of issues.

Now let's suppose that you are a manager over a number of international projects that differ in size and issues. Figure 10.4 shows two projects that differ in size and issues. Where do most managers spend their time? On the larger project. But this is wrong. The other project, B, has many more issues and so should get

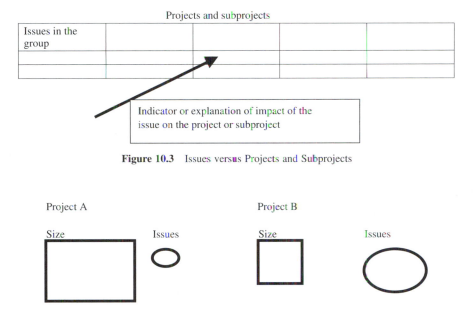

Figure 10.3 Issues versus Projects and Subprojects

Figure 10.4 Example of Two Projects Differing in Size and Number of Issues

more attention. You might want to use this graphic to focus attention on those projects of moderate size, but with many issues.

ISSUE ANALYSIS

There is a great deal that can be done with only a small amount of information in the issues database. Let's restrict our attention to the following data elements:

- Identifier of the issue;
- Type of the issue;
- Status of the issue;
- Date that the issue was discovered;
- Date that the issue was resolved.

In fact, you can export data elements into a spreadsheet to go with the graphs that will be presented. The point here is to emphasize that this is easy to do, has a number of benefits, and can be done without interfering with your regular work. Six different analyses will be discussed using the basic data. You can expand on this by considering other graphs and charts.

Open Issues by Type

At any given time an international project has a number of open, unresolved issues. The mixture of the open issues is very important as you will see. Let's use the following types:

- Team-related issues;
- Work-related issues;
- Vendor-related issues;
- Process-related issues;
- Organization-related issues;
- Management-related issues;
- Policy-related issues;
- Technology-related issues.

Now at the start of an international project, many of the known issues typically relate to requirements, technology, the team, and the work. A typical chart is shown in Fig. 10.5 for a project. Another example is given in Fig. 10.6. These are two spider charts.

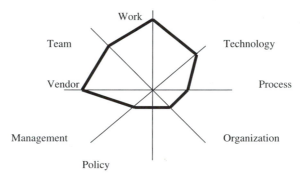

Figure 10.5   First Example of Number of Open Issues by Type

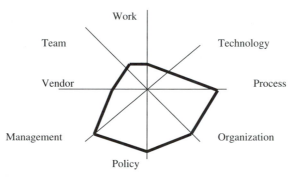

Figure 10.6   Second Example of Number of Open Issues by Type

If you could choose which chart would apply to your project, which would it be? If you picked the first one, you would be correct. Why? In the chart of Fig. 10.5 most of the issues are in areas that you control. In the chart of Fig. 10.6 disaster may loom. Most of the issues that are open are in areas that you don't control. Bad news!

What can do with these charts? They first show that you are on top of the issues. This shows you and the team in a favorable light. Another use is as a tool to press for resolution of some of the issues. However, a major use of the chart is to understand the state of the overall international project. Status, percentage complete, and budget versus actual are OK, but this chart speaks volumes about the project.

You should also redraw and update these charts on a regular basis. They will tell you how you and the team are doing in solving the critical issues and getting these addressed.

TOTAL NUMBER OF ISSUES OVER TIME

Here you only use the date of discovery of the issue. The x axis is time. On the y axis is the number of issues that have been found as of that point in time. You can also do this chart by type of issue. Figure 10.7 gives an example chart with two international projects. The solid line represents a project that is going well. As time progresses, there are few new issues found. There is a spike toward the end to accommodate the seemingly inevitable hidden issues that surface late in the project. The dotted line is another matter entirely. This is a project in trouble where new issues keep surfacing. Note that this chart says nothing about solving the issues. Nevertheless, it is another indicator of the project state.

Open Issues over Time

Let's add the status to the data in the previous chart. You will chart the number of open issues that exist at a particular point in time versus time. Again, you could

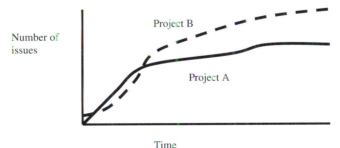

Figure 10.7 Total Number of Issues by Date of Discovery

do this by type of issue as well. Figure 10.8 contains two examples. The solid line for Project A represents a project in which the issues are under control. The dashed line represents a problem project. Note that the number of issues that are open tends to rise and then drop off. It may temporarily pick up and then drop again.

This chart is useful in tracking how the project is doing in resolving issues. It also serves as an early indicator of a project in trouble. If the number of open issues is not declining toward the end of the project, it is possible that the project will fail.

Aging Analysis of Open Issues

Every issue has a discovery date and status. You can determine the percentage of issues that are open by the date of discovery. That is, for issues that were discovered in the past week, the percentage is almost 100%. Meanwhile, the issues that were discovered long ago should be solved—leaving a very small percentage. This is the solid chart in Fig. 10.9. A more difficult situation appears

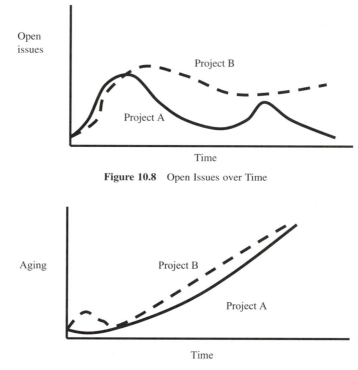

Figure 10.8   Open Issues over Time

Figure 10.9   Aging Chart of Issues over Time

in the dashed graph for Project B. Here there is a bump or jump far back in the project. This means that there are a number of issues that have remained unresolved for some time. This will either cause major problems to the project or even cause the project to fail.

Average Elapsed Time to Resolve Issues

This chart plots the average elapsed time it takes to resolve an issue for all issues discovered up to a specific point in time. Figure 10.10 is an example of this chart. The solid line corresponds to a well-behaved project in which the elapsed time increases as the team, leader, and managers get familiar with solving issues. Then the elapsed time declines until at the end you almost will solve an issue the minute it appears.

Analysis of Open Issues by Impact and Time Urgency

Two factors have not been considered—impact and time urgency. These are subjective, depending on the person who is viewing the issues. Nevertheless, their analysis is useful. Figure 10.11 presents a general chart in which time pressure is the horizontal axis and impact on the project is on the vertical axis. Issue 5 is time urgent, but of low impact. Issue 12 is both time urgent and high impact. It is important. So you should pay attention to the issues in the upper right quadrant.

However, you cannot stop there. While you cannot address all open issues, you can consider those that have less impact, but that are time urgent. This is the lower right quadrant. So if you put this together, you are going to give attention to the issues in the ellipse.

Now let's consider an example. Figure 10.12 shows the open issues on the chart at a specific time. Figure 10.13 reveals the issues at a later time. Note

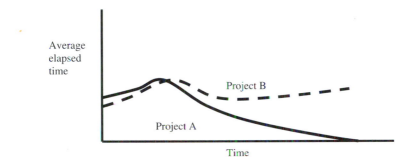

Figure 10.10   Average Elapsed Time to Resolve an Issue

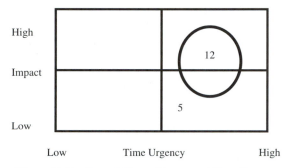

Figure 10.11   General Chart of Impact and Time Urgency

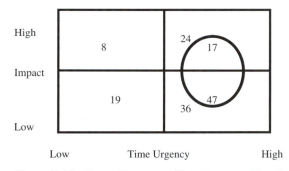

Figure 10.12   Chart of Impact and Time Urgency at Time 1

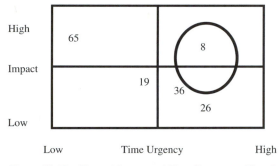

Figure 10.13   Chart of Impact and Time Urgency at Time 2

that focus at the first time was on the issues in the upper right and lower right quadrants. The other issues were left alone. In Fig. 10.13 these issues are removed, but new issues emerged and the position of the other unresolved issues changed.

Some specific notes are:

- Issues 17, 24, and 47 were resolved after the first time and do not show up in the second chart.
  - Issue 36 is still there and didn't change position over the time.
  - Issue 65 appeared for the first time on the second chart.
  - Issue 8 became critical over time.
  - Issue 19 changed but it did not become critical as yet.
  - Issue 26 appeared as low impact, but high time urgency.

What is going on? Over time the time urgency and impact of specific issues may change. This method gives you a useful way to chart these. It is understandable to management and makes an interesting slide show out of what would normally be a boring and arcane subject.

Overall, how do you use these charts? You should consider these as additional templates for issues analysis. These should be produced for each critical and major international project.

CHARACTERISTICS OF LESSONS LEARNED

Lessons learned were defined in the first chapter. Let's delve into this subject more now. A lesson learned is a guideline for doing something. It can be related to the international project. It can be related to management. It can be related to the using the project results in a business process. Lessons learned don't tell you what to do. That is a procedure. Instead, lessons learned tell you how to do the work better. Lessons learned are not a new phenomenon. They go back in time before languages were invented when people used symbols and word of mouth to pass information on. Lessons learned were a critical success factor for the ancient Egyptians, Romans, Chinese, and others. It has been shown by many historians that when a society or civilizations fail to continue to improve through lessons learned, then the society often fails. This was one of the causes for the fall of the Roman Empire. Moving to modern times, lessons learned have shown to be very useful in the military, manufacturing, marketing, and a wide variety of other areas.

Lessons learned cannot just be written down when they are discovered. They have to be discussed and analyzed. It could be that the lesson learned only applies to a unique situation. It may also be capable of being generalized to more situations. Once a lesson learned is defined, it must be organized so that it can be used again. That is why you have the lessons learned database. It serves as a repository of knowledge. However, knowledge doesn't do you much good if you cannot get at it and use it. That is why the lessons learned are cross-referenced to the project templates. You can go back and forth between templates and lessons learned to find those that apply to the upcoming work.

It doesn't stop there. International projects are dynamic. When you attempt to apply a lesson learned, there are several possible outcomes:

- The lesson learned did not apply or did not work in your project.
- Using the lesson learned, you produced work of higher quality or did the work in less time with fewer resources.
- You used the lesson learned and improved upon it.

It is as important to capture this additional experience as it is the original lesson learned. A related guideline here is that you should purge lessons learned that have not been used in a long time. The key idea here is to use the additional experience to update and expand on the lesson learned.

As with issues, there are various types of lessons learned. Here are some examples. Note that you would take the technical category and expand this for the type of international projects that you do.

- Project management;
- Project team;
- Project work;
- Methods;
- Tools;
- Technology;
- Technical;
- Marketing;
- Customer service.

A General Process for Lessons Learned

Figure 10.14 presents the steps in the process of using lessons learned. As with issues, a number of comments are appropriate.

- The maintenance of the lessons learned database and its updating are performed by the coordinator function defined earlier in the book for the multiple international projects.
- The project leaders cannot afford to treat lessons learned lightly. They need to take them seriously and enforce them being considered. Their attitude should be "Why reinvent the wheel again and again?"
- Some might think that this will take time away from the project. Any time spent reviewing and updating lessons learned is more than offset by the increased productivity.

Review current work and extract experience.

Refine the experience and obtain feedback so that you have a lesson learned.

Enter the lesson learned in the lessons learned database.

Cross-reference the lesson learned with the tasks in the project templates.

When any new area of the international project is started, a rule is that the applicable lessons learned (from the template) must be reviewed and used. If they are not used, then the project leader needs to be made aware of the reason.

After the work has begun and the lesson learned applied, the experience is gathered and used to update the lessons learned database and to refine the project templates.

Figure 10.14   General Process for Lessons Learned

GATHER LESSONS LEARNED

How do you get started gathering lessons learned? You don't just ask people for them. You have to reference some tasks and ask how they would go about the work. As they talk about it, consider asking the following questions:

- How did you come across this?
- What did you do before you started using this technique?
- If you did not use this method, what could you do?
- Has the method ever failed?
- Have you had to change the method?
- Have you tried to use the method for other things?

Write down the lesson learned as a sequence of steps. This helps you organize the information. Then you can get feedback from the individuals who provided this.

USE LESSONS LEARNED FOR ADVANTAGE

Lessons learned are useful in almost all lines of work. For many international projects, you can institute lessons learned for the work of the current process. This is what is called a "Quick Hit" or "Quick Win." It is very useful politically because you show that you care about what people are doing. You are showing respect for them and how they do their work. You are also helping them in their future work. It is useful to structure these around established procedures. Consider the following table:

Step	Who	What	Lessons learned

The first three columns constitute the procedures. You will recognize them as playscript. The last column contains the lessons learned on how best to do the work.

You should apply this to your project team. You will get the same benefits. Lessons learned are timeless.

PROJECT MEETINGS FOR LESSONS LEARNED

In the previous chapter on communications, it was indicated that a good strategy is to employ about 1/3 of the project meetings to lessons learned. This is very ambiguous. What are you going to do in these meetings? Here is a useful list of things to do:

• Have team members present their milestones and results to the group. This provides a format that is friendly and routine. It is not done on an exception basis.

• New team members can present lessons learned from their past projects and work. This familiarizes the team members with what that person has done. It also helps to socialize the person into the team.

• Team members who are critical and who may be leaving the project can use the lessons learned to aid in transferring of knowledge of what they have been doing. Using the lessons learned meetings provides a useful, nonthreatening approach for knowledge transfer.

• Vendor staff and consultants can present what they are doing so that knowledge transfer is again facilitated.

• Lessons learned meetings are a good place to collect experience on the use of methods and tools and tips for effective use of these.

EXAMPLES

SAMBAC ENERGY

At Sambac the emphasis was on getting the work done. The attitude changed when it became evident that the same mistakes were occurring again and again. The result was that the approach to lessons learned was applied and the number of mistakes dropped. After each new mistake, lessons learned were collected. This approach was later taken by one of the managers back to the company.

WHITMORE BANK

Whitmore had many issues in their deployment of credit card. Yet, they had no organized approach for issues. There was no numbering or identification system. No one knew how many open issues there were. When the second effort was made at the project, the issues were tracked and labeled. Issue awareness and management were viewed as critical success factors.

LESSONS LEARNED

Here are some things that you can do right away after reading this book

- Identify lessons learned and start building the lessons learned database.
- Create the issues database from the issues in Part IV of the book.
- Establish templates and retrofit the existing projects into the templates.
- Start using a standardized project file approach.
- Employ standardized management reporting.
- Change how project meetings are conducted.
- Begin to use a customized form of the project management software.
- Start emphasizing informal communications.
- Apply the score cards that have been developed in different chapters to your project.

EXERCISES

1. At home sit down with members of your family and gather some simple lessons learned. This will give you hands-on experience in doing this. It will also be beneficial to your family.

2. Use the same approach as the previous exercise for issues.

3. Don't wait for a project to be completed. Get started right away and identify the existing issues in the international project you are working on. Begin to gather lessons learned.

SUMMARY

This chapter has presented an organized approach for dealing with issues and lessons learned. No matter what you do, set up some organized approach. Otherwise, lessons learned are wasted. Issues grow out of control. You should want to use a method such as this for self-interest. Notice also that a number of positive political benefits were identified.

Part III

Types of Global Projects

There have been several examples that have been followed in each of the preceding chapters. In the next part, common issues frequently encountered in international projects are explored. Here the methods and themes of the book are applied to three common types of international projects: software deployment, mergers and acquisitions, and new product introduction. These have been selected from among 30 different types of international projects that we have managed and participated in. These were also picked because they have very different characteristics from each other.

These three chapters are organized around the themes of the book: issues, templates, and lessons learned. In the issue part, a number of specific issues are examined for that type of project. In the template section the major areas of a project of this type are discussed. Finally, there are several lessons learned provided that apply to this type of project. The purpose of these chapters is to give more insight into how to manage types of international projects.

Chapter 11

Multinational Software Deployment

INTRODUCTION

If you go back in time to the 1970s and 1980s, there were few international software packages available. This was for a number of reasons. First, there were fewer mergers and acquisitions on an international scale. Second, the hardware, databases, and other technology were not sufficiently advanced to support the networking requirements for international applications. A third reason was the challenge of trying to create software that could fit a number of different cultures. The most successful software packages tended to be engineering, manufacturing, and assembly-type software that were technically rather than culturally or regulatory based.

The change came in the 1990s with the emergence of enterprise resource planning systems (ERP systems). There are today over 100 significant ERP systems; among the most prominent are SAP, Peoplesoft, BAAN, and J. D. Edwards. ERP and other enterprise software systems offer tantalizing benefits:

- There can be standardization around a region or around the world.
- Management can obtain information with much less effort on a more timely basis.
- There is increased communications among the various users of the software in the company.

Yet, many ERP implementations have either failed or been scaled back. These systems, in addition to the benefits, have the following problems:

- The cost of the overall implementation can be 10–20 times the cost of the software.

- Obtaining qualified consultants to support the implementation is a must. Few firms have had a successful international presence.
- It can be difficult to demonstrate the benefits of the system to in-country managers and staff—creating problems and resistance.

Most companies, however, either are involved in a region or globally seek to implement the same systems in as many locations as possible. Some of the operational benefits of the same software are:

- Simpler and easier sharing of information between locations.

- Centralized support that reduces the overall software cost over the life cycle.
- Capability to take advantage of improved data communications and networking.
- The pressure of e-business to automate transactions with suppliers, employees, and customers.

There are drawbacks in that the local regulatory and cultural factors are difficult to accommodate with the same software. In the longer-term future this situation will improve as software makers adopt object-oriented methods that are more flexible and can accommodate national and regional changes.

Multinational software deployment is complex. Here is a factor that affects this type of project: You cannot do it yourself so that you must rely on consultants and contractors. Now we are not talking about a few people—there could be 20–100 or more of these consultants involved in different locations.

PURPOSE AND SCOPE

TECHNICAL PURPOSE

The technical purpose of software implementation is to complete the installation of the software in as little time as possible without disrupting the business and staying within budget. Another related purpose is that the software correctly reflects the business rules and policies that control the company's operation in each location. This is a very tall order. Let's give an example of a policy. In one Southeast Asian country a package was going to be installed. Before installation, the features of the package were presented to the local management. A key capability of the software package was control. Nothing could be shipped to a customer unless there a signed order was received. A local manager indicated that for valuable, long-time customers they shipped based on a telephone call or fax because of the long-standing relationship. The presenters said that this could not be accommodated. Therefore, they would have to change their local policy. The local manager indicated that they would lose business. He was overridden. When the software was installed, customers started to leave; they refused to fit in with the process imposed by the system. Desperate to keep the company going, the local managers reverted to the old process. They then had a clerk input the data after the fact into the ERP. The result worked, but there were no benefits for the local office—only additional work and pain.

BUSINESS PURPOSE

From a business perspective, the goal is to achieve new, effective business processes and standardization through the installation of the software. The thinking is that it is too hard, if not impossible, to manually control work in remote countries overseas. So if they are using the same system for the standard processes, the software will act to enforce standardization.

This is the correct business purpose. However, it often is not achieved because the implementation is ended almost immediately after the software is installed. There is no follow-up or measurement, and insufficient attention to business process change to mesh the local culture and business rules to those expected and imposed by the software.

POLITICAL PURPOSE

Many firms make the mistake of not having any political purpose; they are satisfied with the technical and business purposes outlined above. It is in these situations where the most problems occur. There are a number of useful political goals, including:

- Build a better understanding at headquarters about operations out in the field.
- Identify clearly the areas where the local rules and factors must be followed. There is some flexibility in that not every local business rule has to be slavishly adopted.
- Create a collaborative environment for the project that will increase communications among locations.
- Support simplification in business processes across the organization, including headquarters.

SCOPE

Scope is an interesting subject. This can be narrow or broad. Narrow scope consists of the software itself. Broad scope might include the software, business processes, policies, and organization structure. Something in the middle would delete the organization from the scope. This middle ground is the most successful.

However, there are factors that get in the way and impact the scope as the project progresses. The two key factors are time and money. Tasks take longer to do. People have to perform their normal tasks as well as work on the software implementation. The budget soars as more consultants climb on board. Together these act to narrow the scope to the software.

END PRODUCTS

The major end product is the software installed, working, and being used effectively as part of improved business processes. Scaled back it might be the software working, but the local business processes are warped and adapted to the software in an ad hoc manner.

Another end product is improved information at headquarters, regions, and countries on a more timely and predictable basis. These are real benefits as well as end products. Why aren't they commonly achieved? Because no one is dedicated to using the information in a structured manner so that much of it goes unused. Another reason is that IT support is required to gain access and manipulate the information.

ISSUES

ISSUE: THERE IS A LACK OF SENSITIVITY TO THE CULTURE FACTORS IN SPECIFIC COUNTRIES

This issue was mentioned, but not addressed. A common thread through the book has been the cultural factors among countries and even parts of a country. Here the issue is applied to software implementation.

Impact

Culture anywhere in the world dictates how you do business and make money. It affects how you interact with customers and suppliers. While there has been some common adoption of some "Western" ways, there remain local nuances and mores. Culture affects the business rules. If the business rules of the software package don't match up or cannot be reconciled, then there are bound to be problems. Something has to give—either the package fails or the business is affected.

Prevention

The best prevention is to understand the culture and business rules in each location at the start. This is a very tall order so let's simplify it. You should identify about 10–20 critical transactions that would be covered by a new system. Then you should examine how these are carried out in each country in detail using the methods from Chapter 2.

Action

You will begin to detect problems when business rules and exceptions start appearing. People will ask "How will the system handle such-and-such a transaction?" When they get an answer, look at their reaction. If they are quiet and don't anything else, you know that there is a problem. They won't discuss it where they are dominated by others. When the problem arises, then you should lower the effort in the software implementation and go back to the transactions and perform analysis.

ISSUE: THE SOFTWARE WAS PURCHASED; HOWEVER, IT CANNOT HANDLE THE REGULATORY REQUIREMENTS IN CERTAIN COUNTRIES DESPITE THE VENDOR CLAIMS

If you are a software provider and you find that you can sell your product in a particular country to several firms, it will be tempting to the marketing staff to indicate that it will work well in the country. However, this may only be for a few industries—not general. Marketing makes the claims that the customer believes and then there are problems.

Impact

Typically, since the software cannot be rebuilt, there are two recourses. One is that you create a workaround using software tables and procedures. Another approach is to create a "shadow system." This can serve as either a front or back end to the system.

Prevention

You really have to evaluate the software more fully during the evaluation work. The true test is to send specific transactions through the system. If the vendor is unwilling or unable to do this, then you will have to resort to having them explain how the transaction would work.

Action

If you did not take preventive action, you are likely to find out about this problem when you are winding up the project in testing. Then suddenly, the crisis hits. Before starting to fix a problem at a time, the best approach is to do an overall assessment to determine how much of the work and transactions are affected.

Issue: A Large Number of Key Personnel May Be Tied Up in This Project for Months

Guidelines for personnel and team members were given in Chapter 4. Recall that you want to have junior people who have energy on the project. Here, the point is that you require senior people with detailed knowledge of the business rules. This is true, but you don't need them all of the time.

Impact

If the critical "king bees" and "queen bees" are taken out of a department, the remaining employees may feel lost. They may not know how to handle certain pieces of work. The employees go to the supervisor or manager who now feels put out that they are coming to her/him. After all, they may not be familiar with that work either. As you can see, the impact can be dramatic and long-lasting. When the senior person returns from the project, he/she is inundated with work. Then back to the project again. They become burned out.

Prevention

The best method for preventing this situation is to involve junior people heavily from the department. Then only pull the senior people in when you require specific business rules. You can measure yourself by seeing the mixture of people and total hours in the project.

Action

If you find that you are becoming overdependent upon senior employees and they are on the project all of the time, then you have to look not at this, but at the reasons why you need the senior employees. What is so arcane and technical? Remember that the package will not be modified. If the senior people are on the project too much, then it is a sign that there may be too much attention to exceptions, workarounds, and shadow systems. Don't assume that this is real productive work. If you get sucked into these exceptions, you may never get out!

ISSUE: THE SOFTWARE DOES NOT INTERFACE EASILY WITH SEVERAL CRITICAL LEGACY SYSTEMS

Software interfaces are a curse of the industry and have been for over 40 years despite all efforts at standardization through EDI (electronic data interchange) and XML (extensible markup language). You could write a whole library of books on this issue. In brief here are some of the problems. Software gets written at different times using slightly different techniques and technology. This makes interfaces more technically difficult. Now programmers come and go so that over 15–20 years (the average life of much of the software out there in operation), the software programs resemble a puzzle—lack of documentation and difficult to understand. Also, hard to make changes. These are just a few of the reasons why interfacing to older, legacy systems is difficult. Why don't people just replace these systems? They work so if it is not broken, why fix it? Next, some of the packages are as old as the customized programs.

Impact

The interface is normally extremely critical. Often, the legacy system feeds the new software package so that it must have the information. Because of the time required to do the interface, it is often on the critical path of the project. Many times it will be delayed—really impacting the project.

Prevention

There is no way to prevent the interface. It must be started early and must be given a high priority by the senior programmers. Anything that can be done to simplify the interface should be evaluated during the design.

Action

If the interface part of the project is suffering, then you have to consider setting up a more limited interface for selected transactions. Putting more people on the interface work will often actually slow the work down.

ISSUE: HEADQUARTERS DOES NOT PROVIDE SUFFICIENT RESOURCES OR MONEY FOR THE IMPLEMENTATION IN REMOTE LOCATIONS

This is a classic issue that we have encountered time and time again. Headquarters expects people in the field to just drop what they are doing and support this as another project—not a good idea. The project leaders at headquarters may not have ever managed a similar project before and are clueless about what is required. If they added on the cost of the staff and managers in the field that will have to support the project, the costs might far outweigh the benefits.

Impact

Local managers will quickly ask what additional resources will be provided to them to do the project. They are often met with vague promises and assurances that there will not be much work. As the local people get sucked into the vortex of the software implementation, then there will be more complaints. Their local work may and likely will suffer. Things will slip. The current processes in the company location will deteriorate—just as they are trying to implement better processes.

Prevention

Planning for the project must be realistic. Also, follow the guidelines of Chapter 5 and use a collaborative approach with the people in the field.

Action

When you start to notice the stress and problems, then you have to step back and determine a more reasonable schedule—if there are no more resources. Instead of slowing everything down, try to implement a module or part of the system.

ISSUE: THE CONSULTANT SELECTED FOR SUPPORTING THE IMPLEMENTATION OF THE SOFTWARE DOES NOT HAVE PERSONNEL IN SOME COMPANY LOCATIONS

Many consulting firms make promises about their international presence. However, what this means sometimes is that when they get business in some country where they really don't operate, they subcontract out to some local firm. These individuals may not be connected at all with the consulting firm. All of the problems mentioned in Chapter 8 come to the foreground.

Impact

The consulting firm either fills in with local people or flies in expensive outside consultants. In both cases, you lose. The costs will be higher. There will be a steep learning curve that wasn't planned. The work may not be of consistent quality.

Prevention

The best method of preventing this problem is to follow the guidelines of Chapter 8 and find out what capabilities they have in each country. In addition, ascertain how they manage multiple locations and people being spread among multiple clients.

Action

You have to track the initial work that a consultant does in a country very carefully. You seek to build up a pattern of behavior between the local office and the consultants working there. Then you have to monitor the consulting firm to see whom they are sending into your offices.

TEMPLATE AREAS

AREA: PLANNING

There are a number of critical decisions to make at the start:

- How will the software be deployed or rolled out?
- Do you opt for one package or several packages from different vendors?
- How will you motivate the employees to support this?

There are a number of approaches for rollout. One way is to deploy the whole system in one country. Another approach is to deploy one part of the system in every country. A third approach is to implement different parts of the system in different locations. The first two are the most popular with the first being the most common.

For packages the trend has been to rely on one vendor. The argument is that you are guaranteed of interfaces that work. You have a simpler management relationship in which you can apply pressure on them due to the size of the order. And it is sometimes simpler.

AREA: SOFTWARE AND CONSULTANT ACQUISITION

General consulting guidelines were presented in Chapter 8. Here we point out that there are a variety of different types of consultants that may be needed for the project. For one package there are actually nine different types of consultants. The basic guideline is to define the outside support that you need when you select the software. Otherwise, you could have selected the software and find that there are few consultants available—making your software decision look pretty bad.

AREA: SOFTWARE IMPLEMENTATION

Here the main guideline follows from Chapters 2 and 5 in terms of how you organize the project. You do not want to organize it by country. In software installation what you learn in one place can be extremely valuable in another country. To facilitate and promote collaboration, set up the project across countries.

AREA: DATA CONVERSION

Data conversion has been a curse for many for years. Data in older systems is often of poor or uneven quality. There may be a lack of completeness and consistency. There may be problems in the timing as to when the data was captured. The problem grows in complexity when there are multiple systems.

The problems get worse when you consider what the new system requires. There are often many new fields of data. But where will this data come from if it is not in the current systems? Will it all have to be entered manually? Will you add the data as you go? Another problem is that a data element may have the same name in both the old and new systems, but have very different meanings. The lesson learned is to pay attention to data conversion early and to create a separate subproject for this area.

AREA: INTERFACES

Interfaces were mentioned earlier in this chapter. This is another subproject. The topics that have to be included in the plan include:

- Timing of the interface;
- Frequency of the interface;
- How validation of the interface will be accomplished;
- Recovery and restart if the interface fails;
- Documentation of the interface;
- Roll back if the data is passed, but later is found to be problematic.

AREA: TRAINING AND CUTOVER

These subjects sound straightforward. After all, the interfaces, data conversion, and other tasks such as testing were handled. However, you would be amazed at what comes up at the last minute. Some users may raise new exceptions and issues—just to delay the implementation. People may have made assumptions about what business rules were—then they found it changed. Keep tracking issues until the very end.

LESSONS LEARNED

- The benefits must be defined and made tangible as to which part of the organization bears the cost of the software and which receives the benefits.

Everyone has heard all of the benefits about new systems. They are easier to use, do away with paper, increase productivity and sales, and reduce costs. However, there is a basic problem—a system cannot do this. A process can. The benefits for systems lie in the business processes in which they are embedded.

Determining the benefits takes several steps. First, you have to define a new business process. In comparing the old and new processes, you obtain the benefits. But will the benefits be realized? You have to dig deeper. Now consider the new system. It is supposed to support the new business process. Will it? Better make sure. You should perform additional analysis to determine if the new system will support the new process. Finally, you want to follow up on the recommendations in Chapters 1, 2, and 10 in conducting reviews of the current and new processes to see if the benefits were achieved.

Remember the approach to benefits. You consider negative benefits as well. That is, you answer the question "What will happen if the new software is not obtained? What will be the impact?" If there is a very old legacy system that is falling apart, then you may have no choice.

- Place as much weight on operations, marketing, and other areas as compared to accounting and finance.

One of the problems that occur in implementing a large-scale system is that one user group or business area tends to step in and dominate the project. They steer the project to their own ends. This happened in one organization where accounting took control. The general ledger was installed fine, but marketing, sales, and operations got very little. An entire new project had to be started up to address their needs.

- Consider hiring a second consultant to watch over the main consultant involved in implementation support of the software package.

You can easily become over-reliant on a large consulting firm. You may even assign project management responsibilities to them. This is not a very good idea. Once you do this you give up not only control, but also a window into what is really going on in the project. A better approach is to hire a second consulting firm on a very limited basis to monitor and assess the first consulting firm. This will promote healthy disagreements and likely uncover unpleasant situations much more earlier—better for you!

• Use the implementation as a means to gather more information on how business is done in different locations.

Repeatedly, we have stressed how you want to piggyback on an international project. On this type of project you want to use the project to review and assess how the organization is performing their work.

SUMMARY

As you have seen, the methods apply easily to multinational software implementations. This type of project is of high risk and has many issues because it involves the core business processes in each location where the company either makes or loses money.

Chapter 12

Mergers and Acquisitions

INTRODUCTION

From a financial view, there are many differences between mergers and acquisitions. However, there are fewer differences in terms of project management. Even in one country many mergers and acquisitions totally and completely fail— not during the negotiations, but after the deal has been completed. Here are some of the common ugly occurrences:

- The acquiring or dominant firm that survives has to write down much of the value of what was acquired.
- The good people leave from both organizations.
- The business processes are not combined so that there are no economies of scale.
- So much attention was placed on the organization that systems, procedures, and policies were ignored.
- Only headquarters units were considered. No one thought of the separate country offices. They were going to sort that out later. It didn't happen. Processes and work fell apart country by country.

PURPOSE AND SCOPE

TECHNICAL PURPOSE

The technical purpose should be to create new processes out of the two organizations that combine the best of both—best of breed approach. Lofty goal, eh?

The real world is that there are often insufficient resources to even approach this goal. So the fallback is to work on the organization and systems. The thinking is that if you get the organization and systems right, then the processes in the middle will work well. Processes are different than that because both systems and the organizations support the processes—they often do not drive the processes.

BUSINESS PURPOSE

The business purpose is to attain the financial and other business objectives that were laid out when the two organizations got together. However, the problem is measurement. If you measure what people do in advance of change, then you have started on measurement. But after the combination of the organizations you find that upper management may not have the taste for measurement. There is too much unpleasant stuff lying around. Also, they will give the reason that the combination is over so there is no point in measuring.

POLITICAL PURPOSE

As with software implementation, there is limited attention to this. But it is very important. You must work to develop a new culture based on the two organizations. You cannot go in and wave a magic wand. How do you develop a common approach? You should get the employees together from both companies in a specific city. Have the individuals from each company discuss each key business process. Then the employees from the other company do the same. Now they discuss how a new process would work. This must be done on the individual transactions level.

END PRODUCTS

The major end products are:

• Results of investigation of the companies. This should include the analysis of specific sample transactions. There should also be a list of potential business, technical, and political issues.
• Business plan for the merger and acquisition; migration plan for the businesses.
  • Financial analysis and proposals.
  • Before-combination measurement.
  • Project plan for implementation.

- After-combination measurement.
- Detailed changes, organization charts, etc.

A guideline here is to not only define these, but also to develop detailed outlines as templates. As was said in Chapter 5, you want to involve employees in the development of these templates. If the employees are involved, there is less anxiety and more commitment.

ISSUES

ISSUE: THE TWO COMPANIES ARE NOT COMPATIBLE IN TERMS OF CULTURE

This is generally the case due to the history and evolution of the firms. Since it is almost always the case, some managers minimize this and state that they can change the culture. After all, they run the company. But culture is deep. There is culture involved at the company, country, and business unit level.

Impact

If the problem is either misunderstood or minimized, then the issue is not addressed. The problems grow and signs show up in terms of clashes at the working level. These are often misdiagnosed.

Prevention

The best approach is to identify a list of potential cultural issues. You can create a table of three columns. The first consists of the issues. The second is the impact. The last consists of comments.

Action

If you start seeing signs of problems, you need to think about culture being behind the situations.

ISSUE: THERE WAS A LACK OF ANALYSIS OF PROCESSES AND SYSTEMS; TOO MUCH ATTENTION WAS PLACED ON ORGANIZATION

It is very interesting that organizations do not generate profits; instead, they generate costs. Where are profits made? In business processes and supporting systems. Yet, the processes and system get so little attention. In some cases, they are treated as afterthoughts. In the real world you want to consider processes first, followed by systems. Then with these defined you can move onto organization—a more consistent approach.

Impact

With the organization fixed and most of the time chewed up in organization analysis, there is tremendous pressure to finish up the processes and systems. Most of the time, the systems part will come through. The process part will not.

Prevention

Start with the processes and transactions. Then move out to systems. After this, then you can consider the organization.

Action

There may be too little time and a crisis. The best thing that we can suggest is to raise examples of problems with specific transactions. Your basic purpose is to raise the spectre of fear and dread to get management's attention.

ISSUE: THE ACQUIRING OR DOMINANT FIRM DOES NOT PAY ATTENTION TO ISSUES AT THE LOCAL LEVEL

In a merger or acquisition there is so much to do and the work falls on the shoulders of too few people. Thus, attention falls at the headquarters level. People often do not want to go out to the field offices because of the fear of being left out of the communications loop.

Impact

If the dominant firm is not paying attention, then they really don't feel that it is important. The employees in that office don't need mind readers to determine what is going on—they get the message. They tend to leave. Then suddenly, the headquarters starts to wake up—too late.

Prevention

You should begin out in the field where the work is done. Then you can work back into the headquarters. There are often many issues that require attention.

During the merger or acquisition process, the work on issues is frozen. The problems build up.

Action

Issues will begin to surface at the local level. They may be dealt with ad hoc responses. This is not systematic. In many cases, the issues are ignored due to the press of other matters.

ISSUE: ORGANIZATION CHANGE IS PUSHED THROUGH WITHOUT THOUGHT OR PLANNING

This arises because management at the headquarters takes a more remote, academic view of the organization. The business processes have not been considered. Often, organization change is based in part upon "deals" or agreements made with certain managers during negotiations. The organization may be warped around the deals. Another situation is that the headquarters part of the organization is defined. However, the structure of in-country offices is left fuzzy—leaving the people there up in the air. The situation is particularly acute in cases where both companies have offices in one city or country.

Impact

The new organization may not fit the business processes—causing problems later. Roles may not be precisely defined. There may be overlap. Where decisions are made or information passed up through the organization may not be clear. If only a part of the organization is defined, then many employees will feel left out. In a time of downsizing, good employees may leave. In some mergers, the company fell apart in a year or two.

Prevention

The first step is to begin where the companies make money—start with in-country and nonheadquarters sites. Define new business processes and then the organizations locally. This gives stability to the processes and work, and guarantees the revenue, sales, and customer service. Then the headquarters organization can be addressed through a combined top down and bottom up approach.

Action

If problems start to arise, you can detect it in the attitude of employees in the field first. One idea here is to freeze the organization at headquarters and not implement change until the processes and local organizations have been addressed.

ISSUE: COSTS ARE NOT REDUCED AS PLANNED

Every merger or acquisition will claim large savings. Overlap in functions is cited. Let's look at the real picture. The people who are doing the sales, distribution, servicing, and other functions, we assume, are productive and are busy. Not much savings here. There could be savings in office consolidation, but even much of this may be lost due to long-term leases on office space. The savings is probably at headquarters. If there are large, bureaucratic headquarters units, then there are large, potential savings. But even here some of the savings may not come true due to deals made during the negotiations.

Impact

Shareholders and investors want the expected savings. Pressure is placed on management to get these savings. Management looks around and finds that they cannot do much more politically at headquarters. So they issue edicts or fiats that the remote offices must make severe cuts. Surprise, the revenue stream diminishes; customers leave and the company shrinks.

Prevention

Overpromising savings often results from an academic, distant look at the organization. If you really want to estimate savings, follow the guidelines of the last issue and begin with the processes and local organization. You can define streamlined versions of these. Then proceed inward toward headquarters and you will find that the headquarters organization can be very small.

Action

Resorting to emergency cuts in costs just creates more problems. Instead, use a combination of trying to raise revenue and looking at the business processes for increased efficiency. Unfortunately, these will take time.

ISSUE: CURRENT WORK IN MANY LOCATIONS IS NEGATIVELY IMPACTED

When there are negotiations going on between two firms, the employees of both firms get very nervous. When there are soothing, general statements from headquarters, the reaction may be panic. In the twenty-first century there is sometimes not a lot of trust in corporate management to tell the truth. Morale starts to go downhill. Customers and suppliers start asking questions of the local, in-country management. When they do not respond adequately, then the customers or suppliers think that local management is out of the loop and may be clueless—not good for customer and supplier relations.

Impact

Lower morale leads to reduced productivity and that in turn rubs off on customers and suppliers. Relations are affected. People may want to wait until the dust settles until they decide what they are going to do.

Prevention

Communications should start with employees, customers, and suppliers. In detail, the companies should indicate the level of service, range of products, and other factors that are tangible and specific to get things calm from the start.

Action

If you start to detect problems in the field through customer and supplier contacts, then you should try to improve relations by stabilizing the field organizations.

TEMPLATE AREAS

AREA: IDENTIFY MERGER AND ACQUISITION CANDIDATES

Tasks here relate to specific investigation activities. Often, politics intervenes at the highest level and a merger or acquisition is pushed from the top. To deal with this, it is wise to include tasks that address the negative aspects of the combination. The milestones in this area are often fuzzy since they are just analysis results. However, what you can do is to develop checklists and question lists to evaluate the work.

Another problem is that the tasks are quite long. You want to know the status of the work during this period. Take the questions and checklists and start applying them before the end of the task to see if the work is proceeding on the right course.

Area: Carry Out Due Diligence and Investigations

This is often treated as financial work. However, it would be useful to take three common business processes that are important to both companies. Investigate in detail these three processes in both organizations. Address the following areas:

- General steps in the process;
- Side-by-side comparison of a process in each company;
- Culture fit of the processes;
- Policy fit of the processes.

Area: Undertake Detailed Planning

In this area, you can expand the review of processes to include the top 10–15 key processes. You can also consider the local, in-country organizations. You can start to identify the new processes and the new or modified local organizations. These steps are done in parallel with the general organization work.

Another task is to develop detailed score cards for the key processes in each company. Why do you want to do this? Because you will want to compare the new, combined process with the scores of the processes in each country. A related idea is to conduct a survey of customers and suppliers.

Area: Perform the Consolidation

When here, you go. Many consolidations fail because they start at headquarters. It is better to stabilize and work with the remote and local offices. Get them set up and combined. Ensure that the processes are working. Now you can move to headquarters. If there is some redundancy at the headquarters units for a while, that is OK. At least, using this approach you ensure sales and service.

Area: Measure Results

Results are often measured by the savings gained per unit of time. After all, this is what looks good to the investment community. It is also a standard measure. There are also the measures of sales and profits. You can also compare the score cards of the processes before and after. Do the same comparison for the customer and supplier surveys.

LESSONS LEARNED

- Try to make sure that you keep key employees.

Now you cannot assume that you cannot detect and determine who is key. Therefore, you should start by assuming everyone is critical. It will take detailed observations and involvement—being passive here may involve employees leaving. Then you have to determine whether they were good. However, they are gone, so you can take no action. It is too late.

- The composition of the team at the start can play a major part in the outcome and success or failure of the merger or acquisition.

The composition of the combination team can make a big impact on the result. For example, if the finance and accounting people dominate the effort, then less attention may be paid to other processes and systems. If human resources is dominant, then they may focus on organization. The inference is that you should have multiple teams involved. Establish action teams across the organizations in different areas that are process focused.

- There is a need to look at potential mergers from different points of view.

You should go beyond management and organization. Other perspectives are: (1) IT organization; (2) key suppliers; (3) important customer segments; (4) business processes; (5) IT systems. Consider different transactions to do comparative analysis.

- There is benefit in collaborative detailed analysis.

The benefit from having collaboration among employees goes beyond the information and analysis that result. You can build a pattern of behavior of working together.

- There is a need to establish a positive, joint attitude at the start.

Attitude at the start of a combination effort is critical. There can be no belief that their processes or organization is the best. There is a need to be positive neutral. By that we mean it is significant to be positive about the result, but neutral about the approach and details.

- Adequate resources should be devoted to process and systems integration.

There is a problem in getting resources to perform these integration tasks. They have to do their normal work so there is little time to engage in this work.

SUMMARY

Mergers and acquisitions often do not yield the planned results. There is a need to do more analysis up front. Too many times events and problems were predicted in advance and then the combination went through—leading to the expected bad results. The importance of politics and establishing a pattern of working together cannot be underestimated.

Chapter 13

Marketing of a New Product

INTRODUCTION

Under the umbrella of new product we also include services, product variations, and the like. You would think that simple consumer products are the same the world over. After all, they are used in the same way by all human beings. This makes sense, but is politically incorrect. Take something simple like hand lotion. Here are some of the things that have to be considered

- The labeling on the container must be sensitive to the culture.
- Government regulations may specify exact labeling rules.
- Cases holding multiple containers may have specific rules as well.
- The colors used on the container and for the product will probably have to be customized to the country.
- Whether to have men, women, children, or pets on the label is another issue.

There is also the issue of the name of the product. One drug store chain changed its name and the new name was offensive to over 40% of the customers. In another case, a new car model was named something that was insulting to the parenthood of a person. Anyone who purchased this model was then viewed as an idiot.

This carries over into the form of advertising and media that will be used. Another factor is whether your firm already has a strong brand name and presence in the country. This will allow you to cross-sell the new product with existing products.

The important lesson learned is that a new product has to be customized to the specific market segment. This is almost part of product development and should be treated as such. Many good products only succeed in one or two markets. In others they have to be withdrawn from the market and then relaunched later.

PURPOSE AND SCOPE

TECHNICAL PURPOSE

The technical purpose is to launch a new product by taking into account as many factors as possible. Completeness is a key technical goal. Related to this the product may have to be certified and accepted in each country through a government agency. The technical goal is that this be done as expeditiously as possible.

BUSINESS PURPOSE

The business purpose is that the new product be successful. However, success is a term relative to specific markets. Therefore, it is important to identify specific business goals for each country. You can use a table like the one below. Here the rows are the general goals and the countries are the columns. The entry is the interpretation and application of the general goal to the specific country.

Countries

General business goal				
		Interpretation of the goal		

POLITICAL PURPOSE

Most of us think of the business and technical goals, but there are political goals as well. One is that the firm wants to show that it is moving to more of an international presence. Another goal is that it is attempting to build families of related products. Both of these help management to show progress of the firm to investors.

END PRODUCTS

Some typical end products are:

* Planning completed for the product for each country.
* Culture and political check and evaluation for the planning.
* Prerollout promotion and advertising for the product.
* Rollout of the product in the countries along with the promotion.
* Gathering of lessons learned and experience to fine tune the marketing for later campaigns.
* Use of lessons learned to improve the product planning process for the future.

ISSUES

ISSUE: THERE IS A FAILURE TO LEARN FROM OTHER PRODUCT LAUNCHES

This occurs when products are assigned to individual product managers and there is a lack of communications among the managers. Also, the organization may not take the cultural factors seriously and so do not emphasize this in product planning.

Impact

The same failures may recur many times before the company becomes aware of the problem and its severity and impact. After the product is launched, the firm may only look at overall sales and ignore the behavior in specific, detailed markets. This risks alienating the people in that country for other products. That is what happened with the automobile and drug store examples.

Prevention

Planning is the key. It must include in-country planning as well as headquarters planning. Focus groups and testing should be considered in specific local markets. You also cannot just test in the capital of a country. Other parts of the country may have different languages and cultures. You have to move out into the field.

Action

If a product starts to run into problems, the immediate question is whether it can be salvaged or whether it should be pulled from the market.

ISSUE: THERE IS A LACK OF CULTURE SENSITIVITY

Many American and European firms still suffer from inflated egos. What sells well in country A should go well in country B. How long was it before American firms began to build cars with the steering wheels on the right-hand side of the car? As soon as they did, sales increased in countries where driving is on the left.

Impact

The first impact is felt in product sales. Then there is sometimes a bigger, negative impact on the company's image. This has occurred with firms who marketed lower-quality products in a market and then found out that sales of all products were affected.

Prevention

You have to get down to the consumer of the product in the specific part of the foreign nation. You have to think like they do. Remember that they have less available money for spending. One good test is to see what they could buy with the same money instead of your product. This can be a real eye opener.

Action

A sign of a problem can be casual statements made by higher-level executives. These can be very damaging. If there is a problem, then it may require a massive effort to recover. The company name and the brands may have to be changed to create new images.

ISSUE: TOO MUCH OF THE ADVERTISING IS GEARED TO AN UPSCALE, WESTERN AUDIENCE

The Internet has increased this issue. People often tend to think of advertising as universal. After all, look at CNN or the BBC. However, for all of this, the local markets are often quite different. The next time you travel overseas, try to view local commercials on television in the local language. These commercials focus on different things and are carried out much differently from western commercials. You may want to think that the world is becoming more homogeneous, but it is still heterogeneous.

Impact

The advertising is often wasted. The impact is not perceptible. The product failed. One flyer that was produced for a market used a variation of the language from another part of the country. The people ignored the advertising because it was not from their area.

Prevention

Testing of the advertising is essential. The true test is to target local media in the local language.

Action

If you see that the advertising is not working, then you want to increase the staff in the country to learn from the problems. Don't just retreat.

ISSUE: HOW THE PRODUCT MARKETING IS HANDLED IS INCONSISTENT BETWEEN COUNTRIES

It is desirable to have product marketing different between countries. That reflects the cultural and language differences. However, consistency is another matter. You must work to have consistency since there is enough communications on the Internet and by other means that a mistake here can be costly.

Impact

People will tend not to believe the marketing if there is an inconsistent message. This can depress sales over time.

Prevention

A good idea is to develop a list of key product attributes and characteristics. Make this the rows of a table. The columns of the table are the countries in which you are going to market the product. The entries are the details of how the characteristic will be marketed. This will improve consistency and can be used to help train people to sell the product in different countries.

Action

Once you detect one inconsistency, you have to assume that there are others. Therefore, it is a good idea to conduct a review of the marketing for all of the countries.

ISSUE: THERE IS A LACK OF COORDINATION DURING THE MARKETING IN DIFFERENT AREAS

Market planning may be centrally coordinated. However, the launch of the product in a specific country may be left with a franchise or local office. They may feel that they are on their own. There may be little contact between and among the various offices during the marketing campaign.

Impact

Lessons learned are lost because of the lack of communications. This may mean that the same mistakes are committed multiple times. It also means that good, valuable lessons learned are lost.

Prevention

There should a forum for sharing information among the countries. An intranet chat room fits this well. Salespeople can log their negative and positive experiences in marketing the new product.

Action

Unless there is a mechanism for sharing information along with management support, there is likely to be little sharing. To test out the situation you can visit several countries and see what their experiences are. You can then infer if there is sharing and can then encourage it.

ISSUE: THERE IS INSUFFICIENT FOLLOW-UP AFTER THE PRODUCT IS LAUNCHED

You are probably thinking here of a follow-up marketing effort. However, what is meant here is gathering lessons learned for later work. In order to do this, there has to be more than management support. There must be a lessons learned database along with a method for using, updating, and applying it on a regular basis. Management must require that this database be employed before the launch of any new product.

Impact

There are missed opportunities. Experience in one country is not gathered and used even for that country. Employees start to feel that each marketing effort is a one-shot deal. Then they begin to think that the company lacks a strategy. Morale starts to sink along with sales.

Prevention

Follow-up should be planned from the start. You want to begin with marketing campaigns and new product launches that are going on now. Management must reward the gathering and use of the experience.

Action

Assuming that there is no follow-up and that you want to do something, one approach is to do limited data collection in several countries where the new product was most and least successful. Develop a list of questions to get started and get going. However, doing this doesn't ensure success. You have to then apply it to the product marketing in all countries. You can also encourage people to volunteer their experiences.

TEMPLATE AREAS

AREA: REVIEW MARKET RESEARCH AND OTHER INFORMATION

The topic that is missed here is the experience of similar products in a specific market. Market research data is very good in developed countries. It is not as available or as high quality in the rest of the world. You have to think about using the local people to collect information that you can get on-line through a service in a developed country. Much of the information may be anecdotal, but it is still useful.

AREA: REVIEW TRACK RECORD FOR SUCCESSFUL AND FAILED COMPETITIVE PRODUCTS

Go beyond your own industry. Look at other international firms and how they launched their products. Go to the Web and look up the same product in different countries at various Web sites. Build a reservoir of this information after you organize it.

AREA: DEVELOP CULTURE PROFILES OF THE PRODUCT FOR EACH MARKET

Of course, the profile depends on the specific product and country. However, you can start by identifying cultural oddities and unique features and characteristics about a specific country.

AREA: PREPARE THE LAUNCH OF THE NEW PRODUCT

This is the planning area that was mentioned earlier in this chapter. The planning should be country specific as much as possible.

AREA: COORDINATE PRODUCT MARKETING AND SALES

Coordinating does not mean just managing. It means facilitating the sharing of information and lessons learned among the various offices.

AREA: GATHER EXPERIENCE AND LESSONS LEARNED

The key here is to implement a structured, routine approach to collect, organize, and use this information. Before any phase of the new product marketing it should be a requirement that the relevant lessons learned be reviewed and applied. Then as more experience is gained, these lessons learned can be expanded.

LESSONS LEARNED

• Understand more about local markets and cultures. This should be started long before a new product is launched. An interesting thing to do is to describe how not to launch the product in terms of the culture. By explaining what not to do, you show people how important culture is and how different this culture is from the one that they are familiar with.

• Set interim milestones and reviews after the new product is launched. Many new product launches run into problems because of the extensive dependencies among tasks across countries. You can literally become lost in the maze of details. There are multiple deadlines in each country, etc. That is why you have to take a relational view of the tasks and look at them from the standpoint of headquarters, local offices, the consumer, etc.

• Ensure that in-country staff and managers are up on the project and part of the sales and marketing team. Many local people have said that they only hear about the product on the eve of the launch. Then any deficiencies and problems noted fall on deaf ears. It is too late.

• Set up a management approach that provides flexibility in dealing with issues and opportunities that surface during the launch of the new product. This has been a constant theme in this book and is very applicable here.

• Implement facilitation, lessons learned, and collaboration among different countries. You may have to do this differently in each country, but it will still result in the same thing. Management should set up a reward system to encourage this collection of knowledge.

SUMMARY

By now you can see that the launch of a new product is similar to many of the other situations that have been addressed in the book so far. Note that failure occurs most often because an international project is treated as a local project.

Part IV

Issues in Global Projects

Chapter 14

Project Issues

INTRODUCTION

This part of the book addresses a variety of issues and opportunities that are likely to be encountered in your international projects. For each issue the following are discussed:

- Impact, if the issue is not addressed. This reveals the effects and importance of the issue.
  - Prevention. Guidance is given for heading off the issue.
  - Action. Specific action items are provided to deal with the issue.

Project issues are those that occur after the project is started. A key lesson learned here is that you should anticipate that some of these issues will likely occur.

ISSUES

ISSUE: INDIVIDUALS IN A COUNTRY ARE PULLED AWAY FROM WORK ON THE PROJECT DUE TO LOCAL NEEDS

Many projects are initiated without sufficient communications with the locations that will undertake the work. The work then begins. People are assigned to the project by local management. Then they are pulled off of the project due to emergencies or other high-priority local work.

Impact

The effect of this is that the project suffers from the lack of team members. However, there are other potential impacts. First, the project leader may not be informed that a person has been pulled off. Maybe, it was felt to be temporary. The project leader was not on top of what the team members were working on. Second, the effect can cascade if people in different locations are removed from the project.

Prevention

Local management may not have been aware of the importance of the project. Certainly, it is often the case that local middle management may not know about the project. If they do, it might seem remote. If you are going to mount an international project, you must visit each location to determine local issues and conditions prior to the project. Then you will need to establish communications to get an early warning of a problem.

Action

If this occurs, then you can be assured that it will happen again. Action should be taken in terms of establishing communications with all locations. There should be a weekly review of resources allocated to the project. Local management need to be encouraged to present potential staffing demands.

ISSUE: THERE ARE DIFFERENT LANGUAGES EMPLOYED AMONG TEAM MEMBERS. THERE IS NO PROVISION FOR INTERPRETERS

In one of most complex projects we have seen, there were four countries involved with five different languages. Almost all team members only spoke one language. Progress reports on the project were submitted in the native language. While interpreters were available to handle documents, translation took much time. A number of problems became much more pressing due to this time delay. This problem may arise because management lacks experience with a multi-lingual project. This problem extends to situations where people speak different dialects or forms of the same language.

Impact

There are delays in getting things done. Misunderstandings arise due to language interpretation. This is important in project management because projects are managed through communications. Nuances are important. Significance of topics and issues depend on tone of voice and words chosen. There are likely to be project delays and substantial rework.

Prevention

One thing to do is to not undertake multilingual projects unless managers are willing to provide additional support. If such a project is to be undertaken, then an organized approach must be taken for communications. Common words and phrases must be given. You must establish symbols. For example, project issues can be green, yellow, or red. This alerts everyone to problems regardless of language.

Action

When language problems crop up, there may be a tendency to overreact and apply too many resources to the problem. This can further slow the project down. Instead, you must endeavor to organize the communications more formally so that problems can be identified. Concentrate on issues and status reports. Then you can move on to milestones and end products.

ISSUE: PEOPLE IN SOME LOCATIONS LACK EXPERIENCE AND KNOWLEDGE ABOUT METHODS AND TOOLS

Often, because people were trained in the same methods and tools, it is assumed that they have a certain common level of knowledge and capability. This is often not the case. The training could have been provided at different times. Perhaps, the training was not put to use so that the people lost knowledge and have no experience.

Impact

As was said repeatedly in this book, a basic problem in international projects is that people make too many assumptions. Management may assume that people have expertise. The local manager may not know what the methods or tools are and want to seem on board. The impact is that there is a lack of progress and a substantial amount of rework. If one location fails to do its part, then other locations may have to step in. Another negative impact is cultural. You can make people feel depressed and down on the project if their lack of knowledge is perceived to be a weakness.

Prevention

Before starting a project, it is important to identify the methods and tools to be employed in the project at all locations. Then you can move down to each location to determine their skills and experience. Gaps in experience may have to be addressed through consultants or employees from other locations.

Action

If the problem arises, you want to step in and conduct an assessment of methods and tools. You may want to simplify and substitute various methods and tools.

ISSUE: COMMUNICATIONS ACROSS THE LOCATIONS ARE POOR

Most of the time people work alone or with people in their own offices. They communicate very little with other locations. The exception here is upper management and some staff positions. So people are not used to communicating with others in different locations. They may never have met or seen these people before—making communications more difficult in many cultures.

Impact

The effect of poor communications is that issues may be left untreated. Problems may occur in one place that are not communicated to others due to pride, concerns about communicating, and other factors. Project issues grow—affecting the schedule and budget of the project.

Prevention

Preventing communications issues is key to successful project management. As the project begins, there must be an effect to establish good communications prior to problems and issues. We have employed simulations of situations and problems to build teamwork across countries. Another important step is to form teams across locations from the start.

Action

In many cases, managers attempt to search for the cause of the poor communications. This is logical, but it takes time away from the project. It is better to work to improve communications by establishing more joint work across locations. In addition, visits among locations should be encouraged.

ISSUE: TECHNOLOGY EMPLOYED IN DIFFERENT LOCATIONS IS NOT COMPATIBLE

People in one location take their technology for granted. Because they are unfamiliar with the systems and technology in other regions, they assume it must be same. After all, everyone has computers and cellular telephones, don't they? This feeling is sometimes spawned by vendors who tell customers that their technology is in wider use than it really is.

Impact

With different technology, the project scope tends to grow. There must be either an effort to establish interfaces or work to implement the same technology in each location. In one example, there were different and incompatible e-mail systems. Messages were lost before people became aware of the problem. Another impact is that the project must now change the infrastructure or at least address infrastructure issues that were not envisioned when the schedule and budget were established.

Prevention

A technology assessment must be undertaken at the start of the project prior to setting the budget and schedule. Interface issues should be identified and addressed.

Action

If this problem surfaces, it may be necessary to scale back the technology in use. In one case, most locations used Lotus Notes. However, because some locations did not have this software, it was decided to resort to e-mail and to database management systems. Simplification of the technology is often an essential part of the early work on a project.

ISSUE: THE PROJECT LEADERS DO NOT HAVE PRIOR EXPERIENCE IN INTERNATIONAL PROJECTS

Project leaders may have been chosen because of their knowledge of the business and of prior project success in one country. These do little to prepare people for dealing with multiple languages and cultures—and different locations.

Impact

Project leaders when thrust into the world of international projects may perform well and rise to the challenge. Or they may fail. In either case, management cannot afford to take the chance. The project leaders may provide a false sense of security and progress about the project. They may hear what they want to hear and then pass it along to upper management. Project issues may worsen. Progress is much less than what is reported. The project loses its credibility.

Prevention

Prevention begins with selecting project leaders more carefully. You can select people with prior international project experience. You can look for individuals who have worked in different countries and speak other languages. In addition, attention must be given to the organization of the project. As was stated in earlier chapters, you should consider having a project leader in each location. Another step is to have the project leaders on the road most of the time in different locations.

Action

One way to address the problem is to substitute project leaders. However, this can slow the project down. Confidence in the project may decline. Instead, you should establish a steering committee for the project and use project leaders in multiple locations. The problem, after all, may not lie with the project leader, but with how the project is organized.

ISSUE: PROJECT TEAM MEMBERS LACK EXPERIENCE AND KNOWLEDGE ABOUT CONDITIONS IN OTHER COUNTRIES

Going beyond the project leaders, problems arise among team members. You can have critical team members in one country who have traveled very little and are unaware of the cultures in other places. They may have been chosen for the team based on their technical or business knowledge. It is too bad that cultural and societal experience turned out to be more important.

Impact

Some team members in projects we have participated in have acted arrogantly and assumed that staff in other locations were dedicated to the project and to them full time. This causes much ill will and antagonism toward the project. The situation often deteriorates rapidly before the project leaders and management are aware of the problem. It surfaces often when the line manager in a location brings the problem up with his counterparts in other locations. People do not respond to the team members. Or they mislead them with optimistic reports.

Prevention

Selection of team members in international projects is a critical success factor in international project management. For international projects, team members must be informed of cultural and other factors in each location. They should be presented with a variety of issues and situations and tested through simulation. From our experience, the result often is to search for new team members.

Action

One action is to replace the team member. However, this can leave a gaping hole in the project. Another, better course of action is to identify other team members or new team members and assign them to joint tasks with the individual who has created the problem. It is not feasible to have the project leader act as a liaison for each and every communication with other locations.

ISSUE: IT IS DIFFICULT TO DETERMINE STATUS OF THE WORK IN VARIOUS LOCATIONS

We encountered one project leader in Singapore who was leading a project involving three countries. She received complete and accurate information from two of the locations and assumed that this was true overall. It was not. Team members would reassure her when she visited them. Then there were no results. She did not know what to do. We suggested that she visit their location without prior notification. This changed the attitude of the team members. She had found that they would hold a meeting prior to her visits generally. The project was turned around.

Impact

When you report on status, it is in the context in terms of culture and language. The impact of not getting proper status means that the project leader and managers are left in the dark. They begin to lack confidence in the project leadership. The project could be terminated or shortened.

Prevention

To prevent this problem, you must address how status will be reported. But this is not enough. You also have to examine how status is verified and checked out. It is clearly insufficient just to get information. Prevention must focus on milestones and end products. If there is not a regular stream of milestones, then the project status is more difficult to determine since you are forced back to consider work in progress.

Action

There are a variety of actions that you can take if status reports are not adequate. One is to provide a template or outline structure for status reports. A second action is to ensure that there are sufficient regular milestones. A third step is to have more reporting on issues. Finally, there is nothing like informal unplanned telephone calls and visits.

ISSUE: THERE IS TOO MUCH ATTENTION ON PROJECT DETAILS THAT MANY ISSUES ARE NOT IDENTIFIED

When an international project gets going, the tasks tend to take over the attention. There is much detailed work to do. Therefore, it is not surprising that with tight deadlines and management pressure, there is little time to consider the big picture and wider issues. This was certainly the case of two firms. One was a drug store chain. The other was an automobile manufacturer. In each case, they rebranded their store name and a model of a car, respectively. Everything was planned out. But no one looked at what the new names meant in one of the local languages. In both cases the names were derogatory. Customers who spoke this language did not patronize the store chain or buy the product.

Impact

Issues left untreated are one of the major causes of project failure. As the team becomes buried in the work, it becomes harder and harder for them to deal with the big picture.

Prevention

At all times the project leader should keep lists and information on larger issues as well as small issues within the team. Team members need to get out to where the project results will be felt. The team overall needs to kept in touch with reality. This can have the benefit of raising the level of awareness of the importance of the project.

Action

If you find that important issues are not being addressed, then you know that the problem is present. The first step is to carry out a project review where you undertake to assess what issues are present and their status. You also should pause the project and have the team consider the larger picture.

Chapter 15

Business Issues

INTRODUCTION

Business issues are those that impact the project and are based in business units. Since all international and regional projects interact with business processes and departments, business issues are often the ones that undermine the project. Business issues are some of the more intractable issues since they are often strongly rooted in the culture of the areas involved. For example, many IT projects involved with rolling out systems run afoul of business issues.

ISSUES

ISSUE: THE INTERNATIONAL PROJECT REQUIRES CRITICAL PEOPLE IN A COUNTRY

This is often inevitable. Traditional project management has for over 50 years emphasized getting the best and most critical people on the team. In general, this has led to the failure of many international projects. There is a need for people with critical skills and knowledge at certain points in the project, but this need does not extend across the entire project.

Impact

When you take a critical person from their regular work and put them into project, you do harm in many ways. First, the department from whence they came is weakened. The department must find a substitute—often impossible. Second, the person may be assigned to the team, but they are pulled off of the project when emergencies or important work arises. Third, they are subjected to many interruptions. Fourth, they derive their power and influence from the status quo. The results of the project may change their importance and weaken it. They are likely to be not as supportive of the project.

Prevention

What do you do? Aim to get people who have some knowledge and experience, but who are eager to participate in the project. Taking these people away will have less impact on the departments. Another step is to have some turnover in the team so that the project is not overly dependent upon one person.

Action

If you have a critical person on the team, then you should assign joint tasks with others. That will protect the project in case they have to leave the project. Another action to take is to restrict which tasks they work on. If you cut down on the tasks, then you can get them back to their home departments sooner.

ISSUE: THE INFRASTRUCTURE IN A COUNTRY IS VERY POOR

This is not just true of emerging nations. It is also true of some developed countries since the infrastructure often deteriorates the further you get from major cities. People often assume infrastructure issues away in the twenty-first century. This is not a good idea. Infrastructure is even more important today. Poor infrastructure has an impact on expectations and what people view as feasible. In some parts of India, for example, the communications are very primitive. Carrying out a project can be very challenging—even if you employ satellite telephones.

Impact

Some of the impacts have already been pointed out. One impact is that logistics support for a project may be seriously underestimated. Another impact is project communications may have to be very limited. In one project in the jungles of southeast Asia this was such a bad situation that the old approach of delegation of authority was used. The manager then left the jungle to report on the project at periodic intervals.

Prevention

An analysis of the infrastructure is very important at the start of the project. The experience of the French and Americans in VietNam point out the importance of this assessment. Contingency plans also need to be established.

Action

An ongoing assessment of infrastructure problems and their impacts should be part of most international projects. There can be improvements as well as deterioration. There can be safety considerations that arise, for example. Consider creating an infrastructure score card in which you assess the infrastructure elements that are relevant to the project in each country.

ISSUE: THE BUSINESS NEEDS ARE DIVERSE IN EACH COUNTRY FOR THE PROJECT

While the project may benefit the company or organization overall, there should be local benefits as well. Each location has its own business needs and concerns. If a project does not address or even acknowledge these needs, then the project will often be seen as negative since it robs resources from dealing with local needs. The project is perceived as an unwelcome diversion. Each location has its own needs. You should not generalize based on one location.

Impact

Ignoring local needs sets the stage for trouble in the project. It will be more difficult to obtain resources. Management in the location will be resistant to the project. They and their employees see the project as just another example of headquarters bullying around the offices. While you cannot have true democracy, you can at least acknowledge local needs.

Prevention

If you want to get people on your side, then you should determine the needs and issues of each location in which the project will be undertaken. Try to map these needs into the project. It may be necessary politically to carry out other projects that provide benefits for specific locations. This will certainly gain more support.

Action

You find that this problem often arises when people are removed from the project. They are pulled off to deal with local problems. Management often reacts by coming down hard on the managers in the location. This is counterproductive and just raises hostility. Instead, you must work to understand the local issues and see how the project can minimize the impact of the project on them.

ISSUE: THE PROJECT DEPENDS UPON VENDORS WHO DO NOT HAVE A STRONG PRESENCE IN SOME LOCATIONS

A vendor or supplier wants to get work. They often state how they have offices and customers in various locations. Potential customers often accept this as a fact. Only later do they find out that the supplier presence in some of the locations is marginal at best. In one case, a vendor claimed that maintenance was available in all 10 countries that the project was going to be implemented in. This turned out to be false. They really only had a presence in 6 of the countries. In the other 4, there was only a sales office. The vendor then had to fly people in from other locations to provide support. Needless to say, the costs were higher and the time to do repairs longer.

Impact

Everyone wants to believe what people tell them. This is the case with vendor claims and statements. If a vendor fails to provide adequate support in one or more locations, the schedule and cost of the project are impacted.

Prevention

You want to determine if this is a problem at the start of the project. For the finalist group of vendors, have the managers in each location carry out an assessment of vendor support in their country. In addition, have each potential vendor identify customers in each location. These can be contacted.

Action

If a vendor fails to perform in one location, treat it as a general problem. This is the principle of "An attack on one is an attack on all." If you don't treat it seriously, then the vendor may think that it is not important. Point out to the vendor that they cannot make up for it by increased support in other locations. Press the vendor to develop an action plan to deal with the problem. Have the local management report on vendor progress.

ISSUE: THERE IS NO PROVISION TO ADDRESS PROBLEMS AND ISSUES IN COUNTRIES AS THEY ARISE

In many projects the project leader identifies and tracks problems that impact the project. However, if the project work is going on in several locations, it becomes more difficult and complex to determine the relevant issues in each location. Some project leaders may not treat an issue as significant if it only affects one location.

Impact

During the course of a project, many issues and problems arise. Some of these occur within the project itself and so are more easily recognizable. Others occur in other departments or externally in one location. The project leader may not be geared up to find these and figure out what to do. The project leader may not have the experience or skills to recognize the potential impact on the project. The result is that the project team may be hit "blind-sided" and not be aware.

Prevention

At the start of the project it is important to identify local issues and problems that exist. Work to discover issues that may on the surface bear no relation to the project. Then you need to actively track these and uncover new issues as time goes on. Seek input from local management on the importance of an issue.

Action

If you find an issue that catches you by surprise, you must do several things. First, you can work to deal with the issue. Second, you should immediately determine what local issues are present in each location. Present to management an expanded list of issues.

ISSUE: THERE IS A WIDE VARIETY OF BUSINESS PROCESSES IN DIFFERENT COUNTRIES

A business process is a business process, right? Yes and no. While many processes that do the same thing are similar, they are not likely to be identical.

Take an office products supplier in Asia. They were directed by their parent firm to implement an ERP system. The system selected was quite rigid. When the system was analyzed, it was determined that there were differences in almost all processes supported by the ERP. As an example, the ERP does not allow products to be shipped to customers without the proper paperwork and transactions. In this country the paperwork always follows the shipping since there is a history of trust and confidence. In the end the ERP could not be installed—but not before over US$ 1 million was wasted!

Impact

If you don't pay attention to the unique way transactions are carried out in various countries, then the project may be implementing solutions that will not fit in the specific country. The results of the project may never be able to be used. Rather than fight with headquarters, many local managers will try their best and then eventually give up. They do not want to be perceived as negative. The project is successful, but the results of the project fail. Overall, the result is failure.

Prevention

It is necessary to identify which business processes will be touched by a project. Then you can undertake to have each location conduct an assessment of the processes in their location. This will surface a number of problems and issues to be addressed. Do not stay at the level of a general business process. Instead, get down to the level of specific transactions.

Action

If you find that a business process issue arises, you should have the specific location examine the other processes that are touched by the project. You should have someone independent of the team do an assessment of the business processes as they will be impartial. They may also uncover ways to get around the problems without changing the project in a major way.

ISSUE: PROBLEMS IN ONE COUNTRY ARE NOT SEEN AS SUFFICIENTLY IMPORTANT IN HEADQUARTERS

Each location has individual problems and situations. Management at headquarters may not want to hear about these things. They rely on the managers put in place in the location to deal with the situations. This was the only way centuries ago when communications were poor. Remote managers and governors were given wide discretion on what to do. The problem is exacerbated by local managers who want to get promoted and so tend to push local problems "under the rug" if they cannot deal with them.

Impact

Many very large problems start out as simple issues at the local level. There could be a small chemical leak or a problem with employee security. Then it turns out that the problem expands. This was the case with the renegade employee at the trading firm in Asia who caused the parent company in Europe to go under. The signs were fairly plain to see locally, but went unreported.

Prevention

Independent of the projects going on, management at headquarters must make the effort to be informed of local issues and problems. Managers at various locations should be encouraged, not discouraged, to present problems. This often is a major culture problem in companies. It requires a degree of openness that is not common or inherent in the culture of the firm.

Action

When a problem surfaces, it is often treated as unique. This is not the proper course of action. When you kill one termite, you can assume that there are many others. Here it is the same. You should institute an effort to uncover local issues. You should visit the locations and work with Human Resources to encourage people to come forward with problems and situations.

ISSUE: IT IS TAKING TOO LONG TO HAVE DECISIONS MADE

Suppose you have an international project that is based at headquarters. The project leaders are there as well. So you would think that if the project leader required a decision on a situation, it would be straightforward. This is often not the case. Discussing and dealing with the situation may require a great deal of coordination with several locations. There may be many managers involved. All of these factors tend to stretch out decision-making.

Impact

Delayed decisions have the obvious impacts on a project in terms of work. However, there are additional side effects. First, people may infer that management must not care about the project. Otherwise, they would have made decisions. Second, some may feel that the problems must be so important that the project work should be stopped until there is resolution. In all of these the project suffers.

Prevention

A defined method for generating decisions should be established at the start of the project by the project leader. The project leader should then test out this method by surfacing an issue. Informal methods of communication need to be set up and tested as well. Management should be kept informed of issues before they become serious.

Action

If a decision is being delayed, then the project leader should work informally to determine what the problem is. It is possible that the issue is perceived to be bigger in scope than what the project needs to have addressed. An effort should be made to restrict the scope of the decision required to get action. It does little good to raise panic about the project. Then managers will question the project leader's abilities.

ISSUE: THERE IS SUBSTANTIAL TURNOVER OF STAFF IN ONE LOCATION

In one project we were involved with there were 4 countries involved. There was virtually no turnover in 2 countries. There was some turnover (about 25%) in another. However, in the fourth there was over 50% turnover. This was due to the labor market in the area. It was also due to weak local management. Employees were really turned off. The project could not address the local management problem except to bring this to management's attention. The approach was to construct the project so that the work in the country was of very limited scope. Work was transferred to other locations.

Impact

The direct impact of turnover is to create a shortage of resources to the project. Knowledge is lost. Experience is lost. The project work in the location can grind to a halt.

Prevention

Before starting the project carry out a review of the management and employee turnover in the locations of the project. If you find one problem location, then you need to carefully consider what work is assigned to the location. When you organize the project in the location, you should mete sure most tasks are jointly performed. This will give you backup in the event of loss of staff. You should institute short tasks and milestones.

Action

If you find that there is a turnover problem, then you should go to the location and start managing it directly. Hands-on management can give you more information. It also reveals to the employees how important their involvement in the project is. Another step is to reorganize the work in the project there along the lines discussed above.

Chapter 16

Management Issues

INTRODUCTION

Management issues tend to be of larger scale than business issues. Many management issues are often accepted as constraints. That is, they are treated as a fact of life and there is nothing that can be done. You just have to accept the situation. While you cannot change the situation, we feel strongly that you can take steps to mitigate the impact and effect upon the project.

ISSUES

ISSUE: WORK IS PERFORMED IN ONE COUNTRY AND THEN SENT TO ANOTHER COUNTRY FOR FINISHING

This is a natural way of doing business in many industries. Examples are the clothing and garment industry, the software industry, and manufacturing. When you look at this issue, you may be tempted to say "So what?" After all, that is the way life is. True. However, you can examine the situation and make a stab at determining potential issues that will arise due to the situation.

Impact

When work is handed off from one organization to another, there are bound to be discrepancies and disagreements as to what was shipped and what was received. This is natural. If you are doing a project in such a situation, you should identify potential issues in the handoff. You may want to create a separate subproject that deals with the interface between the departments or locations. This will draw attention to the handoff and surface issues earlier.

Prevention

Setting up a separate subproject is one step. Another step is to involve the two locations in joint tasks to improve and facilitate the handoff. The important thing here is not to place blame for problems; it is to get the problems solved quickly. Issues related to interfaces should be tracked separately from other issues since they tend to be more severe in their impacts.

Action

Often, problems in handoffs are detected too late. It is this way in manufacturing where subassemblies are made by contractors in one country and then shipped to another country for final assembly. One automobile manufacturer had to delay the introduction of a new model because the radiator assembly was faulty. Unfortunately, this was not detected until over 50,000 vehicles had been produced. They all had to be mothballed until new assemblies were received and tested.

ISSUE: MANAGEMENT EXPECTATIONS ARE CENTERED UPON HEADQUARTERS WITH A LACK OF ATTENTION TO LOCAL NEEDS

High management expectations are a leading cause of project failures. A project is more than the sum of its parts. Projects represent the culmination of a major effort in many different locations. Expectations are also often too vague to address in the project and so are ignored. In one company management thought that a new manufacturing method would revolutionize work around the world at 11 plants. However, in practice due to the varied activities of each plant, only 5 plants were ultimately affected by the project. The impact at these 5 was positive, but management viewed the project as a failure since there were no benefits at the other 6 plants!

Impact

The impact of high management expectations tends to create depression among team members. How can they live up to these? The project may be viewed as doomed at the start. Moreover, the project team can only do so much. It is often the management and employees of each location to take the work of the project and turn out the benefits. A critical success factor is to realize that it is the benefits that occur after the project is completed that count—more than the project itself. This is epitomized in the expression from medical science, "The operation on the patient was a success, but the patient died."

Prevention

One sure way to deal with management expectations is to dampen them at the start. Issues can be raised to depress anyone. Next, expectations should be placed on the people who will use the results of the project—not the team. The team is responsible for completing the project on time and within budget. They are not responsible for changing the organization or culture in a specific country.

Action

If there are high management expectations during the project, the project leader should work to lower these and redirect them to the business units who will use the results of the project. This can be done by encouraging an additional project to be started to monitor how the results of the project are used.

ISSUE: THE PROJECT IS APPROVED WITHOUT RECOGNIZING OTHER PROJECTS AND EFFORTS

In some companies, a high-level manager goes to a seminar, reads a book, or hears about some wonderful concept for a project. The manager returns to the organization and presses for the immediate start of the project. No one wants to take on the manager and explain that there are limited resources. So the project is approved. We have seen this occur again and again.

Impact

By introducing one more project, management may unknowingly not only undermine the new project, but also the current projects. All of the projects then suffer as resources are robbed from regular work and other projects. In one company the result was bankruptcy.

Prevention

This situation can be prevented by undertaking a review of all projects and new ideas for projects every 3–4 months. New ideas for projects can be suggested prior to this meeting and analyzed in terms of resource requirements. The resources in each location can then be assessed to see what level of resources can be brought to bear on all of the projects.

Action

If a new project is given a high priority, it will likely demand many already committed resources. So the first step is to assess the resource requirements of the new project. Then the current projects can be studied to see if any can be cancelled or deferred. A resource allocation method can then be performed to prioritize the work. If you just overlay the project with other work, the projects will start to be affected one at a time.

ISSUE: THERE IS A LACK OF CONTROL SINCE THE PROJECT IS A JOINT VENTURE

There are many instances where the operations in specific locations are jointly owned and controlled by several firms. These firms typically have very different cultures and methods of management. Managing a joint venture project is very challenging for these reasons. Since the project is being carried out by equal partners, it is very difficult to establish control. Instead, firms typically create coordination. Unfortunately, this is not the same as control. When actions are required, it may take too long to get decisions since each party must understand the situation and agree on what is to be done—a very tall order.

Impact

The joint venture sounded like a good idea. The problem was that little thought was given to how things other than daily work would be done. When confronted by a project, just getting the project started is a major challenge. In one such firm, it took 3 months to get any substantial project approved. Managers in the field quickly learned that they had to work informally and not call the work a project—to avoid the bureaucracy. The impact is that the work is driven underground.

Prevention

At the time a joint venture is established, the ground rules for projects as well as the daily management of work need to be established. It is recommended that several sample projects be dry run so that guidelines for projects can be set up. In one joint venture each partner firm supplied managers in alternate years. This sounded like a good idea in theory since it established formal authority. However, many problems arose. The cultures of the two firms were almost diametrically opposite. In one there was a formal structure; in the other managers were encouraged to be entrepreneurial. This led to differences in project reporting, control, and direction. If a project spanned the period of the end of the year, there were likely to be many changes to the active projects due to this major cultural difference.

Action

It is better to surface a number of smaller issues to the management of both firms than to wait until a major crisis arises. This will pave the way for better ways of addressing problems later. An active project can be used as an example and standardized reporting and review methods established.

ISSUE: THE COMPANY IN ONE COUNTRY IS JOINTLY OWNED WITH A LOCAL FIRM

A variation of the previous issue is the situation where an overseas firm must take on a local partner in order to operate in the country. This is often the case in Asia, for example. The potential problems in projects go beyond project management. In some cases, the local firm gains expertise and sets up a duplicate operation to make even more money by cutting out the foreign partner. In some countries it is difficult for the foreign firm to pursue remedies in the local courts. This indicates that firms should be very cautious when they embark on projects. At the heart of this is what expertise and knowledge is the foreign firm willing to transfer to the local firm?

Impact

If the project is started as a partnership like a joint venture, then there can be many cultural and political problems. The local firm may try to exert the final say on all issues. The foreign firm may seem helpless. The impact can be a failed project or one that just goes on and on. The foreign firm does not want to kill the project; the local firm gets money from the foreign partner. In one case, the obviously failed project went on for 3 years.

Prevention

The foreign firm must define the range of projects it is willing to undertake in terms of risk. Once this is completed, the next step is to define how the projects will be managed. Some specific questions include the following:

- What will be the role of the local firm?
- How will decisions be made?
- Can the project be broken down in phases so that the project can be changed or killed at the end of a phase?
  - How much of the work will be performed locally?
  - How many employees of the foreign firm will be involved in the project?
  - How will the results of the project be managed?
  - How will performance of the local firm be measured and tracked?
  - How will decisions and issues be addressed?

Action

If there is a project underway and problems arise, there are only a limited number of options available. One is to kill the project. This is difficult, if not impossible, to do without loss of face. A second approach that we have employed is to change the direction of the project and scale it back. The project can be divided into local and foreign parts. The project then can be allowed to wilt away. If the project is very important, then an increased foreign presence in the project is warranted.

ISSUE: MANAGEMENT APPROVAL WAS ONLY OBTAINED AT HEADQUARTERS WITHOUT INVOLVEMENT OF LOCAL MANAGEMENT

A project was formulated either at headquarters or in one of the locations of the firm. Staff at headquarters then take the project idea and develop a plan. However, they do so without the knowledge of local conditions or involvement of regional management. This actually happened in southeast Asia where a cement plant was conceived by bureaucrats in the country, giving the aid. The plant was then constructed along with docks and supporting facilities by the foreign government. It failed miserably. The climate in the foreign country was cold; the climate in the other country was very humid. The cement was produced and put on the dock. However, the ship to pick up the cement was delayed due to mechanical breakdowns. The cement hardened on the dock and the dock collapsed. Then the cement in the plant froze up. The plant was worthless.

Impact

What was a good idea turned out to be a bad idea when planned from headquarters. As the preceding example shows, the result can be total failure. More importantly, the experience puts a damper on any future projects.

Prevention

The best approach is to develop the plan as a collaborative effort between the local and headquarters management. Both local and headquarters goals need to be spelled out along with potential issues, roles, and issues.

Action

If a project gets started from headquarters and starts to go bad, one course of action is to kill the project. However, there is often too much invested in the project to do this. There is a lack of will. A better approach is to redirect the project toward local goals.

ISSUE: THE METHOD FOR MANAGING THE PROJECT OVERALL IS TOO BUREAUCRATIC

In some companies projects are run tightly from headquarters. After all, this worked in the past before the firm expanded internationally. When you are dealing with one location, getting decisions made and dealing with bureaucracy can be tolerated. They are part of the job. When the project is international, then there are more problems. This happens in some construction and engineering projects.

Impact

The effect of the bureaucracy can lead to delayed decisions and issues hanging for months. The project gets bogged down. If the rules are not relaxed, then there are likely to be continuing problems. The project will fail.

Prevention

To prevent this problem it is essential to develop project guidelines and rules for international projects. There should be a side-by-side comparison of the rules for headquarters and for local projects. This will ensure that people are aware of the different rules. However, it goes beyond this. People selected for the project must be more flexible and not rigid. Often, this means that new people from outside the organization must be recruited since they are not "tainted" by the bureaucratic procedures. This method was followed by the East India Company and by most of the European powers in the nineteenth century.

Action

If a project is underway and is being buried under bureaucracy, then the entire project should be reviewed. The likelihood of failure should be determined and used as a club to get changes in project management.

Issue: The Manager Who Was behind the Project Moves to a New Position

It is often the case that projects are started by one manager who may have been stationed overseas. The project idea was a good one. Work is proceeding on the project. Then the manager leaves. There is a vacuum. People at headquarters may not be aware of the project. They left it to the now departed manager to direct the work.

Impact

When the manager leaves, work in the project continues. Then issues arise and decisions are required. Requests for support are made to headquarters, but there is no one assigned to the project since it was going along OK. The project gets assigned on an emergency basis to a middle-level manager. This person lacks the authority to get decisions made on a timely basis. The project goes into a state of crisis.

Prevention

It is never a good idea to depend on one manager. The manager should endeavor to involve other managers and to establish a steering committee at headquarters to support the project. This will ensure that there are other interested and informed managers on hand. There should also be a transition if the manager is about to leave.

Action

In the event that a manager leaves, all of the projects that the manager was involved with should be reviewed. There should be visits to headquarters and the local locations as well to build communications and knowledge.

ISSUE: MANAGEMENT APPEARS TO LOSE INTEREST IN THE PROJECT DUE TO OTHER COMMITMENTS

Many projects are started, but few finish. This is true of project management in general. It is even more true with international projects. Management at head-quarters is subject to many demands on their time. If the project seems to running along without problems, it may be left alone. People may forget about the project due to other priorities and pressing issues.

Impact

If management loses interest, the project manager may begin to lose interest as well. This is more frequent when the project leader lacks experience in previous large projects. The project leader may begin to search for another job. The project team may begin to drift away from the project.

Prevention

How a project is to be managed and coordinated over an extended period of time must be defined at the start of the project. It should be assumed that management will lose interest. This is not a bad thing; it is a fact of life. The project support should come from the people who will benefit from the project results. That is, in the end, what keeps the project going. To maintain management interest, a useful approach is to keep feeding status and issues to managers.

Action

To rekindle management interest, the project leader can undertake to showcase some of the recent milestones of the project. This will create interest. This can be followed up by surfacing issues.

Chapter 17

External Issues

INTRODUCTION

External issues are those that arise from government, competition, and other factors that are not within the organization. Hence, there is a lack of control. Often, management is caught by surprise by these issues. They have trouble reacting to the situations.

ISSUES

ISSUE: LOCAL LAWS ARE IMPACTING THE PROJECT

Many firms make assumptions regarding local laws. They sometimes assume that the laws in the country are compatible with their own. Companies can get into such difficulties that they are forced to withdraw from the country for some time.

Impact

If a firm does not give attention to local laws and customs, then projects tend to run into barriers. The project team is forced into a reactive mode. Work on the project stops and the issues raised by local laws are dealt with. The project may just unravel.

Prevention

Understanding of local laws requires more than a few local attorneys. You have to get at the interpretation of the laws in the specific location of the country.

In China, for example, each province can interpret rules and regulations differently. You should look for similar projects that ran into trouble and succeeded. Draw lessons learned from these experiences.

Action

If a problem with local regulations surfaces, try to address the issue while keeping the project going. You do not want to draw off personnel from the project team unless it is absolutely necessary. Start another project to deal with the local regulations.

ISSUE: COMPETITION IS MUCH MORE INTENSE IN A SPECIFIC COUNTRY

Competition impacts a company's operations in terms of what products and services they offer. It also affects such areas as advertising. People get the impression that just because a project is not involved in competition that there is no impact. This is often not the case. Competitive pressures require responses and generate many activities by the managers and staff at the specific location. This then denies the use of the resources for the project. In one soft drink bottling company several major construction projects as well as IT efforts had to be postponed because the attention had to be given to ensuring customer satisfaction and in feeding the distribution channels. Headquarters may not be aware of the pressures that one location is feeling. Management may still insist that the project be done.

Impact

The above discussion pointed to the negative aspects of competition where projects are deferred or put on hold. There can be a positive impact. If, for example, a competitor adopts some technology or embarks on some project to expand their market share, then this is an opportunity for a new project. This happened recently with one retail chain that detected major store upgrades in the works at a competitor. It triggered a response to upgrade their stores—thereby preserving their share of the market.

However, the situation can arise where the management in the field propose a new project in response to competitive pressure to headquarters. Headquarters may not be interested or willing to start the project. The local office is then left with trying to carry out smaller efforts to stem any damage. Only later does the management at headquarters wake up to find out the opportunity that was missed.

Prevention

Headquarters management should take several proactive steps. First, they should encourage each location to undertake a regular competitive assessment. In some industries this should be done once a year. In other more aggressive settings it should be done more frequently. Headquarters should provide guidelines and training in how to generally go about this while leaving the detailed structure of the work to the individual location's management.

The second step is to encourage each location to submit ideas for new projects and efforts. Many times this is restricted to an annual basis. However, business changes much more dynamically so that a better approach is to do it on a quarterly basis.

Action

If there is a competitor who is getting more aggressive, then the local office can be encouraged to collect the information about this effort. Headquarters can then poll the other locations to find out what is going on. A concerted response can then be planned and taken in one or more locations.

Issue: Savings from a Project Are Not Attainable Because of Local Laws

There are many local regulations that inhibit the attainment of savings. One example is a restriction on currency conversion and transfer out of the country. The savings may have to remain in the country. A second case is where there are strong labor laws that protect jobs and make it difficult to downsize. That is why, for example, many European firms first downsize and obtain economies in other continents. Their labor laws are much less restrictive. While the short-term benefits are obvious to the job market, the long-term effect is to shift employment to countries where the labor laws are more flexible.

Impact

In many projects there is little thought given to how the benefits and savings will be realized. People assume that there will be the same benefits as at headquarters. They later find out to their dismay that there are no savings in some locations. Management may then try to force economies. Future projects are then discouraged.

Prevention

Prevention is really simpler than it first appears. The firm needs to be aware of the local laws and regulations. Then they can plan how to take advantage of the savings in other ways. For example, if there is a currency restriction, then other uses of the funds from the project results can be found in the country. Charitable projects might be undertaken. Parts of a plant can be expanded. In the case where people cannot be terminated, then the employees can be redirected into other work. In one southeast Asia country we organized such an effort. Both quality and overall productivity improved.

Action

If a project is started and the benefits are not thought through, then a possible action is to initiate another project to determine how the benefits can be used locally.

ISSUE: ECONOMIC CONDITIONS IN ONE COUNTRY WORSEN

Many economies of the world behave in harmony and sympathy due to globalization. However, it can still happen that one or more locations may be in recession or worse. The question is whether to pursue projects in these countries. While the first answer would seem to be no, there is the argument that a downturn is a good time to make the situation better in the company's operations so that when the recovery occurs, the company can take advantage of the new and improved situation.

Impact

The initial impact of a downturn has been in the past to put new projects on hold and to scale back on current projects. Many projects today are on a larger scale so that scaling back or stopping is not an economically attractive option. Then the decision is made to continue.

Prevention

There is a need to gather economic information as well as internal business information in each area in which a company operates. This will provide an early warning system to potential problems that may affect projects.

Action

If there is a sudden downturn, then there should be an organized assessment of all of the locations to determine if other ones will be impacted. You really don't want to wait for a crisis to occur. You should have a proactive approach ready when the problem surfaces.

ISSUE: THE OPERATIONS IN ONE COUNTRY HAVE MORE URGENT WORK THAN THE PROJECT

An organization may have many far-flung operations. Each location has its own individual needs and problems. When headquarters initiates a project that does not really benefit many of the business locations, then people at the local offices become quite resentful. Morale may suffer. Productivity may drop. The company may appear to many as being mismanaged. This was certainly the case when many firms rolled out ERP systems.

Impact

Morale and productivity are affected. More importantly, the new project robs resources in each location that could have been employed to address local problems. Moreover, management attention becomes focused on the new project so that there is less time to deal with local issues.

Prevention

Companies exist in a global environment. Making decisions based on one location, even if it is the headquarters, is very short sighted and tends to result in more problems. Projects should be planned across all offices in a proactive way as opposed to reacting to specific situations. The most successful firms are often those that are highly sensitive to local conditions.

Action

If a project is started at headquarters, an assessment of the impact and benefits at each location should be undertaken. Perhaps, the project should only be undertaken in a few locations. Later, it can be expanded when the situation warrants action.

ISSUE: NEW TECHNOLOGIES APPEAR IN SOME LOCATIONS THAT OFFER NEW OPPORTUNITIES

Technology advances relentlessly. The pace of technology tends to be uneven due to the unpredictability of breakthroughs. While there have been many successes, it can be argued that there have been many failures. Widespread deployment of PCs in the 1980s often led to lowered productivity without networking. More recently, the adoption of portable, handheld devices has found to be wasteful since there were no real business applications. To take advantage of new technology requires a company to assess the following:

* What are the real benefits of the technology?
* If the technology is not pursued, what are the impacts?
* Are competitors likely to use the technology soon?
* Is the technology sufficiently mature to be able to be placed in many countries around the world?
* Is there sufficient infrastructure of support available?

Answering these questions can lead you to defer the new technology until it has matured.

Impact

New technology has benefits, but it is also disruptive. Everything around the technology is affected. Thus, it has been the case that while there are long-term benefits, the short-term effects of the new technology are quite negative.

Prevention

There should be a technology watch capability in companies of substantial size. This provides an early warning to new technologies. The company can then be more selective and follow a proactive approach to the selected technology. Unfortunately, much technology is adopted in a reactive mode that is not fully thought through.

Action

If a technology has been adopted for use in a company, one of the parts of the project should be an assessment to determine the readiness of each company location to accept and use the technology.

ISSUE: IT IS DIFFICULT TO LINE UP QUALIFIED SUPPLIERS IN SOME COUNTRIES

When you undertake a new project, you often have to rely on contractors and suppliers to provide labor, material, and expertise. In a multinational firm there are likely to be a number of locations where there is no local support available. The alternative then is to relocate supplier staff to remote locations—very expensive.

Impact

Without qualified suppliers a project may languish and flounder in some locations. Local management may be blamed for not getting the project off of the ground.

Prevention

Before any new project is started, an assessment is necessary to determine how the project will be rolled out in different countries. It may be determined that some countries may have to have the project deferred for several years.

Action

If the project has already started and contractors are on board, an effort needs to be undertaken with the contractors to determine how each location will be supported. If there are gaping holes, then deferment is almost a necessity.

ISSUE: THE CULTURE IN A COUNTRY IS NOT COMPATIBLE WITH THE RESULTS OF THE PROJECT

A project produces results that should benefit the business in each location. However, the culture of the country may be such that the results are counter-culture. A simple example occurred when a fast food firm rolled out a new product worldwide. Too bad that the firm did not realize that the religious sensitivities of the citizens of the country were offended. There were street demonstrations and several stores were destroyed by arson. The firm had to retrench. It took over three years to recover to the sales level before the disaster product was launched.

Impact

The example points to the problems when projects are carried out without sufficient thought and sensitivity. The result extends to more than failure of the project.

Prevention

All of the aspects of a project need to be explained to local management prior to the start of the project. Managers should be encouraged to voice any concerns. This must be done long before the project is started. If it is done too close to the project start, then there is too much momentum to make changes.

Action

If a project is started without the analysis, then the project should be reviewed as soon as possible in each location. The firm must be willing to halt the project in specific countries.

ISSUE: THERE ARE MANY DIFFERENT CULTURES AND LANGUAGES IN A COUNTRY

In most countries of the world now there are many different religions, cultures, and languages. If the company pays too much attention to the characteristics of the dominant group, then they risk alienating other groups.

Impact

The impact in direct terms is lost sales. These sales are often lost forever or for a long term regardless of what the firm does. The people feel that the company is a agent of the dominant group.

Prevention

The specific steps depend on the individual company and project. However, one approach is to create alternative versions of the project that address different audiences.

Action

If the problem arises, consideration should be given to halting or redirecting the project.

Appendix 1
The Magic Cross Reference

(continued)

Appendix 2
Web Sites

International Project Management Association: www.ipma.ch

International Journal of Project Management: www.ipma.ch/new1.htm

Project Management Institute: www.pmi.org

ESI International, training in project management around the world: www.esi-intl.com

Project Management Forum: www.pmforum.org

International Cost Engineering Council: www.icoste.org

Earned value management: www.acq.osd.mil/pm/

Guidelines: www.ssie.binghamton.edu/ipm/introduction.htm

Association for Project Management: www.apm.org.uk/pub/journal.htm

Links to project management sites: www.infogoal.com/pmc/pmcorg.htm, www.business2.com

New Grange Center for Project Management: www.newgrange.org

AFITEP, French Project Management Association: www.afitep.fr

Asociacion Espanola de Project Management: www.aepm.org

Australian Institute for Project Management: www.aipm.com.au

Center for International Project and Program Management: www.iol.ie/~mattewar/CIPPM

Projekt Management–Austria: www.p-m-a.at

Swedish Project Management Society: www.projforum.se

Barnes and Noble Professional, Technical, and Business Bookstore: http://btob.barnesandnoble.com

GANTTHead: www.gantthead.com

Appendix 3
References

Bennett, J., *International Construction Project Management: General Theory and Practice*, Butterworth-Heinemann, London, 1991.

Cleland, D.L. and R. Gareis (Eds.), *Global Project Management Handbook*, McGraw-Hill, New York, 1994.

Kangari, R. and C.L. Lucas, *Managing International Operations: A Guide for Engineers, Architects, and Construction Managers*, American Society of Civil Engineers, Reston, VA, 1997.

Keeling, R., *Project Management: An International Perspective*, Palgrave, New York, 2000.

Lientz, B.P. and K.P. Rea, *Project Management for the 21st Century*, 3rd ed., Academic Press, San Diego, 2001.

Miles, D., Constructive Change: *Managing International Technology Transfer*, International Labor Office, Washington, DC, 1999.

Price, A.D.F., *International Project Accounting*, International Labor Office, Washington, DC, 1999.

Stallworthy, E.A. and Kharbanda, *International Construction and the Role of Project Management*, Ashgate, Burlington, VT, 1985.

Index

The letters "ff" indicate the reader should also see the following pages.